*Companion to Good
Health*

The Wordsworth
Companion to Good Health

–

Carol Ann Rinzler

Wordsworth Reference

First published 1991 as *Are You at Risk?* by Facts on File, Inc,
460 Park Avenue South, New York NY 10016.

This edition published 1996 by Wordsworth Editions Ltd,
Cumberland House, Crib Street, Ware, Hertfordshire SG12 9ET.

ISBN 1-85326-362-1

Printed and bound in Great Britain by Mackays of Chatham PLC.

A NOTE TO THE READER

The material in this book, which is drawn from sources current as the book was written, is presented for your information only.

It is not intended as a substitute for your own doctor's advice nor should it be adopted without his or her consent.

Your doctor is the person most familiar with your own medical history and current health. Therefore, he or she is the person best qualified to offer medical advice regarding your personal risk of specific illnesses and medical conditions.

Please note that some of the product names used in this book are registered trademarks.

CONTENTS

viii   Contents

FOREWORD

We now know many, but not all, of the reasons people become sick, and have found ways to prevent some diseases. Unfortunately, this information is not always easy to come by. If you are intent on minimizing the chances of acquiring certain illnesses, it is possible to wade through the medical jargon of the local library's texts (if they are up to date) or visit your personal physician with a list of concerns. Neither of these options is an efficient use of time or resources, however.

What might you need to know to decrease your risk of disease? Certainly understanding the cause of a disease can help you realize what can be done to prevent it. For example, the means of preventing emphysema and influenza are entirely different. Although both diseases affect the lungs, emphysema is largely caused by smoking, whereas influenza is a viral infection. It follows that avoiding tobacco smoke is the best way to reduce your risk of the former, whereas receiving the influenza vaccine is the best prevention for the latter. Knowing the symptoms of an illness can be helpful. If you recognize the symptoms of a disease early you can consult your physician in a more timely fashion. Getting all of this information is going to take a very long time in the library or an unusually patient personal physician.

This book goes a long way toward solving the problem. Carol Ann Rinzler has addressed all of these issues, and more, in *Are You At Risk?* Ms. Rinzler has an impressive ability to distill complex information about important and timely topics. In addition to providing us with the standard information in a readable fashion, she has been careful to include information based on the most recent medical research.

The information in *Are You At Risk?* can be retrieved in two ways. If you are interested in a certain disease, you can look under that heading to see whether you are at risk and what can be done to decrease that risk. Alternatively, if your life-style includes high risk behaviors, it is possible to check to see what illnesses might result. There are some chapters in this book that almost everyone should review, such as those concerning vaccination for preventable illnesses (tetanus, rubella, whooping cough etc.). Other sections, such as those on breast and cervical cancer, may be primarily of interest to women. Each of the chapters thoroughly reviews what is know about the illnesses and what can be done to decrease the chances of suffering from such an illness.

It is important to emphasize that there are two factors to be considered about how diseases may harm you. Obviously, the first is whether or not you will get it: No one chooses to develop an illness. Of almost equal importance, however, is how a disease affects you. While it may be devastating to find out you or a family member has breast cancer, hypertension or phenylkentonuria, these are all treatable conditions. If diagnosed early enough, treatment has the potential to preserve both the quality and the length of life. Because early diagnosis of disease is sometimes more important (or more practical) than prevention, Ms. Rinzler has carefully outlined measures you can take to decrease your chances of *suffering* from some diseases that cannot always be prevented.

The discussion of each illness not only includes information about its known causes and symptoms, but also data on tests you might undergo.

While this book is not intended as a substitute for physician visits, people heeding the advice provided could make more efficient use of fewer visits. Keeping fit, eating sensibly and not smoking could reduce the number of doctor visits in between those important for preventative reasons (vaccinations, blood pressure monitoring etc.). This should have the added benefit of reducing the cost of health care.

If you are interested in maintaining your health by avoiding risks, I believe you will enjoy this book. Many people would like to know what they can do to stay healthy, especially if certain diseases run in their families. The information in *Are You At Risk?* should help.

Michael D. Jensen, M.D.
Mayo Clinic
Rochester, Minnesota

ACKNOWLEDGMENTS

I am grateful to the following people and organizations, among others, who were kind enough to provide information or share with me their expertise regarding the material in this book: Dennis Bowman, Charles Ebel, Derrick Jeffers, Michael D. Jensen, M.D., Steven Koenig, M.D., Doug Lasky, Richard Leavitt, Louis Linn, M.D., Glennis McNeal, Julius Obin, D.D.S., Adele Paroni, Creighton Phelps, Ph.D., Lester Shapiro, M.D., John P. Utz, M.D., and The Alzheimer's Disease and Related Disorders Association, the American Cancer Society, the American Diabetes Association, the American Heart Association, The American Social Health Association, the Arthritis Foundation, the Epilepsy Society of New York, the Gay Men's Health Crisis, the March of Dimes Birth Defects Foundation, the Muscular Dystrophy Association, the National Psoriasis Foundation and the Pharmaceutical Manufacturers Association.

INTRODUCTION

When is a health risk risky for you?

Sometimes it's obvious. *Everyone* who swallows a large enough dose of cyanide will die. A hot poker will burn *anybody's* skin. *Everyone* whose diet is deficient in vitamin C will eventually develop scurvy.

But the risk of developing any one of dozens of serious illnesses can vary dramatically from person to person. Although problems such as birth defects, cancer, diabetes, heart disease, osteoporosis and infectious diseases such as AIDS may seem to threaten us all, the truth is that our real risk depends on a variety of specific individual characteristics, including (but not limited to) our age, our gender, our work, our family history, our behavior and our body chemistry.

We call these characteristics "risk factors."

Some risk factors are statistical. They accurately describe trends among large groups of people but may not say a lot about what will happen to us as individuals, one at a time. For example, waiting until you are 30 to have your first baby is a risk factor for breast cancer, but nobody seriously believes that every woman who has her first child after she is 30 will develop cancer of the breast.

Other risk factors might be described as "causative" because exposure to them has a direct effect on whether or not you will get sick. If you are bitten by a mosquito while you are traveling in a part of the world where malaria is endemic, your risk of getting malaria rises. If you have unprotected intercourse with someone in a high-risk group, your risk of acquiring the HIV virus that causes AIDS also increases.

Does the impact of these risk factors really vary from person to person? Absolutely. Having a serum cholesterol reading higher than 240 ml/dL is a statistical risk factor for heart disease, but it's only a part of the story. In order to figure out just how threatening your cholesterol reading really is, you also need to know the ratio of "good cholesterol" (high-density lipoproteins/HDLs) to "bad cholesterol" (low-density lipoproteins/LDLs) in your blood, as well as your levels of another kind of blood fat called triglycerides, and whether or not you have additional risk factors such as smoking or diabetes or being overweight.

In many cases, we can reduce the impact of individual risk factors. In other words, how we behave can go a long way toward keeping us alive and healthy. If you are obese, losing weight will reduce your risk of diabetes. If you are traveling to a place where malaria is endemic, taking preventive medication will protect against the organisms transmitted in a mosquito bite. Practicing safe sex will reduce your risk of acquiring HIV.

And when prevention is impractical, early detection may save your life. Right now, there is no medically certain way to prevent breast cancer, but women can reduce their risk of succumbing to the disease by having regular mammograms to find any tumor as early as possible before it spreads. The same thing goes for people who have a family history of colon cancer. You can't change your genetically determined risk factor, but early detection *can* save your life.

How to use this book

The material in this book is organized into individual entries for 128 diseases and medical conditions listed in alphabetical order.

Each entry begins with a list of the *Known risk factors*, each marked "yes" if it affects your risk of this particular condition, and "no" if it does not. These risk factors are:

Age: A "yes" here means that how old you are affects your risk of getting sick. It does not necessarily tell you among which age group most cases of this illness will occur. For example, being an adolescent increases your risk of developing acne, but being young does not increase your risk of chicken pox or measles. Although more children than adults get these two diseases, the risk factor is their lack of immunity, not their age.

Gender: A "yes" here refers to your risk of getting the disease in the first place, not necessarily to its effects once you get it. For example, men and women are at equal risk for the sexually transmitted disease chlamydia, but women are more likely than men to suffer serious consequences such as sterility if they get it.

Race/ethnic group: A "yes" here defines the risk of a person to get a disease because he or she belongs to a specific group whose genetic inheritance raises its risk for specific medical conditions. For example, the gene for Tay-Sachs disease occurs most commonly among people of Jewish ancestry; the gene for sickle-cell disease, among blacks.

Family history: A "yes" here refers to the risk posed by the presence among your relatives of clearly inherited conditions as muscular dystrophy or the vulnerability to depression. It does not refer to behavioral problems, such as the link between a woman's drinking heavily while pregnant and her infant's risk of fetal alcohol syndrome.

Diet: A "yes" here refers to the risk posed by specific foods, beverages (including alcoholic beverages), food additives and nutrients. It means that the things you eat raise your risk of getting sick, not that what you eat may make your symptoms worse. For example, consuming contaminated seafood or water raises your risk of getting cholera. On the other hand, eating something to which you are allergic won't cause asthma even though it may make your existing asthma worse.

Smoking: A "yes" here refers to the hazard posed by any one of a number of tobacco products: cigarettes, cigars, pipes and smokeless tobacco. For example, using smokeless tobacco increases your risk of oral cancers.

Drugs & medical procedures: A "yes" here refers to the risk inherent in specific medical drugs and medical procedures such as X-rays or surgery. For example, some anti-cancer drugs used to treat other cancers may increase your risk of developing leukemia.

General health: A "yes" here means that other medical conditions may increase your risk of getting this one. For example, being overweight increases your risk of diabetes; having diabetes increases your risk of developing heart disease.

Environment: This includes all environmental influences such as air pollution, altitude, climate, animals, plants and weather. A "yes" means that environmental conditions can cause the illness, not simply that they make it worse. For example, specific kinds of air pollution can cause emphysema, but not hay fever, although they can make the hay fever worse.

Occupation: A "yes" here means that some of the conditions that go with a specific job can cause illness, not simply make it worse. For example, working with a vibrating tool such as a chainsaw can cause Raynaud's disease; being exposed to the cold will make it worse, but it doesn't cause the condition in the first place.

Next, under the heading *Are you at risk?* you will find a short essay listing the incidence of the condition (how many people have it) and describing the specific statistical and/or causative risk factors for each illness or medical condition. In some cases, there will also be a statistical picture, in words, of the person most likely to develop the disease. For example, under Heat Stroke: "The most common victim of heat stroke is an athlete who neglects to replace the salt and water lost while working out in the sun."

After this is a section on early detection, which explains, often with the use of statistics on survival, the value of early detection. For example, 88% of the people with bladder cancer whose tumor is found early, before it has spread, will be alive five years later. Only 41% whose tumor is found after it has spread to other organs will survive five years. This section also includes a description of various diagnostic tests such as urinalysis (to detect microscopic amounts of blood in the urine, the earliest warning sign of bladder cancer) and cystoscopy to view the inside of the bladder.

Each entry ends with a list of things you can do *To lower your risk* of getting the condition the entry describes. These precautions range from the obvious (stop smoking to reduce your risk of lung cancer, cancer of the pancreas and heart disease) to the less familiar (practice safer sex to reduce your risk of cervical cancer).

In the end, remember this: Not everything threatens everybody. Not everyone is equally at risk. If you frequently drive in a car but never travel to a place where cholera is endemic, your risk of dying in an automobile accident dramatically outweighs your risk of dying from cholera. If you are immunized against polio but still smoke, your risk of dying from lung cancer is high; your risk of polio is virtually nil.

In short, the point of being aware of risks is not to fear everything but to have the information you need to identify the things that truly threaten you and to adjust your way of living so as to reduce their potential for harm.

I hope this book will help you do that.

Carol Ann Rinzler

ACNE

Known risk factors

Age:	Yes	Smoking:	No
Gender:	Yes	Drugs & medical procedures:	Yes
Race/ethnic group:	No	General health:	Yes
Family history:	Yes	Environment:	Yes
Diet:	No	Occupation:	Yes

Are you at risk?

Acne, which shows up first at puberty, is linked to biological changes in the skin triggered by rising levels of the male hormone testosterone that make the sebaceous (oil) glands in the skin larger.

The people most likely to develop acne are adolescents, girls first, around age 14, followed by boys about two years later. Males and females both have male hormones and female hormones, but because males have more testosterone than females do, a teen-age boy's acne is likely to be more severe. Getting older doesn't mean an end to acne. During their childbearing years, women may develop acne that gets worse right before menstruation starts and clears up after. Their acne may also get better—or worse—during pregnancy and at menopause.

Because identical twins often have identical cases of acne, some people believe there is a genetic component involved. Some drugs, such as steroid hormones and iodides, can trigger a rash that looks like acne. Some people develop acne-like eruptions from their cosmetics. This condition, known as *acne cosmetica*, occurs in about one-third of all women who use cosmetics. Hair dressings that contain mineral oil or petrolatum (petroleum jelly) may cause whiteheads and blackheads on the forehead and temples.

Does what you eat affect your acne? Not necessarily. Although American Academy of Dermatology agrees that some people find that their acne gets worse when they eat certain foods, such as chocolate and fats, it's strictly an individual reaction.

Early detection. Acne is diagnosed by its characteristic appearance.

To lower your risk of acne

Avoid oily cosmetics and hair dressings. Petrolatum (petroleum jelly) and mineral oil soften the skin but they may also block pores, causing whiteheads and blackheads. If there is a specific cosmetic that makes your face break out, avoid that, too. Over the years, a number of cosmetic ingredients, such as isopropyl myristate, have been called comedogenic because they produce comedones (whiteheads and blackheads) when applied full-strength to the sensitive inner skin of a rabbit's ear. However, there is some question about whether these ingredients produce the same effect when diluted for use in cosmetics.

Wash but don't scrub. Washing with warm water and gentle soap or cleanser eliminates oil and dirt, but scrubbing irritates the skin and can make your acne worse. So can picking at your face, which increases the likelihood of infections (pustules).

Don't wear tight-fitting hats, chin-straps or scarves. The fabric rubbing against your forehead or chin can irritate and aggravate your acne.

Monitor your diet. Diet alone won't cure acne, but if you find that certain foods aggravate the condition, the American Academy of Dermatology's sensible solution is to avoid the aggravating foods.

ACQUIRED IMMUNE DEFICIENCY SYNDROME (AIDS)

Known risk factors

Age:	No	Smoking:	No
Gender:	Yes	Drugs & medical procedures:	Yes
Race/ethnic group:	No	General health:	Yes
Family history:	No	Environment:	No
Diet:	No	Occupation:	No

Are you at risk?

In 1991, six years after AIDS first forced its way into the American consciousness, The Federal Centers for Disease Control counted 161,073 cases diagnosed in the United States, with 100,777 people dead of the disease. Estimates of Americans infected but not yet showing any symptoms ranged from 800,000 to 1.3 million. Worldwide, the World Health Organization (WHO) believes that as many as 5 million to 10 million people may be infected with the human immunodeficiency virus (HIV) that causes AIDS.

The statistical portrait of the American most likely to test positive for HIV is a 28- to 49-year-old homosexual or bisexual man, or an intravenous drug user. (In Africa, a woman's risk is the same as a man's, perhaps because anal intercourse is more common or because of the increased incidence of sexually transmitted diseases [STDs] thought to raise the risk of acquiring HIV.)

A relatively small number of AIDS patients are hemophiliacs or people who have had blood transfusions; 1% are heterosexual partners of people with AIDS. Although doctors, nurses, dentists, laboratory technicians and other health professionals are often considered at higher risk because they may be exposed to infected body fluids at work, the actual number of such people who have contracted HIV through their jobs is extremely small.

It is not easy to acquire HIV. You are not at risk from donating blood or if you live with someone who has AIDS or if you eat food prepared by someone who has AIDS or if you go to school or work with someone who has AIDS or if someone who has AIDS sneezes or coughs in your presence or if you share a toilet or bar of soap or washing machine with someone who has AIDS.

Outside the body, HIV is vulnerable to common sanitary procedures. It can be killed by exposure to hot (135-degree Fahrenheit) water for 10 minutes in a dishwasher or washing machine or exposure to the steam or chemicals used in dry cleaning or to sterilize medical equipment, or to ordinary household disinfectants such as hydrogen peroxide, chlorine bleach or rubbing alcohol or to germicidal skin cleaners such as povidone iodine.

What does increase your risk is exposure to semen or blood from a person who has HIV. You are at high risk if you engage in anal intercourse, perhaps because the lining of the rectum is easily torn during intercourse, permitting HIV in contaminated semen to enter your blood stream. You are also at risk if you get blood transfusions, although more stringent, finely drawn testing for HIV antibodies in blood has reduced this risk significantly in the past few years. A child born to a woman who had HIV while pregnant is likely to acquire the virus in the womb and to die of the disease within a few years after birth.

Early detection. Although AIDS is still considered a fatal disease, there are two valid reasons for finding it as early as possible. First, early detection cuts down the risk that a person with HIV will inadvertently transmit the virus to someone else. Second, early detection followed by medical treatment may significantly postpone the development of full-blown AIDS.

The standard screening test for HIV is the ELISA (*e*nzyme *l*inked *i*mmuno *s*orbent *a*ssay) test to detect antibodies to the AIDS virus in an infected person's blood anywhere about two to 12 weeks after infection occurs. A more refined test, submitted for Food and Drug Administration (FDA) approval in 1989, identifies antigens (the substances that trigger the immune system's production of antibodies) in blood plasma about two weeks sooner, at a time when the results of an ELISA test would still likely be negative.

To lower your risk of AIDS

Practice safer sex. In a post-AIDS world, this means avoiding any unprotected (latex condom–free) oral, anal or vaginal intercourse, unless you are in a long-term monogamous relationship with someone whom you know to be HIV-free.

Using condoms correctly begins with storing them properly in a cool, dry place to protect the latex from drying out. Put it on gently to avoid tearing and leave room at the tip to accommodate the ejaculate. After ejaculation, withdraw the penis with the condom still in place, holding it close against the base of the penis to avoid spilling any ejaculate. Discard all used condoms; never try to wash them out and use them again.

According to the American Social Health Association, you may increase the protective effect of a condom by using a spermicidal foam that contains nonoxynol-9. In laboratory studies, nonoxynol-9 appears to kill HIV on contact. But the two contraceptives must be used in tandem; on its own, the foam is not considered adequately protective.

If you are scheduled for elective surgery, consider a "self-transfusion." Although more stringent testing for HIV antibodies and antigens has significantly increased the safety of our blood supply, you can cut your risk of acquiring HIV from a transfusion to zero by donating and storing your own blood in advance.

If you are at risk, do not become pregnant without having an HIV test first. If you test positive after you are already pregnant, you may wish to talk with your doctor about the advisability of abortion.

Avoid intravenous drugs. At the very least, it is important to avoid sharing intravenous needles. The chance of acquiring HIV by sharing a toothbrush, razor or other implement that may be contaminated with blood is presumed to be minimal, but it's a risk that can easily be reduced to zero by using your own.

ALCOHOLISM

Known risk factors

Age:	Yes	Smoking:	No
Gender:	No	Drugs & medical procedures:	No
Race/ethnic group:	No	General health:	Yes
Family history:	Yes	Environment:	No
Diet:	No	Occupation:	No

Are you at risk?

Alcoholism is an addictive, chronic disease that becomes progressively worse if untreated and may eventually be fatal. An important risk factor for alcoholism is being the child of an alcoholic. Although most of the early research in this area focused on the sons of alcoholics, later studies have shown that daughters of alcoholics have pretty much the same risks. What sets children of alcoholics apart from the rest of us is that they seem to be less susceptible to the physical effects of alcohol consumption. In laboratory tests, for example, they are less likely than other people to sway back and forth on a moving platform after consuming a few drinks. They have a higher tolerance for alcohol and tend to consume more because they never get the signal that says, "I've had enough."

Other strong predictors of alcohol abuse are psychological problems such as depression or a lack of self-esteem, especially among people who use alcohol as self-medication (to feel better). Sexual problems such as impotence or failure to experience orgasm may increase the risk of alcohol abuse, and in all cases, the risk is highest among the young. Men are most at risk for alcohol abuse when they are teen-agers; women, when they are 21 to 34 years old.

Women also seem more at risk for alcohol's intoxicating effects in the days immediately preceding menstruation, when the concentration of alcohol in their blood is highest, suggesting a cyclic disruption in the enzyme systems that normally metabolize and eliminate alcohol from the body. (Many Orientals also have an unusual metabolic response to alcohol. Because their bodies have only an inefficient form of a liver enzyme needed to metabolize and eliminate alcohol, a large amount of acetaldehyde, an alcohol by-product, piles up in their bloodstream, producing a flushed face, headache and nausea—but not alcoholism, since the obvious response to this set of symptoms is to drink less, not more.)

Early detection. Right now, there is no fool-proof test to determine who is (or will be) an alcoholic, but someday soon there may well be a simple blood test to predict susceptibility. In 1988, the National Institute on Alcohol Abuse and Alcoholism (NIAAA) in Bethesda, Maryland, suggested that measuring the activity of two specific enzymes in the blood can identify potential alcoholics. In testing blood samples from known alcohol abusers and people known to be non-alcoholics, the NIAAA researchers found that the activity of both enzymes (monoamine oxidase and adenylate cyclase) were markedly reduced in the blood of alcoholic abusers. The enzyme abnormality may mark an inherited genetic inability to metabolize alcohol and a consequent susceptibility to alcoholism.

Lacking this kind of definitive test as to who is an alcoholic, we are left to rely on simple observation, which can be tricky because it is often subjective. For example, is a person who has one drink each night with dinner an alcoholic? How about a person who has three drinks, but only drinks on Saturday night? Or a person who only drinks once a year, on New Year's Eve, but drinks to excess on that one night? Clearly, when it comes to describing alcoholic behavior, people brought up in a tradition that takes alcohol beverages with meals for granted would not use the same standards as some neo-prohibitionists who frown on any alcohol consumption at all.

A valuable set of guidelines regarding unhealthy use of alcohol is these three patterns established by the American Psychiatric Association: (1) drinking every day or drinking large amounts of alcohol on a regular basis, (2) drinking heavily only on the weekends, or (3) going for long periods of time without drinking at all and then drinking heavily, sometimes for weeks or months at a time.

One additional guideline suggested by the National Council on Alcoholism can help to clarify the issue: What makes people who abuse alcohol different from people who use alcohol safely and in moderation is that when alcohol abusers start to drink, they cannot know what will happen next, whether they will be able to stop or whether they will inevitably progress to inebriation. As a result, their drinking, which is beyond their control, interferes with their professional and personal lives.

To lower your risk of alcohol abuse

Know your own risk factors. Being the child of an alcoholic raises your risk, but it does not inevitably doom you to a similar fate. Despite the suggestion of a genetic predisposition to alcoholism, no one has yet found a gene for it. Clearly you can modify the effects of your family history by modifying your behavior. Your state, county or city health department can provide information about local treatment and prevention programs.

Avoid using alcohol to "feel better." It is safer and far more effective to seek psychological help for emotional problems than to bandage them over with alcohol.

ALTITUDE SICKNESS

Known risk factors

Age:	Yes	Smoking:	No
Gender:	Yes	Drugs & medical procedures:	No
Race/ethnic group:	No	General health:	Yes
Family history:	No	Environment:	Yes
Diet:	Yes	Occupation:	No

Are you at risk?

As the altitude increases, the amount of oxygen in the atmosphere decreases. Because every breath you take brings less oxygen into your body, the amount of oxygen circulating in your blood decreases. Eventually, the lack of sufficient oxygen will cause a multiplicity of symptoms, including headache, fatigue, nausea, vomiting, sleep disturbance, ringing in the ears and difficulty breathing. These symptoms are known collectively as acute mountain sickness (AMS). People with a more serious form of altitude sickness, high altitude pulmonary edema (swelling of the tissues of the lungs (HAPE), may also develop irregular heartbeat and a cough that produces a frothy, sometimes bloody sputum. High altitude cerebral edema (HACE), which may occur along with either AMS or HAPE, can cause mental confusion, double vision, and clumsiness in arm and leg movements.

Acute mountain sickness may occur at altitudes as low as 6,500 feet above sea level. Within 24 to 72 hours of climbing to more than 9,000 feet above sea level, 10 percent to 25 percent of all climbers will have symptoms of altitude sickness, including pulmonary edema. According to the *Mayo Clinic*

Health Letter, at 10,000 feet, 50 percent of all people who are not long-time residents of high-altitude locations will experience problems; at 12,000 feet above sea level, virtually everyone is affected; at altitudes higher than 17,000 feet above sea level, the lack of oxygen is severe enough to cause hemorrhages in the retina of the eye.

It is difficult to predict with certainty who will develop altitude sickness. Contrary to popular belief, physical fitness offers no protection; the fit are as likely as the slothful to suffer at high altitudes. Having climbed to high altitudes previously with no problems does not guarantee that the next trip will be symptom free. On the other hand, once you have had altitude sickness, your risk is increased the next time you are at high altitudes.

Children, particularly those younger than six, are more susceptible than adults to all forms of altitude sickness. Women in the premenstrual phase of the menstrual cycle may also be at higher risk, as are men, women and children who have lived for long periods of time at higher altitudes and return home after a short stay at a lower altitude.

Note: The relative lack of oxygen at high altitudes may be hazardous for people with sickle cell disease, who are at increased risk not from altitude sickness but from an acute episode of sickle cell disease. The oxygen-poor environment may also be hazardous for people with heart or lung disease.

Early detection. If you develop symptoms of altitude sickness, it is imperative to seek medical help as quickly as possible. Sometimes, the condition may worsen precipitously if the victim does not descend immediately to a lower altitude. In cases of high altitude pulmonary edema, coma and death may follow within hours of the first symptoms.

To lower your risk of altitude sickness

Ascend slowly. The first step in preventing altitude sickness is to climb slowly. In general, it is safest to ascend no more than 1,000 feet a day when you are between 5,000 and 10,000 feet above sea level, and safest to go up even more slowly after this. If your ski trip or climb takes you to altitudes higher than 10,000 feet during the day, it is prudent to spend your nights sleeping at altitudes lower than 8,000 to 9,000 feet. (At night, when your breathing is shallower, the level of oxygen in your blood will fall even faster in an oxygen-poor, high-altitude environment.)

Drink plenty of water. Every time you breathe out, your body loses some water; breathing the dry air at high altitudes increases this natural water loss. To prevent dehydration, which can worsen the symptoms of altitude sickness, drink more water than usual.

Avoid alcoholic beverages and excessive amounts of caffeinated liquids. Alcohol and caffeine are both mild diuretics; they increase the body's loss of water.

Ask your doctor about preventive treatment. If you have already experienced altitude sickness or are planning a trip that includes a rapid ascent or are a member of a group at risk for problems at high altitudes, check with your doctor before planning your trip. There are a number of drugs used to prevent or mitigate the effects of high altitude in the body. In the United States, the drug used most frequently is acetazolamide (Diamox). Preventive treatment with acetazolamide must begin before you leave and continue during your trip.

ALZHEIMER'S DISEASE

Known risk factors

Age:	Yes	Smoking:	No
Gender:	?	Drugs & medical procedures:	No
Race/ethnic group:	No	General health:	No
Family history:	?	Environment:	No
Diet:	No	Occupation:	No

Are you at risk?

Ask Americans which disease they fear most as they grow older and Alzheimer's is sure to be high on the list. Approximately 15% of all Americans older than 65 have some form of dementia; an estimated 4 million adults have Alzheimer's disease, the most common dementing illness. Although it may occur in people as young as 25, most cases show up in people past 60.

Women appear to be at high risk. They are a clear and disproportionate majority among Alzheimer's victims. Whether this is the result of their gender or simply perhaps because they live longer than men and are thus more likely to survive to the age when Alzheimer's appears remains to be seen.

Is Alzheimer's a genetic condition? Maybe. Is a tendency to Alzheimer's inherited? In some case, the answer may be yes.

In some families early onset Alzheimer's Disease is associated with specific "markers" on chromosome 21. (Some of the degenerative physical changes that occur in the brain of a person with Alzheimer's are remarkably similar to the destruction of cells and the consequent clumps and spaces in brain tissue found in the brain of a person with Down's syndrome, also linked to chromosome 21.)

There have been instances of Alzheimer's in two or more generations of the same family, and several years ago scientists at the University of Pittsburgh found that Alzheimer's patients with excessively fluid surface membranes on their blood platelets got their symptoms earlier and had more severe symptoms than patients without the abnormality. The parents and siblings of these patients were more likely than other people to have this same abnormality. Relatives who had the abnormal platelet membranes and who developed Alzheimer's disease also got it about five years earlier than Alzheimer patients whose platelet membranes were normal. Whether or not the abnormal platelet membrane will become a "marker" for Alzheimer's disease remains to be seen.

To date, there is no proof that anything we eat or drink or anything in our environment can cause Alzheimer's disease.

Over the past 15 years, scientists have discovered that people with Alzheimer's seem to accumulate larger-than-normal amounts of aluminum in the brain. As a result, there has been a continuing scientific effort around the world to determine whether the aluminum we get in food and water raises our risk of getting Alzheimer's. In January 1989, for example, the British medical journal *Lancet* carried the results of a government study suggesting that people who drink water high in aluminum (aluminum sulfate is one of the chemicals used to purify water) appear to be at higher risk.

However, there really is only one scientific way to confirm or disprove a link between aluminum consumption and Alzheimer's. That is to set up an experiment in which people are given large amounts of aluminum and then wait to see what happens. Unthinkable? Of course. But it turns out that this unthinkable experiment actually happened not just once, but twice. Both times the results were negative: no apparent connection between the aluminum and the disease.

The first such "experiment" involves the millions of people with ulcers and heartburn who, over the years, have taken billions of doses of over-the-counter antacids containing aluminum compounds such as aluminum carbonate, aluminum hydroxide, aluminum phosphate and dihydroxyaluminum aminoacetate with absolutely no reported increase in the incidence of either senile dementia or Alzheimer's disease.

The second such "experiment" occurred early in the 1970s, when groups of kidney dialysis patients in Great Britain and the United States were inadvertently dialyzed with water containing toxic amounts of aluminum. Many patients eventually experienced severe neurological disturbances attributed to aluminum poisoning and some died. When autopsies were performed, the levels of aluminum in their brains were even higher than the levels found in the brains of Alzheimer's patients, but none who had been dialyzed with the aluminum-packed solution had Alzheimer's disease.

Early detection. There is currently no effective treatment but early diagnosis allows you to rule out other conditions such as depression, nutritional imbalances, drug reactions, malfunction of the thyroid gland, infections, tumors or blood clots, all of which may cause dementia but are treatable. Among the tests used to rule out illnesses that might cause symptoms similar to Alzheimer's disease are a cranial CT-scan, an electroencephalogram (EEG), an analysis of the spinal fluid and magnetic resonance imaging (MRI).

To lower your risk of Alzheimer's disease

At present there is no known way to reduce your own chances of developing Alzheimer's disease.

AMYOTROPHIC LATERAL SCLEROSIS (ALS)

Known risk factors

Age:	Yes	Smoking:	No
Gender:	Yes	Drugs & medical procedures:	No
Race/ethnic group:	No	General health:	No
Family history:	?	Environment:	No
Diet:	No	Occupation:	No

Are you at risk?

Amyotrophic lateral sclerosis (ALS), also known as Lou Gehrig's disease, currently affects approximately 20,000 Americans; about 5,000 new cases are diagnosed each year.

ALS destroys motor neurons, the nerve cells in the spinal cord that transmit impulses to our muscles. It does not affect intelligence or our ability to feel and think, but it progressively wipes out our ability to control any muscles other than the ones we use to move our eyes and to control the rings of muscle (sphincters) at the opening of the anus and the urinary bladder. ALS is a disease of late middle age that seems to be growing more common as our population ages. It rarely shows up before age 40, and its early symptoms, such as weakness and cramps in the hands, may be discounted as the ordinary aches and pains of growing older, thus delaying a diagnosis. ALS is more common among men than among women, and about 10% of its victims have a family history of the disease.

Early detection. Among the tests used to diagnose ALS are electromyography (EMG), a recording of the electrical impulses running through an active muscle (in ALS, these impulses decline); muscle biopsy (which shows a thickening of muscle fibers if ALS is present); and a blood test to determine the level of creatine phosphokinase (CPK), an enzyme that makes it possible for your muscles to contract (blood levels of CPK rise up in patients with ALS).

Right now, there is no treatment for ALS, but it is important to pinpoint a diagnosis as early as possible. This is so that you can differentiate ALS from a number of other conditions, such as postpolio syndrome or chronic lead poisoning or thyrotoxicosis (an overproduction of thyroid hormone), whose symptoms may be similar but can be treated. The following tests may be used to rule out these and other possible causes of muscle loss: a CT-scan of the skull, a spinal CT-scan, an analysis of the spinal fluid and tests to determine the blood levels of calcium and phosphorous (which rise with some forms of cancer).

To lower your risk of ALS

Genetic counseling. Like Huntington's disease, ALS is a treacherous condition that rarely shows up until a person is well into or even past the childbearing years. There is presently no known way to reduce your own risk of acquiring ALS, but if you have any relatives with the disease, you may wish to seek genetic counseling. No one has yet identified a specific genetic "marker" for the disease, but an experienced counselor can help you calculate your risk of unwittingly passing ALS along to your children.

APPENDICITIS

Known risk factors

Age:	Yes	Smoking:	No
Gender:	Yes	Drugs & medical procedures:	No
Race/ethnic group:	No	General health:	Yes
Family history:	No	Environment:	No
Diet:	?	Occupation:	No

Are you at risk?

Appendicitis is a bacterial infection of the vermiform ("worm-like") appendix, a 3-to-6-inch-long organ in the lower right-hand part of your abdomen. The older you get, the less likely you are to end up with appendicitis. Most cases (78%) occur in people younger than 40; the person most likely to develop a "hot" appendix is a young man age 15 to 24. After 40, your risk drops dramatically (14% of all cases). Only 8% of all appendicitis attacks occur in people older than 60. Nobody really knows why appendicitis is more common among the young or why boys have a higher risk than girls.

On the other hand, it's easy to see why your risk rises when you have an abdominal inflammation (the infection can spread to the appendix), when you have abdominal cancer (the cancer can obstruct your intestines, collect bacteria and trigger an infection) or when you have intestinal parasites (infection, again).

Early detection. How can you tell if the pain in your belly is appendicitis? Surprisingly, location is not the best guide since the pain of an infected appendix may bounce around your abdomen and body.

If you are obese, your doctor may have a hard time localizing the pain. When you are pregnant, the pain of appendicitis may seem like normal cramping. If you are older than 60 or if you are taking corticosteroid drugs, the pain may be so muted that the infection can actually chew through (perforate) the wall of your appendix and spill into the abdomen to cause the general infection we call peritonitis before you even feel a twinge.

A more reliable guide to acute appendicitis is a diagnosis of pain plus an elevated white blood cell count. (White blood cells proliferate when you have an infection.)

Naturally, there's an exception to this rule. When you are pregnant, your white blood cell count normally rises, so a blood test may be as unreliable a guide as a pain in your right side. This makes diagnosis difficult and, not surprisingly, the death rate from appendicitis (actually, the failure to diagnose it properly) is higher during pregnancy or right after delivery, when appendicitis is also more common.

Approximately 272,000 appendectomies are performed each year in the United States, making this our sixth most common surgical operation. The mortality rate (the number of people who die from the surgery) is about one in 500, two times as high as the death rate from hysterectomies but five times lower than the death rate for a gallbladder operation.

To lower your risk of appendicitis

Eat more high-fiber foods. Because the appendix is located in the abdomen, people have often tried to pin the infection on something they ate, most commonly a fruit seed that "got caught in the appendix." That's hardly likely, but there is now some speculation that a low-fiber diet that allows food to linger in your intestinal tract may increase the risk, while a high-fiber diet that speeds food through your body may be protective. The theory remains to be proven.

ARTHRITIS

Known risk factors

Age:	Yes	Smoking:	No
Gender:	Yes	Drugs & medical procedures:	No
Race/ethnic group:	No	General health:	No
Family history:	Yes	Environment:	No
Diet:	No	Occupation:	No

Are you at risk?

The most common form of arthritis is osteoarthritis, also known as degenerative joint disease. Although it seems reasonable to assume that putting stress on a joint over a long period of time will raise the risk of developing osteoarthritis, this is far from certain. On the one hand, osteoarthritis of the shoulders and knees is more frequent among coal miners. On the other hand, neither runners nor people who spend their working hours at heavy physical work have a higher-than-normal risk of osteoarthritis. Injuries to joints, however, do increase risk.

Arthritis experts have long known that osteoarthritis often seems to run in families, but how it passed from one person to another remained unclear. In 1990, a team of researchers at Thomas Jefferson University in Philadel-

phia announced a possible lead. In a study of 19 members of three generations of a family in which nine people had osteoarthritis, the researchers
were able to isolate a defective gene for collagen II, a protein that strengthens the cartilage that cushions joints. People with the defective gene had
the amino acid cysteine rather than the amino acid arginine in their collagen
II. This single change in the lineup of the more than 1,000 amino acids
normally found in collagen II showed up in all family members who had
osteoarthritis. It did not appear in any family member without osteoarthritis.

Gender plays a small role in deciding who is at risk for osteoarthritis.
Before age 45, a man's risk is slightly higher than a woman's. After age 55,
the picture is reversed. By age 75, almost everyone has some painful joints.

The second well-known form of arthritis is rheumatoid arthritis (RA), a
chronic immune disorder that affects about 1% to 2% of all Americans. RA
commonly appears simultaneously in several joints, usually on both sides
of the body—that is, both wrists, shoulders, ankles or knees. Unlike osteoarthritis, which is generally a penalty of old age, rheumatoid arthritis can
show up in 20-year-olds; 85% of the people who eventually get RA are first
diagnosed when they are age 25 to 50. Women with RA outnumber men
with RA three to one.

Close relatives of RA patients run a risk four times that of people whose
relatives do not have RA. If one identical twin has RA, the other twin born
from the single fertilized egg will also have RA about 30% of the time. Among
fraternal twins—babies born at the same time but from two different fertilized eggs—rheumatoid arthritis affects both twins only 5% of the time.

Using oral contraceptives or the cholesterol-lowering drugs cholestyra-
mine (Questran) and clofibrate (Atromid) may increase the risk of RA.

Does what you eat affect your risk of developing arthritis? No. But there
is evidence to suggest that some foods can relieve or worsen the symptoms
of existing arthritis for some people.

The idea that that certain foods can provoke symptoms of rheumatoid
arthritis has always hovered in a kind of never-never land of myth and
magic. Although several studies had shown that people with arthritis often
feel better after fasting, there was none to prove a relationship between
specific foods and arthritis pains or to show that arthritis could be affected
by food allergies.

Now there is.

In 1987, researchers of the University of Florida College of Medicine found
that a small minority (5%) of people with arthritis have a definite uptick in
symptoms when they consume milk, milk products and foods such as cakes
and cookies that contain milk. The study concentrated on adults, who com-
prise 80% of the patients with rheumatoid arthritis. This study has not, as
of yet, been confirmed, and there is no information yet on whether children
with rheumatoid arthritis suffer the same symptoms when they drink milk.

However, eating a food to which you are allergic can cause your body to produce antigens and antibodies, chemicals known to trigger inflammatory reactions. The opposite occurs when you eat cold water fish such as salmon that contain omega-3 polyunsaturated fatty acids. Omega-3 fish oils contain chemicals that inhibit inflammation. Some studies suggest that omega-3 fish oils can alleviate the symptoms of rheumatoid arthritis, but this remains unproven.

As with many other nutrients, it's best to get your fish oils from real foods, not capsules. According to the *Tufts University Diet & Nutrition Letter*, studies have shown that fish oil supplements may lower the levels of high-density lipoproteins (HDLs), the fat-and-protein particles that help carry cholesterol out of your body, and may cause digestive problems such as belching and loose stool.

Early detection. Osteoarthritis is often diagnosed by its symptoms. Another diagnostic device is an X-ray of the affected joint. As arthritis progresses, the X-ray may show a deformed joint or a narrowing of the spaces around the joint or cyst-like deposits of bone around the joint.

A diagnosis of rheumatoid arthritis may begin with a blood test to detect an increase in the erythrocyte sedimentation rate (ESR), the time it takes for blood cells to settle to the bottom of a test tube. An increased ESR is a common sign of inflammation (from any cause).

The blood test may also show an increase in rheumatoid factors (RF), proteins that increase the tendency of particles in blood to clump together. In its early stages, RA may also be identified by swelling around the joint; an analysis of the synovial fluid (the fluid in the tissues around the joint) will show an increase in white blood cells, another common sign of inflammation or infection. As RA progresses, an X-ray may show a narrowing of the spaces around the joint and a loss of cartilage and bone.

According to the American College of Rheumatology, people with Classic RA have seven of the following symptoms. Symptoms in the first group of five must be present for at least six weeks to count:

1. Stiffness in the joint when you first wake up in the morning.
2. Pain or tenderness when you move or touch the joint.
3. Swelling of the tissue around the joint.
4. Swelling and tenderness in the same joint on the other side of the body.
5. Swelling or tenderness in at least one other joint within three months.
6. Lumps under the skin at bony places such as the wrist.
7. Inflammation in these lumps.
8. A loss of bone tissue that shows up on an X-ray.
9. A blood test positive for RF.
10. An increase in white blood cells in the synovial fluid.
11. A decrease in the rate at which certain chemicals separate from the synovial fluid.

Having five of these symptoms merits a diagnosis of Definite RA. If you have three of these symptoms, the diagnosis is Probable RA.

To lower your risk of arthritis

Control your weight. Although the tendency to rheumatoid arthritis appears to be inherited and thus cannot be changed, there is some evidence to suggest that keeping your weight within normal limits reduces the stress on hip and knee joints and may lower your risk of developing osteoarthritis in these joints as you grow older.

ASTHMA

Known risk factors

Age:	Yes	Smoking:	Yes
Gender:	Yes	Drugs & medical procedures:	No
Race/ethnic group:	No	General health:	Yes
Family history:	Yes	Environment:	Yes
Diet:	No	Occupation:	Yes

Are you at risk?

Asthma is a chronic condition characterized by spasms of the bronchi, the air passages between the trachea [windpipe] and the lungs.

Some experts estimate that there may be more than 10 million asthmatics in the United States, including 3 million children. According to 1990 figures from the Federal Centers for Disease Control, from 1980 to 1987 the incidence of asthma incrased from 31.2 to 40.1 cases per 1,000 people. From 1980 to 1987, the death rate from asthma rose from 1.3 to 1.7 for each 100,000 people; there were 4,360 asthma deaths in 1987 vs. 2,891 asthma deaths in 1980.

Your risk of developing asthma rises if you or someone in your immediate family already have a history of allergic reactions such as hay fever, hives or eczema. People who develop asthma may have an inherited or acquired imbalance in the chemicals known as neurotransmitters that regulate impulses in nerves that control opening and closing of air passages. When these people experience physical or emotional stress from causes as various as respiratory allergens, irritants or very cold air, a viral infection, strenuous exercise, certain foods or drugs or even a change in barometric pressure, the result may be an acute asthmatic attack.

No single racial or ethnic group is more likely than any other to develop asthma, but blacks and Hispanics are more likely to die from it. In New York City, for example, a 1989 United Hospital Fund study found that a black person with asthma was five times more likely than a white person with asthma to die of the disease; a Hispanic's risk of dying from asthma was three times higher than a white's.

Allergic asthma almost always appears first during childhood, and it is more common among boys than among girls. Asthma that shows up after age 40 is sometimes caused by continuing exposure to a chemical irritant at work or in the air.

Asthma is on the increase among people who live in urban areas, and a growing list of substances are now known to trigger occupational asthma. Among the groups at risk: bakers (who are exposed to flour dust); brewers and detergent manufacturers (who are exposed to biologic enzymes); food processors (who are exposed to green coffee beans and various vegetable gums); leather tanners (who are exposed to dyes and formaldehyde); metal workers (who are exposed to chrome, nickel and platinum dust); paint and plastics workers (who are exposed to dyes and plasticizers such as phthalic anhydride); pharmaceutical workers (who are exposed to antibiotics); textile workers (who are exposed to dyes and textile fibers); and woodworkers (who are exposed to oak and western red cedar dust).

Some medical drugs and food additives may precipitate an asthmatic attack in sensitive persons, but they don't cause asthma. Among the drugs and additives known to trigger asthma attacks are aspirin (which is most likely to affect adults), *beta*-adrenergic blocking agents used to treat heart disease and high blood pressure, coloring agents (including tartrazine, a yellow dye used in many pharmaceuticals) and sulfites (used to preserve some wines and keep fresh vegetables and shrimp from darkening).

People with asthma who are sensitive to aspirin may also be sensitive to other non-steroidal anti-inflammatory drugs (NSAIDs) such as fenoprofen (Nalfon), indomethacin (Indocin), ibuprofen (Advil, Medipren, Midol 200), mefenamic acid (Ponstel) and naproxen (Naprosyn).

Early detection. Asthma is a chronic condition that can ordinarily be controlled with proper drug therapy. If your doctor suspects that you have asthma, he or she may first wish to rule out other possibilities such as a respiratory infection or tuberculosis via blood tests or X-rays. If these are negative, a test measuring your pulmonary function (the ability to breathe air in and then expel it from your lungs), usually reduced in people with asthma, can confirm his or her diagnosis.

To lower your risk of asthma

Reduce your exposure to airborne allergens and pollutants. There is no way to reduce your inherited susceptibility to allergic asthma, but you may be able to reduce the incidence and severity of acute asthma attacks by wearing a protective mask when the air is heavily polluted, by wearing a scarf or mask over your nose and mouth to warm and moisten very cold air before it enters your lungs or by cutting back on strenuous activity when the weather is very cold or the air is very polluted. You can also reduce the risk of asthma attacks by avoiding known allergens.

If your work puts you at risk of occupational asthma, you can reduce the risk by wearing protective equipment that filters the air you breathe.

It goes without saying that no one with asthma should smoke.

ATHLETE'S FOOT

Known risk factors

Age:	Yes	Smoking:	No
Gender:	Yes	Drugs & medical procedures:	No
Race/ethnic group:	No	General health:	Yes
Family history:	No	Environment:	Yes
Diet:	?	Occupation:	No

Are you at risk?

Athlete's foot is our most common fungal infection. Theoretically, anybody who walks barefoot on a surface contaminated with the fungus or wears fungus-infested shoes or socks or uses a towel that's been used by someone who already has athlete's foot is at high risk, and according to the American Academy of Dermatology, as many as 90% of all Americans may be affected at one time or another.

On the other hand, exposure to the fungus doesn't guarantee immediate infection. Active athlete's foot may be six times more common among men than among women, and adults seem to be more susceptible than children. People with diabetes are at high risk; so are people who are poorly nourished or who don't keep their feet clean and dry, or who have a cut, scrape or other skin injury that would allow the fungus a toehold. Once you've had athlete's foot, you may have some resistance to the next attack. Or you may not: For some people, one attack produces a kind of chronic inflammation.

Early detection. The symptoms of athlete's foot may resemble those of contact dermatitis (a local reaction to material in your shoes or socks), psoriasis or eczema. Your doctor can make a conclusive diagnosis by taking small scrapings of infected skin and examining them under a microscope where the fungus will be clearly visible.

To lower your risk of athlete's foot

Practice good hygiene. It's boring but true: The best way to prevent athlete's foot is to keep your feet cool and dry.

Dry thoroughly after bathing. Dust your feet and between your toes with a drying powder every time you change your socks. Whenever possible (and safe) walk barefoot to expose your feet to air and sunlight. Pick shoes and socks that allow perspiration to evaporate. Open sandals are good; so are leather shoes and thin cotton socks. Some socks made of synthetic materials are specifically designed to pull perspiration away from your skin, but wearing rubber soled canvas sneakers with any kind of thick socks (cotton, wool or synthetic) may allow perspiration to pool inside your shoes. Let your shoes air out between wearings. Change your socks every day. If you (or someone in your household) already has athlete's foot, change towels frequently. Wash your towels in hot water and dry them completely before you use them again. Drying them outside on a clothesline in the sun is a great idea. Not only will the towels smell wonderful, but the ultraviolet radiation in sunlight is a natural antiseptic that can destroy the fungi. Keep your shower and bathroom floor clean by washing frequently with a solution of household bleach and water, an effective disinfectant when prepared as directed on the container. And ask your doctor about the value of non-prescription fungicidal powders for your feet.

BLADDER CANCER

Known risk factors

Age:	Yes	Smoking:	Yes
Gender:	Yes	Drugs & medical procedures:	Yes
Race/ethnic group:	Yes	General health:	Yes
Family history:	No	Environment:	?
Diet:	?	Occupation:	Yes

Are you at risk?

In 1990, the American Cancer Society estimated that there would be 49,000 new cases of bladder cancer in the United States, with an estimated 9,700 people dying of the disease. Overall, a man's risk of bladder cancer is four times as high as a woman's. The older the man, the greater the risk; about 90% of all bladder tumors in men occur in men older than 50.

One possible explanation for this gender difference may be the fact that more men have smoked for longer periods of time. Tobacco smoke contains benzo[a]pyrene and other known carcinogens eliminated through the kidneys and bladder. The American Cancer Society estimates that smoking may be responsible for 47% of the bladder cancers in men and 37% in women.

The chronic irritation from bladder stones may increase risk of bladder cancer. So may the use of the anti-cancer drug cyclophosphamide (Cytoxin). In the body, cyclophosphamide is metabolized to acrolein and phosphoramide mustard, two chemicals associated with a higher risk of bladder cancer. Where you live and how you earn your living also affects your risk: Bladder cancer is more common in urban areas and among dye, rubber and leather workers who are repeatedly exposed to carcinogenic chemicals at work.

There is no proven link between diet and bladder cancer. The artificial sweetener saccharin is a weak carcinogen that has caused bladder tumors in laboratory rats who were given saccharin in amounts equivalent to what a human being would get by drinking 800 cans of saccharin-sweetened diet soda a day. However, three major studies since 1980 have failed to demonstrate any link for human beings between consuming saccharin and developing bladder cancer.

Early detection. The five-year survival rate for people whose bladder cancer is found early, before it has spread, is 88%. Only 41% of the people whose cancer is found after it spreads will be alive five years later.

Right now, the standard screening test for bladder cancer is a urinalysis to detect microscopic amounts of blood in the urine, the earliest visible sign of the disease. If this test shows blood in your urine, your doctor may advise a second urinalysis to confirm the first or an examination of other cells in the urine to determine whether there are cancer cells present, or he or she may advise cystoscopy, the insertion of a flexible tube into the bladder to allow him or her to see the surface of the bladder or obtain tissue for biopsy.

This series of tests may soon be replaced by a single, more sensitive urine test. In 1988, the National Cancer Institute (NCI) announced the development of a new screening test that identifies bladder cancer by detecting minute amounts of autocrine mobility factor (AMF) in urine. AMF is a protein in cancer cells that makes it possible for the cancer to spread throughout the body. In one study of 47 patients, the new test correctly identified the 22 who had bladder cancer. NCI expects it to take two years until the test is refined enough to be used in large-scale clinical trials.

To lower your risk of bladder cancer

If you smoke, stop. According to the American Cancer Society, a smoker's risk of bladder cancer may be double that of a non-smoker.

BREAST CANCER

Known risk factors

Age:	Yes	Smoking:	No
Gender:	Yes	Drugs & medical procedures:	Yes
Race/ethnic group:	Yes	General health:	?
Family history:	Yes	Environment:	No
Diet:	?	Occupation:	No

Are you at risk?

As of 1990, the American Cancer Society estimates that there are 150,900 new cases of breast cancer each year in the United States, and an estimated 44,300 deaths (44,000 women; 300 men). The most important risk factor for breast cancer is being a woman older than 50. Having a close female relative—sister, mother, grandmother—who had breast cancer before reaching menopause increases the risk for young women, but a study of 9,000 women at Rush-Presbyterian-St. Luke's Medical Center in Chicago released in late 1990 showed that by age 60, the risk is nearly the same for all women, whether or not they have relatives with the disease. Women who became pregnant for the first time after age 30 or who have not been pregnant at all, or who had their first menstrual period early (before age 12) and/or reached menopause late (after age 52), are also at increased risk.

Does using the pill raise your risk? Nobody really knows for sure. The information on the link between oral contraceptives and breast cancer is contradictory. For example, one British study suggested that women who use the pill for more than four years before having their first child may be three times more likely to develop breast cancer before they were 45 than women who had not used the pill. But in 1985 the National Institute of Child Health and Human Development (NICHD) in Bethesda, Maryland, announced the results of a controlled study of 4,000 women between the ages of 20 and 45 showing no increased risk of breast cancer for women who used birth control pills. Then a 1989 study of menopausal Swedish women who used estrogen to prevent osteoporosis suggested that the longer the women used the estrogen, the higher their risk of breast cancer appeared to be.

The question is further complicated by the fact that the link to breast cancer may depend on the dose and variation of estrogen a woman takes. For example, the risk appears to be lowest with conjugated estrogens, the form of estrogen most commonly prescribed in the United States. And the dose of hormones in oral contraceptives has decreased steadily over the years. At the University of Southern California (USC) School of Medicine in Los Angeles, for example, researchers found that women who used pills with high doses of progesten for four years before age 25 appeared to have a four times higher risk. It is uncertain whether or not this finding would also apply to women who have been taking the newer low-dose pills. Clearly, this is a question begging for a definitive answer.

Exposure to radiation (including medical X-rays) in childhood and adolescence may increase the risk of breast cancer later on. In 1989, researchers at the University of Rochester (New York) School of Medicine and Dentistry released the results of a study of 1,201 American women who had been given X-ray treatments as children to shrink an enlarged thymus gland. The women who had been given the radiation were 3.5 times as likely to develop breast cancer as their non-radiated sisters. No similar study has ever shown an increased risk of breast cancer among older women who undergo low-dose mammography to detect early breast tumors.

Risk factors for breast cancer are considered cumulative; the more factors you have (or are exposed to), the higher your risk. But the real question is, once you know about the risk factors, can you actually predict whether or not you will develop breast cancer? In a word, no.

First, as many as 55% of the women who develop breast cancer have *no* known risk factors. Second, risk factors for breast cancer are strictly statistical. None has been conclusively shown to have a straightforward cause-and-effect relationship with the disease. Worse yet, again with the exception of birth control pills, these are risk factors you can't do anything about. You're stuck with your gender and your relatives and your menstrual pattern and the fact that you're thirty years old and haven't yet been pregnant.

That's the bad news. The good news is that your real risk of breast cancer is almost certainly lower than you think it is. Although you have heard over and over that one out of every ten (now, one in nine) American women will develop breast cancer at some time in her life, the fact is that this familiar but misunderstood statistic applies only to the complete lifetime risk for all women in the United States from birth to death.

The true risk of developing breast cancer changes with your age. At 40, the real annual incidence of breast cancer is about one in 1,000 women; at age 60, about one in 500. At age 35, the chance that any one woman will develop breast cancer over the next 10 years is about one in 120. At age 50, it is one in 54. At age 65, it is one in 32.

Early detection. The odds on your surviving breast cancer rise dramatically if the cancer is found early. Ninety percent of the women whose cancers are found before they have spread to the lymph nodes will be alive five years later; if the cancer has spread before it is found, the five-year survival rate falls to 60%. The ACS recommends monthly self-examination, annual examinations by your doctor and a regular schedule of mammography beginning with a baseline picture at age 35 to 39 for women who have no symptoms and are not considered high risk, followed by mammography every one to two years from 40 to 49, and once a year after age 50.

One intriguing question that deserves a serious study is whether where you live affects your chances of surviving breast cancer. Right now, the states with the highest death rates for breast cancer (54.5 or more per 100,000) among white women 35 to 74 years old are Connecticut, Delaware, Hawaii, Maryland, Massachusetts, New Jersey, New York, Ohio, South Dakota and the District of Columbia. The states with the highest death rates for breast cancer (56 or more per 100,000) among black women age 35 to 74 are Kentucky, Michigan, New Jersey, Ohio and the District of Columbia. The question of why this should be so remains a mystery.

To lower your risk of breast cancer:

Eat less fat. Does a high-fat diet increase the risk of breast cancer? The evidence is mixed. Some studies have shown a link; others have not. Right now, both the American Cancer Society and the National Cancer Institute continue to recommend that you reduce fat intake to about 30 percent of total daily calories and maintain a normal body weight.

Keep your weight normal. Being obese may influence the course of breast cancer. For as-yet-unexplained reasons, breast cancer patients who are more than 20% overweight appear to have a lower chance of surviving their disease than patients who are "normal" weight.

Drink only in moderation. A 1987 study reported in *The New England Journal of Medicine* suggested an increased risk of breast cancer among women who had as few as three drinks a week. The following year, though, the results of a five-year study of more than 6,200 women conducted by the Centers for Disease Control found no association at all between breast cancer and moderate use of alcohol. Additional studies have also presented mixed evidence.

Exercise regularly. Beginning to menstruate early, having regular menstrual cycles fewer than 26 days apart or reaching menopause late are all signs that a woman's body is producing lots of estrogen and may raise her risk. The body ordinarily produces two kinds of estrogen, an active form that triggers cell division and an inactive form that does not. The active form of estrogen may be implicated in breast cancer.

Some researchers believe that women athletes who have their first periods later than age 12 (the current national average), have long or irregular cycles and get to menopause later have higher levels of the inactive estrogen. In two separate studies involving 11,000 college students and college graduates, scientists at the Harvard University School of Public Health found that women who exercise regularly twice a week, starting with two weekly sessions of ordinary college sports such as tennis, field hockey and modern dance, also have a lifelong lower rate of breast cancer. Even for those who have not been exercising twice a week since adolescence, it's never too late to start. For women, the heightened risk of most serious disease begins at menopause. Since the average age of menopause for American women is now 52, it is possible to begin exercising at age 35 and still have an average 17 years of lowered estrogen production.

CANKER SORES

Known risk factors

Age:	No	Smoking:	No
Gender:	Yes	Drugs & medical procedures:	Yes
Race/ethnic group:	No	General health:	Yes
Family history:	?	Environment:	No
Diet:	Yes	Occupation:	No

Are you at risk?

The good news about canker sores (apthous ulcers) is that they are not believed to be herpes infections nor are they early signs of oral cancer. The bad news is that these sores, which usually occur on the tongue or the inside lining of the mouth, are very common. Twenty percent of all Americans get them at one time or another.*

Susceptibility to canker sores may run in families. If one or both of your parents had them, you probably will too. Women suffer from canker sores more often than men do, but emotional and physical stress increases the risk for everybody. For example, canker sores are most common among students at exam time.

Nutrition counts. A small number of people may develop canker sores because they have a folic acid, iron or vitamin B_{12} deficiency. Eating chocolate, citrus fruits, and nuts may trigger an attack in people who have had canker sores in the past, but eliminating these foods from the diet won't prevent or cure the sores.

Any illness stresses your immune system and increases the chances of your developing canker sores. Mouth sores are a common side effect of several major anti-cancer drugs including asparaginase (Elspar), carmustine (BiCNU), chlorambucil (Leukeran), cyclophosphamide (Cytoxan), cytarabine (Cytosar-U), dacarbazine (DTIC-Dome), dactinomycin (Cosmegen), daunorubicin (Cerubidine), doxorubicin (Adriamycin), etoposide (VP-16), fluorouracil (Adrucil), floxuridine (FUDR), hydroxyurea (Hydrea), lomustine (CeeNU), mercaptopurine (Purinethol), methotrexate (Mexate), mitomycin (Mutamycin), procarbazine (Matulan, Natulan), vinblastine (Velban) and vincristine (Oncovin).

Early detection. Like the common cold, a true canker sore lasts about seven days if you treat it and a week if you don't. If yours lasts longer, check with your dentist to rule out the possibility that what looks like a canker sore may actually be an early oral cancer.

To lower your risk of canker sores

Brush or floss with care. A major cause of canker sores is minor trauma such as scratching your gum while flossing or hitting your gums or tongue with a toothbrush.

CATARACT

Known risk factors

Age:	Yes	Smoking:	?
Gender:	No	Drugs & medical procedures:	Yes
Race/ethnic group:	?	General health:	Yes
Family history:	?	Environment:	Yes
Diet:	?	Occupation:	Yes

*Fever blisters, which usually occur on the non-moving parts of the mouth—the gums and the roof of the mouth—are herpes infections. (See HERPES.)

Are you at risk?

A cataract is a loss of transparency in the lens of the eye, which, if left untreated, may lead to blindness. Cataracts may be congenital (present at birth) or they may be acquired, caused by a metabolic disease, an injury to the eye, exposure to radiation or certain drugs or simply the result of aging. They are most common among people older than 65. In fact, nearly two-thirds of all Americans age 65 to 75 have some signs of cataract; more than 3 million have cataracts serious enough to impair their vision.

Babies born to women who had herpes, rubella or syphilis while pregnant are at risk for congenital cataracts. Infants born with galactosemia (an inherited inability to digest galactose, a common sugar) may develop cataracts within weeks after birth. People with diabetes often develop cataracts at an earlier age than other people and their cataracts "mature" (grow opaque) more quickly.

Cataracts are more common in the tropics than in the temperate zones, at higher elevations and among people who work outdoors. According to the National Institute of Environmental Health Sciences, the color of your eyes may also influence your risk of cataracts. People with dark (brown, hazel) eyes who are born with more melanin in their eyes have a higher risk of cataracts than people with light eyes (blue, gray and green). The common link may be exposure to the sun's radiation, but that remains to be proven.

Does what you eat affect your risk of cataract? Maybe.

It is already known that taking very large doses of vitamin D over long periods of time can raise the risk. On the other hand, a 1989 study from the University of Western Ontario, Canada suggests that regular daily doses of the anti-oxidant vitamins C and E may be protective. The Ontario scientists compared the vitamin intake of 175 cataract patients with those of 175 people without cataracts. They found that people who had taken at least 400 IU of vitamin E a day (13 times the USRDA) had 50% fewer cataracts than people who took no vitamins at all. People who took 300 mg of vitamin C a day (the amount of vitamin C in 2¾ cups fresh orange juice) had 70% fewer cataracts. So few people took both vitamins that it was impossible to tell whether the combination would work better than either vitamin alone. It remains to be seen whether smaller doses of the vitamins will also protect against cataracts.

Finally, a word about smoking: Don't. In 1989, researchers at Johns Hopkins University released a study of 838 Maryland fishermen age 30 to 94 showing that the risk of developing cataracts by age 70 was two times higher among smokers than among those who had quit. The exact mechanism of the link between smoking and cataracts remains to be identified.

Early detection. Cataracts are detectable during an ordinary eye examination. When the lens becomes so clouded that it interferes with vision, the cataract can be removed and replaced with a permanent clear plastic lens.

In 1989, scientists at the Georgia Institute of Technology and the Joslin

Diabetes Center in Atlanta developed a laser instrument that measures the concentration of the proteins in the lens that predict the development of cataracts long before the cataracts are visible during an eye examination. A two-year clinical study has been scheduled in an attempt to set standards by which to judge the predictive value of different rates of formation and levels of proteins in the lens.

To lower your risk of cataract

Wear protective sunglasses. In 1989, acting on the theory that exposure to sunlight plays a part in cataract formation, the Food and Drug Administration and the Sunglass Association created a voluntary labeling system for rating the protection you get from non-prescription sunglasses. The color of the lenses is not important in judging whether a pair of sunglasses will protect your eyes from sun damage, but it is a safety factor for drivers. Blue lenses, which distort red and green (the color of traffic lights), are considered unsafe; gray, green and brown distort colors least.

Label Term	Level of Protection	Use
"Cosmetic"	Will block at least 70% UVB; 20% UVA; 60% visible light	Not in direct sunlight
"General purpose"	Will block at least 95% UVB; 60% UVA; 60% to 92% visible light	In moderate sunlight
"Special purpose"	Will block at least 99% UVB; 60% UVA; 97% visible light	In bright sunlight

CERVICAL CANCER

Known risk factors

Age:	Yes	Smoking:	?
Gender:	Yes	Drugs & medical procedures:	No
Race/ethnic group:	Yes	General health:	?
Family history:	No	Environment:	No
Diet:	No	Occupation:	No

Are you at risk?

Cancer of the cervix (the opening of the uterus into the vagina) is the second most common malignancy of the female reproductive organs. It strikes approximately 13,500 American women every year. Most cases occur among women older than 55, with the highest rates among women older than 65. This cancer is more common among poor women, perhaps because they do not have access to a yearly gynecological test to detect pre-cancerous changes in the tissues of the cervix. In America, Hispanic women have a risk twice that of white women; the risk for black women and American Indian women is slightly higher.

Your chance of developing cervical cancer may also rise if you are infected with human papilloma virus (HPV), but the herpes virus, once thought to be implicated as a cause of cervical cancer, has been exonerated. There is no known connection between this virus and cancer of the cervix.

There are more than 50 different types of papilloma viruses, some of which are known to cause venereal warts. Others have been found inside cancer cells from 90 to 95 percent of all women with cancer of the cervix, but it is not yet certain whether the virus entered the cell before or after it became cancerous. Being sexually active with more than one partner increases your risk of cervical cancer, probably because it increases your risk of acquiring HPV. Multiple pregnancies may also increase the possibility of your acquiring an HPV infection, perhaps because immune function is reduced during pregnancy or because an injury during delivery allows an HPV infection to take hold.

In 1989, the National Cancer Institute (NCI) released the results of a study of women in four South American Countries, which showed that women who had experienced 10 or more pregnancies had a risk of cervical cancer four times that of women who had only been pregnant once or twice.

Is cervical cancer a smoking-related disease? Maybe. Most of the more than 10 studies of smoking and cervical cancer suggest that women who smoke are at higher risk. At least one study has also suggested that passive smoking (being exposed to other people's cigarette, cigar or pipe smoke) may also raise the risk.

In a 1988 study of 670 women, 266 with cancer of the cervix and 408 healthy controls, researchers at the University of Utah Medical School found that women who smoke or are exposed to other people's smoke for three hours or more every day had a risk of cervical cancer three times higher than women who were not exposed to smoke. The unanswered question is whether inhaling the carcinogens in tobacco smoke makes the cervix more vulnerable to infections that trigger cervical cancer or whether women who smoke (or associate with people who smoke) are likely to behave in ways that increase their chance of acquiring an infection in the first place.

Early detection. Seventy-seven to 99% of all women whose cervical cancer is identified when it is confined to the cervix will be alive five years later. The figure drops to 65% for women whose cancer is diagnosed when it has moved beyond the cervix, but has not invaded the pelvic wall; 25% for women whose cancer has spread into the wall of the pelvis; and 5% for women whose cancer has spread beyond the pelvis.

The screening test for cervical cancer is the Papanicolaou (Pap) test, during which your doctor scrapes a sample of cells from the cervix for examination under a microscope. The results are classified as Class I (no abnormal cells); Class II (some atypical cells, perhaps due to an infection); Class III (some cells that suggest cancerous changes); Class IV and V (cancer cells present).

If the Pap test shows suspicious cells, your doctor will want to examine the cervical area more completely by culdoscopy, the introduction of a flexible lighted tube into the area, or to obtain more tissue for biopsy by removing a small sample of tissue (punch biopsy) or a cone-shaped section of the cervix (cone biopsy). The cone biopsy may cure as well as diagnose if it removes all the affected tissue.

To lower your risk of cervical cancer

Have a Pap test once a year. In the mid-1980s, the American Cancer Society issued a controversial recommendation that women age 20 to 65 did not need to have a Pap test more than once every three years after having two negative tests one year apart. (Women who are sexually active before age 20 were advised to begin the Pap test earlier.) The recommendation, which was considered cost-effective, was defended on the basis that cervical cancer is ordinarily a slow-growing cancer that can take two to ten years to progress from localized (*in situ*) to invasive disease.

Be that as it may, there are atypical cases that spread more quickly. As a result, many gynecologists continue to recommend a Pap test every year, especially for women who are sexually active with more than one partner. This point of view is bolstered by the fact that the Pap test, which can find more than 90% of all early cancers of the cervix, is believed to have reduced deaths from cancer of the cervix by more than 50% among American women. Many experts believe that deaths from cervical cancer could be eliminated entirely if every woman had a Pap test once a year.

Today, the ACS recommends that after three or more consecutive normal Pap tests, the test may be performed less frequently at the discretion of the doctor.

Practice safer sex. Your risk of cervical cancer may depend not only your sexual behavior but upon your partner's as well. The 1988 NCI South American study suggested that monogamous married women whose husbands admitted to more than 25 different sex partners had a risk of cervical cancer twice that of monogamous married women whose husbands had six or fewer sexual partners during their lifetimes. Whether or not the men were circumcised did not seem to alter their partner's risk one way or the other.

Your partner's use of a condom may reduce your risk of acquiring HPV.

The correct use of condoms begins with storing them properly in a cool, dry place to protect the latex from drying out. The condom should be put on gently to avoid tearing. Leave room at the tip to accommodate the ejaculate. After ejaculation, your partner should withdraw the penis with the condom still in place, holding it close against the base of the penis to avoid spilling any ejaculate. Discard all used condoms; never try to wash them out and use them again.

CHICKEN POX (VARICELLA)

Known risk factors

Age:	Yes	Smoking:	No
Gender:	No	Drugs & medical procedures:	No
Race/ethnic group:	No	General health:	No
Family history:	No	Environment:	No
Diet:	No	Occupation:	No

Are you at risk?

Anyone who has not had chicken pox is at risk anytime he or she is exposed to someone who has chicken pox or shingles and can transmit the varicella virus that causes both diseases. The itchy, uncomfortable illness is highly communicable in the 10 days to three weeks after infection. Newborn infants often have a transient immunity from maternal antibodies acquired in uterus that protects them for the first six months of life.

In children, chicken pox is usually an uneventful disease, but it can be severe or even fatal for leukemia patients or people who are taking steroid drugs. In newborns or adults, it may lead to pneumonia.

Early detection. Chickenpox is diagnosed by its characteristic crusty, itchy rash.

To lower your risk of chicken pox

Studies to produce a vaccine to protect against chicken pox are currently under way, but right now, there is no long-term immunization available. Chicken pox can be prevented or its effects ameliorated by administering serum made from the blood of people who are recovering from chickenpox or herpes zoster (see SHINGLES), but this treatment is usually reserved for people with leukemia or whose immune system has been weakened by medication or a viral infection.

CHLAMYDIA

Known risk factors

Age:	No	Smoking:	No
Gender:	No	Drugs & medical procedures:	No
Race/ethnic group:	No	General health:	No
Family history:	No	Environment:	No
Diet:	No	Occupation:	No

Are you at risk?

Chlamydia is a sexually transmitted disease (STD). According to the American Social Health Association, it may affect 4 million Americans a year, three times as many as get gonorrhea, and 40 times as many as get syphilis. Like other STDs, chlamydia is most prevalent among young, unmarried men and women, not because they are more susceptible, but because they are more sexually active. The wider the circle of sexual contacts, the higher the risk. Both sexes are at risk, but chlamydia is more common among women and its consequences are likely to be more severe.

Early detection. Untreated chlamydial infections may be extremely painful conditions that cause permanent damage to the reproductive system, including infertility. Women who have chlamydia while pregnant may miscarry or pass the infection along to their babies who pick it up as they travel through the birth canal. In a newborn, chlamydia is a potentially fatal infection that most commonly causes infections of the eye, ear and lungs.

Chlamydia may cause symptoms such as a discharge from the penis or vagina, a burning discomfort when you urinate, abdominal pain and a low-grade fever that resemble those of many other STDs. But it may also develop silently, which is why it is important to be tested if you are sexually active.

To lower your risk of chlamydia

Practice safer sex. Limiting the number of people with whom you have sex and using a latex condom plus a spermicidal foam containing the ingredient nonoxynol-9 every time you have sexual intercourse can reduce your risk of acquiring chlamydia.

Using condoms correctly begins with storing them properly in a cool, dry place to protect the latex from drying out. Put it on gently to avoid tearing and leave room at the tip to accommodate the ejaculate. After ejaculation, withdraw the penis with the condom still in place, holding it close against the base of the penis to avoid spilling any ejaculate. Discard all used condoms; never try to wash them out and use them again.

CHOLERA

Known risk factors

Age:	Yes	Smoking:	No
Gender:	No	Drugs & medical procedures:	No
Race/ethnic group:	No	General health:	No
Family history:	No	Environment:	Yes
Diet:	Yes	Occupation:	No

Are you at risk?

Cholera is disease of societies with poor sanitation. It is endemic in parts of Asia, Africa and the Middle East. Cholera is acquired only by consuming food or water contaminated with the bacterium *Vibrio cholera*, which is found in the excrement of infected people who may (or may not) have symptoms such as profuse diarrhea, intestinal cramps, vomiting and dehydration.

Your risk of getting cholera rises or falls depending on where you live, work or travel. In Asia, the Middle East and Africa, where cholera is endemic, you are at high risk. Although there are pockets of imported cholera throughout southern Europe, you are generally at low risk in western and northern Europe, and you are at lowest risk in the United States, where sanitary waste disposal and adequate purification of water systems have virtually eliminated the disease except along the Gulf coasts of Louisiana and Texas where since 1978 more than 40 people have developed cholera after eating seafood from these coastal waters that had been inadequately cooked or drinking water that had been inadequately purified.

In areas where cholera is endemic, the largest outbreaks are likely to occur in the spring and summer; a child's risk is 10 times that of an adult whose repeated exposure to the disease has given him some immunity. Because *Vibrio cholera* is sensitive to stomach acid, people who produce large amounts of stomach acid are at lower risk.

Early detection. A diagnosis of cholera is confirmed by the discovery of the *Vibrio cholera* organisms in a stool sample. The quicker the confirmation, the faster treatment with antibiotics can begin to wipe out the cholera organisms that cause the profuse diarrhea that can lead to dehydration and, in extreme circumstances, death.

To lower your risk of cholera

Practice proper sanitation. Eat carefully when you travel. If you are in an area where the sanitation is dubious, follow all the protective rules to the letter: Avoid uncooked fruits and vegetables, never drink any water that isn't boiled, take your cold drinks without ice, brush your teeth with bottled water. Wherever you are, always wash your hands after using the bathroom.

Vaccination. If you are planning to travel to an area where cholera is endemic, consult your doctor about cholera vaccination. The vaccine gives only temporary protection, though; you will need booster shots every four to six months. If, despite precautions, you find yourself in a household where there is a person with cholera, ask your doctor about taking tetracycline to prevent a cholera infection.

CLEFT PALATE

Known risk factors

Age:	?	Smoking:	No
Gender:	No	Drugs & medical procedures:	Yes
Race/ethnic group:	?	General health:	No
Family history:	Yes	Environment:	No
Diet:	No	Occupation:	No

Are you at risk?

Cleft lip and palate are among the most common of the major birth defects, occurring in one in every 700 to 800 babies born live in the United States. In this country, cleft palate occurs most frequently among Oriental babies, less frequently among white babies and least frequently among blacks. Your family history affected your own risk of being born with, or having a baby with, cleft lip or palate. If your mother or father had a cleft lip or palate, with no other birth defects, you had a 4% chance of being born with one. If one of your parents or a sister or brother born before you had a cleft lip or palate with no other birth defects, your risk nearly doubled to 7%. Naturally, the same odds apply to any children you may have.

Whether or not a pregnant woman's use of certain drugs can increase her chances of producing a baby with cleft lip or palate remains open to suspicion. Pregnant laboratory animals fed amphetamines, chlordiazepoxide (Librium), corticosteroids and diazepam (Valium) were more likely than others to give birth to offspring with this defect, but there there is no evidence that the same effect occurs in human beings.

Early detection. Both cleft lip and cleft palate can be identified in the fetus by sonography or in a newborn at birth. Both can be corrected surgically.

To lower your child's risk of cleft palate

Avoid unnecessary drugs while pregnant. Although there is no absolute proof that drugs taken while pregnant can cause cleft lip or palate in the fetus, this is a sensible precaution.

Seek genetic counseling. If you have a family history of cleft lip or cleft palate, you may wish to speak with a genetic counselor who can realistically evaluate your risk of having a baby with a cleft lip or palate and discuss treatment options.

COLORECTAL CANCER

Known risk factors

Age:	Yes	Drugs & medical procedures:	No
Gender:	?	General health:	No
Race/ethnic group:	No	Environment:	No
Family history:	Yes	Occupation:	No
Diet:	Yes		

Are you at risk?

There are an estimated 155,000 new cases of colorectal cancers in the United States each year and an estimated 60,900 deaths, which makes the death rate from colorectal cancers second only to that of lung cancer. Cancer of the colon is more common among women, while cancers of the rectum are slightly more common among men. In 1990, the American Cancer Society predicted an estimated 58,000 new cases of colon cancer among American women compared with 52,000 new cases among American men. Twenty-seven thousand women were expected to die of the disease, making colon cancers the third leading cause of cancer deaths among women, right behind lung cancers and breast cancers. At the same time, the ACS predicted 24,000 new cases of cancer of the rectum among men, and 21,000 new cases among women. For both men and women, the risk rises with age; colorectal cancers are most common after age 50.

Both men and women are considered at high risk for colorectal cancer if they or their close relatives (mother, father, sister, brother or grandparents) have colon cancer or colon polyps or inflammatory bowel disease, and recent Japanese and British studies of patients with the hereditary disease called familial polyposis *coli* (also known as familial adenomatous polyposis) show that people with this condition, who develop multiple non-cancerous polyps in their intestines, are also at high risk. The family predisposition to colorectal cancers seems to involve an extremely complex series of events that lead to the loss of anti-cancer genes ("anti-oncogenes") on several different chromosomes. In a 1988 study of colon tumors at Johns Hopkins University in Maryland, researchers found that about half of the more advanced tumors contained mutated versions of the *ras* genes (a gene often associated with tumor formation), suggesting that cancers of the colon and rectum may be triggered by genetic changes that set off the *ras* gene while blocking the protective effect of anti-oncogenes.

There is a clearer link between diet and colon cancer than between diet and other forms of cancer. Colon and rectal cancers show up most frequently in societies where people eat foods low in fiber and high in animal protein, fat and refined carbohydrates. Some experts suggest that a high-fat diet may be hazardous because it contains natural carcinogens. Others believe that a diet high in fat triggers a greater secretion of bile acids, which, while necessary to the digestion of fats, have also been shown (in laboratory animals) to increase the growth of tumors in the colon. Still others theorize that the bacteria that live naturally in our digestive tract may turn something in the high-fat foods into carcinogens.

A high-fiber diet seems to be protective, perhaps because it reduces the harmful effects of bile acids or because it speeds food and waste through our bodies before the bacteria can act on them. However, still unanswered are questions about which kinds of fiber are truly protective and whether they work on their own or only in conjunction with a low-fat diet.

In studies with laboratory animals, for example, the soluble fiber in oat bran and fruits actually seemed to increase tumor formation by increasing the secretion of bile acids, while the insoluble fiber in whole wheat products consistently helped to reduce tumors. In a 1988 University of Utah School of Medicine study of 622 white, predominantly Mormon Utah residents, half of whom had colon cancer, found that men seemed to reduce their risk of colon cancer best by eating a diet high in fruit; women seemed to reduce their risk by eating a diet high in vegetables; and neither got any particular protection from a diet high in grains.

In an effort to resolve the issue, the National Cancer Institute (NCI) in 1988 announced a three-year project designed to analyze the specific fiber content of 400 common foods. Based on these analyses, later research may finally figure out which kinds of fiber are protective and which are not.

Early detection. The earlier a colorectal cancer is found, the better your chances of survival will be. The five-year survival rate for people whose colon cancer is found before it spreads is 90%; for cancers of the rectum, 80%. The rates fall to 40% and 30% respectively if the cancers have spread.

In order to find these cancers early, before any symptoms appear, the American Cancer Society recommends a digital rectal exam every year after you reach age 40; a guaiac test for hidden blood in your stool every year after you get to be 50; and proctosigmoidoscopy—an examination during which your doctor inspects your rectum and colon with a hollow, lighted, rigid scope or a longer flexible tube—two years in a row after age 50, then every three to five years after you get two cancer-free results.

If you have a close relative (grandmother, grandfather, mother, father, sister or brother) who has had a colorectal cancer, you should talk with your doctor about the advisability of making this regime a part of your regular medical care regardless of your age.

To lower your risk of colorectal cancer

Reduce the amount of fat in your diet. How much fat raises your risk of colorectal cancers? Nobody knows for sure, but it is reasonable to assume that more is worse and less is better. The American Heart Association's guidelines, which suggest that you keep the fat in your diet to 30% or less of your total calories, is almost certainly an acceptable starting point.

COMMON COLD

Known risk factors

Age:	Yes	Smoking:	No
Gender:	?	Drugs & medical procedures:	No
Race/ethnic group:	No	General health:	Yes
Family history:	No	Environment:	Yes
Diet:	No	Occupation:	No

Are you at risk?

If you think the season affects your risk of catching a cold, you're absolutely right. From December to March, during the three winter months, at least 50% of all Americans will have caught cold, some of us more than once. In summer, by contrast, only 20% of us get colds. Children younger than five are the most likely candidates for a cold; they have an average of six to 12 each year.

There is a simple scientific reason for this. Every time you have a cold, you acquire immunity to the virus that caused it. There are nearly 200 different viruses now known to cause colds, and it takes time to run through the list. Young children have had less contact with these viruses; therefore, they have less immunity and more colds. By the time a person gets to be 25 to 30, the average number of colds he gets each year drops to six. After 30, it goes down to two or three. Boys catch cold more often than girls, but mothers get more colds than fathers do, probably because they are more likely to be home with the sick child. Regardless of age and sex, your chance of catching a cold rises with fatigue, emotional stress or respiratory allergies. Women are most vulnerable at the mid-point in their menstrual cycles.

Early detection. If your cold lasts longer than a week or is accompanied by a high fever or a cough that brings up blood or green or yellow mucus, see your doctor who can distinguish between a cold and an allergy or a bacterial infection, each of which requires specific medication.

To lower your risk of a common cold

Wash your hands. One common way to acquire someone else's cold is to shake hands with him or her or use his or her towel or touch or drink from a glass he or she has used and then touch your own mouth, nose or eyes (all ports of entry for the cold virus). By the same token, you may pass your own cold along to others by failing to wash your hands after covering your mouth or nose when you cough or blow and then touching other people.

Eat well, sleep well and live well. The better you feel, the better your chance of resisting the cold virus. Not a single scientific study has shown that taking massive amounts of vitamin C every day will reduce your risk of catching a cold, but after you have one, it's a different story. A number of studies, both here and in Europe, have suggested that taking large amounts of vitamin C as soon as you get a cold may shorten the time you are sick by a day or so.

But check with your doctor before self-medicating. Massive doses of vitamin C may increase the likelihood of kidney stones or constipation. Pregnant women who take amounts of vitamin C in excess of the recommended dietary allowance (RDA) may give birth to babies who need larger-than-normal amounts of vitamin C and who temporarily develop scurvy on a diet containing a normal amount of the vitamin.

CONSTIPATION

Known risk factors

Age:	Yes	Smoking:	No
Gender:	No	Drugs & medical procedures:	Yes
Race/ethnic group:	No	General health:	Yes
Family history:	No	Environment:	No
Diet:	Yes	Occupation:	Yes

Are you at risk?

According to the National Center for Health Statistics, about 3.6 million Americans a year report frequent constipation, our most common gastrointestinal complaint.

The risk of being constipated rises when you do not consume enough high-fiber food, a common problem with young women on reducing diets. Being pregnant increases a woman's chance of being constipated. As the pregnant uterus gets bigger, it presses against the rectum and colon, making defecation less comfortable. And during pregnancy a woman's body secretes additional progesterone, a hormone that relaxes the smooth muscles in the intestinal tract, slowing the passage of food and waste through the body.

Getting older may also increase the risk of constipation. Food is pushed through the digestive tract by rhythmical, regular intestinal contractions known as peristalsis. As we get older, these contractions may become less forceful, and food takes longer to move along. Once your doctor has confirmed that your constipation is the result of normal aging, not a medical problem such as an underactive thyroid (which can slow down body functions) or a cancer of the colon (which might block the digestive tract), the simplest remedy may be an increase in dietary fiber. Healthy people who are free of complicating gastrointestinal disease, who stay active and continue to eat a diet rich in fiber are unlikely to be constipated, no matter how old they are.

People with psychological problems, particularly depression, are more likely to be constipated. How we feel about the process of elimination can also cause problems. If we either ignore our body's natural signals to defecate or become obsessively concerned with maintaining a rigidly regular schedule in the bathroom, constipation is likely to be the consequence.

Finally, a whole slew of medicines can cause constipation. Among the most common are the analgesics codeine, propoxyphene (Darvon), pentazocaine (Talwin) and meperidine (Demerol); the antacid aluminum carbonate; the antispasmodics atropine, benzotropine, dicyclomine, propentheline (Pro-bantine) and tridihexethyl (Pathilon); some antihistamines such as diphenhydramine (Benadryl, Benylin, Compoz, among others) and pheniramine (Citra forte, among others) and tripelenamine (PBZ); tricyclic antidepressants such as amitryptiline (Elavil, Endep) and doxepin (Adapin, Sinequan); the MAO inhibitor tranylcypromine (Parnate); and tranquilizers including chlordiazepoxide (Valium) and diazepam (Librium).

Early detection. First, a definition. Constipation is not simply the failure to have a bowel movement every day. There is no single "healthy" pattern of defecation; a normal pattern can range anywhere from three times a day to three times a week. Constipation is any decrease from your own pattern.

There are some serious diseases and medical conditions that can make you constipated. An obstruction in the rectum or the intestinal tract, for example, may cause pencil-thin stools. Bleeding from a colorectal cancer or an intestinal irritation may make stool bloody or black. These symptoms, as well as any case of sudden, severe constipation, any constipation with pain, or any prolonged unexplained constipation should be reported to your doctor.

To lower your risk of constipation

Consume enough fiber-rich food. People who go on a reducing diet occasionally cut their food intake so drastically that they just don't eat enough fiber to produce a daily bowel movement. Insoluble fiber (the fiber in wheat bran, fruit and vegetable skins and those small hard granules in pears) relieves constipation by producing bulky stool that moves more quickly through your intestines. Soluble fiber (the fiber in oat bran, beans, barley and the flesh of fruits and vegetables) is thought less likely to do this, but individual reactions to specific fibers can vary. Some people find soluble fiber just as effective as insoluble fiber.

Don't forget to drink water. It helps bulk up stool and move it through the intestinal tract. As for that old-fashioned home remedy, a glass of warm water first thing in the morning: It may work by stimulating gastric juices and producing a mild laxative effect.

Do not use laxatives unless absolutely necessary. Using laxatives too often can impair the normal function of your bowel so that you become dependent on the laxatives and cannot defecate without them.

If you choose to use laxatives occasionally, the FDA Advisory Review Panel on OTC Laxative, Antidiarrheal, Emetic and Antiemetic Drug Products recommends using those that contain safe and effective bulk-forming ingredients such as psyillium, the active ingredient in Metamucil and Konsyl.

CYSTIC FIBROSIS

Known risk factors

Age:	No	Smoking:	No
Gender:	No	Drugs & medical procedures:	No
Race/ethnic group:	Yes	General health:	No
Family history:	Yes	Environment:	No
Diet:	No	Occupation:	No

Are you at risk?

Cystic fibrosis, which causes obstructive sticky mucus in the lungs and interferes with digestion, is the most common fatal hereditary disorder among white people in the United States. One in every 20 to 25 white Americans carries the CF gene; approximately one in every 1,600 to 2,000 white American babies is born with CF. Black Americans are at much lower risk, with an incidence of one in every 17,000 births. The disease is virtually unknown among African blacks. Among Orientals, it occurs approximately once in every 90,000 births. There are approximately 30,000 Americans with cystic fibrosis; 400 new cases are diagnosed each year.

Early detection. Cystic fibrosis is caused by a recessive gene. If you inherit the gene from one parent but not the other, you won't show any symptoms but you can pass the gene along to your children. If you have a brother or sister with cystic fibrosis, there is a 66% chance of your having the gene. If you marry a person who also has a gene for cystic fibrosis, there is a 25% chance that any child you conceive will inherit two genes for cystic fibrosis and develop the disease.

If you have had one child with CF, you know that you and your partner are CF carriers. If you become pregnant again, it is usually possible to diagnose or rule out CF in the fetus by amniocentesis or chorionic villa sampling that allows a direct gene analysis or a comparison of the fetal genetic pattern with that of your affected child and yourselves.

It is possible to diagnose CF soon after birth. Early diagnosis may help minimize CF lung damage (most children who die of cystic fibrosis, die of an infection that began in the lungs) and to treat the digestive problems that can keep a child from growing and developing. In newborns, cystic fibrosis can usually be diagnosed by measuring the amount of sodium and chloride in the babies' sweat (higher-than-normal levels confirm the disease). Getting enough perspiration from a newborn baby can be difficult, and the sample must be sent to a special laboratory for analysis, which can be time-consuming.

A newly invented "skin patch" (a disposable piece of plastic containing chemicals sensitive to sodium and chloride) can be strapped on the baby's arm and read instantly. The device, which is currently in development, could eventually make tentative diagnosis a snap. Another screening method is to measure the amount of immunoreactive tryptinogen (IRT), a blood protein, in a blood sample such as a drop of blood on a piece of laboratory paper.

In older children, cystic fibrosis might be mistaken for asthma, bronchitis, pneumonia or other respiratory problems and its digestive symptoms can mimic those of some inherited metabolic conditions such as celiac disease. A diagnosis of cystic fibrosis can be confirmed by the sweat test.

To reduce your child's risk of cystic fibrosis

Genetic counseling. If you have a history of CF, genetic counselors can help you calculate your risk of having a child with CF (see above).

In 1988, researchers at the University of Michigan at Ann Arbor announced the identification of the CF gene. It is expected that this discovery will soon lead to a simple test to identify most CF carriers before they begin to have children.

DEPRESSION

Known risk factors

Age:	Yes	Smoking:	No
Gender:	Yes	Drugs & medical procedures:	Yes
Race/ethnic group:	No	General health:	Yes
Family history:	Yes	Environment:	?
Diet:	No	Occupation:	No

Are you at risk?

Although depression may occur in people who have no family history of the illness, the single most important risk factor is having had relatives who suffer from depression. When one identical twin suffers from depression, 33% to 75% of the time the other will, too. If your mother, father, sister or brother has had depression, your risk is increased.

What you inherit is a vulnerability that appears to make you susceptible to depression when you are faced with a loss such as that of a loved one or the loss of a job or the loss of control over your life due to a serious illness.

No one has yet shown exactly how the vulnerability to depression is transmitted from one generation to the next. Many researchers suspect that the inherited defect may be an abnormality in the mechanism that regulates neurotransmitters, chemicals that are considered important in determining mood because they transmit impulses within the brain. Anti-depressant drugs work by boosting the action of specific neurotransmitters linked to the prevention of depression.

At present, the person most likely to develop depression is middle-aged and female. Women seem to be at highest risk between the ages of 35 and 45; after that, their risk declines. A man's risk of depression, on the other hand, rises with age.

There are several theories as to why women appear to be at higher risk. Some explanations focus on the physical fact of a woman's more volatile hormone system—the endocrine changes that come with the menstrual cycle, pregnancy and menopause. Women also have more variable production of thyroid hormones and higher levels of monoamine oxidase, an enzyme that acts on neurotransmitters.

Other explanations focus on the psychological and cultural effects of a society that once devalued motherhood and home-making ("women's work") while denying women the opportunity to develop other avenues to self-esteem. Women whose only source of self-esteem is raising their children may be vulnerable to depression when the children leave to make lives of their own (the "empty nest syndrome"). It may be significant that as women have developed other avenues to self-esteem, including but not limited to work outside the home, the incidence of reported depression among men has begun to move very slowly upward, toward equality between the sexes.

Right now, there is no known relationship between your social class, your educational level, your race or your occupation and your risk of clinical depression. On the other hand, your family's cultural heritage may affect how you behave when you are suffering from a mood disorder.

Regardless of your background, some physical illnesses, such as hepatitis, influenza, multiple sclerosis, pancreatic cancer and vitamin B deficiencies may change your body in ways that raise your risk of depression. So may some medications, such as those used to treat high blood pressure. People who have severe heart disease or emphysema may be depressed because of a lack of oxygen, as well as the psychological effects of the disease. People who are obese may be depressed because of a poor body image.

Early detection. People who suffer from depression are not just having a bad day or week. In fact, their misery may seem wildly out of place because their lives seem so successful. According to the American Psychiatric Association, a diagnosis of depression requires that at least four of the following symptoms be present for at least two weeks or more:

1. A change in appetite. You may be eating much more (or less) than normal or you may have lost (or gained) a significant amount of weight.
2. A dramatic change in sleep patterns. You may be suffering from insomnia that keeps you from falling asleep or that wakes you up early in the morning and keeps you from falling asleep again, or you may be sleeping unusually long hours.
3. A sudden loss of energy that leaves you tired all the time.
4. A loss of pleasure in work, family or friends and a dramatic decrease in your desire for sex and the pleasure you get from sex.
5. An unreasonable, overwhelming feeling of worthlessness and guilt.
6. An inability to concentrate or think clearly.
7. An increased preoccupation with death and suicide, that may include suicide attempts.

To lower your risk of depression

Seek treatment. There is no way to eliminate your inherited vulnerability to depression, but both medication and psychiatric or psychological counseling can reduce the incidence and severity of depressive episodes.

Exactly how psychotherapy (the "talking cure") relieves depression remains a mystery, but the action of the anti-depressant drugs is clear-cut.

Tricyclic anti-depressants such as amitriptyline (Elavil) work by keeping the nerve cells that release serotonin and a second neurotransmitter, norepinephrine, from re-absorbing these chemicals so that they continue to transmit messages through the nervous system. Monoamine oxidase inhibitors (MAOIs) such as Nardil and Parnate inactivate enzymes that would otherwise destroy serotonin and norepinephrine. A new class of antidepressant drugs such as fluoxetine (Prozac) works like the tricyclics but targets only serotonin.

For as-yet-unexplained reasons, some people find that regular exercise relieves some depression.

DIABETES (DIABETES MELLITUS)

Known risk factors

Age:	Yes	Smoking:	No
Gender:	Yes	Drugs & medical procedures:	No
Race/ethnic group:	Yes	General health:	Yes
Family history:	Yes	Environment:	?
Diet:	No	Occupation:	No

Are you at risk?

More than 11 million Americans have diabetes. An additional 500,000 cases are diagnosed each year, and 150,000 people die of the disease, making diabetes our sixth leading cause of death.

The tendency to diabetes is inherited. You are at risk if you have close relatives who have diabetes, although nine out of every 10 people who have a brother or sister with diabetes do not develop diabetes themselves. Your risk is higher if you are Native American, Hispanic or black. In some Indian tribes, 20% of all the adults have diabetes; 20% of all people with diabetes are Hispanic or black.

Giving birth to more than one baby who weighed more than nine pounds at birth may be an early symptom of diabetes; perhaps the baby gained weight in the womb because it absorbed extra sugar circulating in your bloodstream. (This excess sugar is in your blood because your diabetes makes it impossible for your body to metabolize all the sugar you eat. Although people who have diabetes may need to restrict their sugar intake, a diet high in sugar does not cause diabetes in the first place.)

Women are also at risk for gestational diabetes, a temporary form of glucose (sugar) intolerance that appears in the last six months of pregnancy and usually goes away once the baby is born.

Ninety percent of all Americans with diabetes have non-insulin dependent diabetes (also known as Type II diabetes or NIDDM), the form of the disease that usually shows up in people older than 40. Being overweight is a definite risk factor, perhaps because excess body fat interferes with the body's ability to use the insulin it produces. (The high incidence of diabetes among American Indians seems to correlate with their equally high incidence of obesity.) Being fat above the waist ("apple-shaped") is considered a greater risk than being fat below the waist ("pear-shaped").

Ten percent of the Americans with diabetes have insulin-dependent diabetes (also known as Type I diabetes or IDDM), the more serious form of the disease. Type I diabetes is usually diagnosed in childhood. Some experts believe that it is triggered by a viral infection or a reaction of the immune system, and in 1988, the Diabetes Epidemiology Research Group released the results of data from 15 countries showing that a child's chance of developing insulin-dependent diabetes is higher in a cold climate than in a warm one. For example, in the United States, the incidence of diabetes among children younger than 15 ranges from a low of 9.4 per 100,000 in San Diego, California, to a high of 20.8 per 100,000 in Rochester, Minnesota. This is the second study to show a clear, but as yet unexplained link between climate and the risk of IDDM.

Early detection. Because having diabetes increases the risk of blindness, heart disease, kidney disease, circulatory problems and miscarriage, as well as birth defects in babies born to women who have diabetes while pregnant, it is important to find and treat the disease as early as possible.

The basic screening test for diabetes is a urinalysis to detect higher-than-normal levels of unmetabolized sugar in your urine. If your urinalysis shows high levels of sugar and you have other symptoms of diabetes such as frequent urination and recent, unexplained weight loss, continuing thirst and fatigue, the next diagnostic step is a blood test to measure the level of glucose (sugar) in your blood. For adults who are not pregnant, a blood glucose level higher than 200 mg/dl after eating normally or higher than 140 mg/dL on two occasions after fasting or higher than 200 mg/dL on two occasions after drinking 2.5 oz of a special glucose solution indicates diabetes.

To lower your risk of diabetes

Keep your weight down to a normal range. Statistics from the U.S. Department of Health and Human Services (HHS) show that 85% of the people with non-insulin-dependent diabetes are at least 20% overweight. Although some people with Type II diabetes do need insulin injections, many others find that when they lose weight, their diabetes is controlled or disappears entirely.

DIPHTHERIA

Known risk factors

Age:	No	Smoking:	No
Gender:	No	Drugs & medical procedures:	No
Race/ethnic group:	No	General health:	No
Family history:	No	Environment:	No
Diet:	No	Occupation:	No

Are you at risk?

Calculating your risk of catching diphtheria when you are exposed to someone who has it is pretty much a cut-and-dried affair. With immunization, your risk is virtually nil. Without it, your risk is high.

Where you live can be a factor in determining whether or not you are likely to be exposed. Diphtheria infections of the respiratory system are principally a disease of the temperate zone, passed from person to person by breathing in the bacteria. Infections of the skin (cutaneous diphtheria), transmitted by skin contact with a diphtheria patient's nasal secretions, were once exclusive to tropical areas. But since 1980, for reasons that have not yet been explained, pockets of infection have begun to appear among indigent adults in the American and Canadian northwest and American Indians in the southwestern United States.

Early detection. Diphtheria organisms flourish in the tissues of the nose and throat, producing toxins that spread through the bloodstream to damage other organs such as the heart, the liver, the nervous system and the kidneys. The toxins may paralyze the cranial nerves that enable you to speak and swallow, the muscles of the diaphragm that facilitate breathing and the muscles that control arms and legs. Untreated diphtheria can cause death by respiratory or heart failure. People who recover without being treated with antimicrobial drugs may still harbor diphtheria organisms in their respiratory system. They are symptom-free carriers who can pass their infection on to other people.

The characteristic sign of respiratory diphtheria is the appearance of a membrane-like tissue growing across the back of the throat. The sores of cutaneous diphtheria resemble infected mosquito bites or the sores of the bacterial infection impetigo, small and round with a thick, yellowish crust. A diagnosis of diphtheria is confirmed by finding the diphtheria organism, *Corynebacterium diphtherium*, in a culture of these tissues.

To lower your risk of diphtheria

Immunization. You can be immunized against diphtheria with a series of five injections of toxoid (toxin that has been treated to destroy its ability to harm you while retaining its ability to prod your body into producing antibodies to the diphtheria bacteria). Diphtheria toxoid is usually given to children in combination with pertussis (whooping cough) and tetanus toxoid. The combination is known as DPT. Previously immunized adults should get a booster shot every 10 years or when exposed to the disease.

EATING DISORDERS

Known risk factors

Age:	Yes	Smoking:	No
Gender:	Yes	Drugs & medical procedures:	No
Race/ethnic group:	Yes	General health:	Yes
Family history:	?	Environment:	No
Diet:	No	Occupation:	No

Are you at risk?

Millions of us go on reducing diets, lose weight and then go back to eating normally while trying to hold onto our newly slim figures.

A small percentage of dieters will begin to enjoy losing weight so much that they push it past the limits of good health to the pathological refusal to eat known as anorexia nervosa. Among women, the dividing line between normal dieting and anorexia nervosa is crossed when the dieter loses so much weight that she ceases to menstruate. At that point, anorexia nervosa has all the hallmarks of an addiction to losing weight.

Anorexia nervosa and bulimia (self-induced vomiting) occur almost exclusively among young, affluent women in cultures where skinniness is admired. They are rarely found among black and Oriental women, in areas where there is a real threat of famine or among men (who account for only 5% of the reported cases). The people at highest risk are middle- and upperclass young women who may be compulsive or meticulously neat or have psychological problems that involve a fear of growing up as evidenced by a desire to retain a child's slim body.

Overall, anorexia is estimated to occur in about one person in every 100,000, but the incidence among psychologically vulnerable young women may run as high as one in every 100 to 250. The incidence of bulimia is harder to pin down because the condition can be hidden, but some experts estimate that as many as one in every five women college students may be bulimic. As many as 50% of all anorectics will develop a form of bulimia that involves periodic binge eating.

Early detection. Anorexia and bulimia are potentially fatal conditions. Two to 6% of anorectics will die from their disease, either from the effects of starvation or by suicide. Bulimics are even more likely to die as suicides. They may also suffer from dental problems caused by the constant exposure of the teeth to acidic stomach contents, as well as kidney stones, lung damage and imbalances in salts that can damage the heart.

Anorexia is almost always diagnosed after a severe loss of weight; bulimia, often by accident. The treatment for both is primarily psychological and may include the use of anti-depressant drugs.

To lower your risk of eating disorders

Recognize the symptoms. Eating disorders such as anorexia nervosa are most likely to show up after a girl first begins to menstruate. Because anorectics seem to have a fear of growing up, they need an encouraging environment to get through adolescence unscathed. If a family is unable to provide this and symptoms of anorexia nervosa appear, psychological help is required. In some cases, anti-depressant drugs have seemed to help. (See also OBESITY.)

EMPHYSEMA

Known risk factors

Age:	Yes	Smoking:	Yes
Gender:	Yes	Drugs & medical procedures:	No
Race/ethnic group:	No	General health:	No
Family history:	Yes	Environment:	Yes
Diet:	No	Occupation:	Yes

Are you at risk?

Emphysema is a condition in which the lining of the air sacs in the lung loses its elasticity and is unable to expand, which means that the lungs cannot provide enough oxygen to the body.

The person most likely to develop emphysema is a man older than 45 who is a heavy smoker, but this gender difference is likely to disappear as more women continue to smoke for longer periods of time.

In experiments with laboratory animals, ozone and nitrous oxide—chemicals that occur in the gray-blue exhaust from motor vehicles and are present in polluted air—have been shown to cause changes in lung tissue similar to those seen in people with emphysema. Not surprisingly, emphysema is more common in large cities and highly industrialized areas.

Genetics plays a large role in determining which of us is at greatest risk for emphysema. Our bodies maintain a steady balance between proteases (substances that attack disease organisms and fight inflammation but also damage tissue) and the enzymes that inactivate proteases and protect us from unlimited tissue damage. Some of us are unable to defend our bodies against the proteases either because we are exposed to continuing insult, such as smoking, that provokes an unending formation of proteases or because we are genetically unable to manufacture enzymes such as *alpha*-1-antitrypsin that protect the lining of our lungs. The inability to produce sufficient amounts of *alpha*-1-antitrypsin is inherited, which may be why emphysema sometimes seems to run in families. People who inherit this defect are more likely than the rest of us to develop emphysema and to develop it at an earlier age even if they don't smoke and are never exposed to environmental or occupational chemicals that damage the lungs.

Early detection. Emphysema can be diagnosed by a chest X-ray that shows characteristic changes such as large air spaces in the lungs or a flattened diaphragm. Pulmonary function tests, which measure your ability to move air in and out of your lungs, may show reduced capacities.

To lower your risk of emphysema

If you smoke, stop. No half-way measures will do. All smoking is equally hazardous. Cigars, pipes and all cigarettes, including the ones labeled "low-tar" or "low-nicotine," irritate and inflame your lungs, provoking the constant formation of proteases.

When the air is polluted, don't run. Or bicycle. Or play tennis. Or engage in any strenuous activity that increases your exposure to noxious chemicals in the air.

ENDOMETRIAL CANCER

Known risk factors

Age:	Yes	Smoking:	?
Gender:	Yes	Drugs & medical procedures:	Yes
Race/ethnic group:	Yes	General health:	No
Family history:	No	Environment:	No
Diet:	?	Occupation:	No

Are you at risk?

Every year, about 47,000 American women develop cancers of the uterus. Twenty-nine percent of these (13,500) are cancers of the cervix (see CERVICAL CANCER); the rest (33,000) are cancers of the endometrium, the lining of the uterus.

The women at highest risk for endometrial cancer are native Hawaiians, whose risk is twice that of white, black or Hispanic women. The group at lowest risk is women of American Indian descent.

Endometrial cancer is most common after 50. Your risk is higher than normal if you do not have children (either by choice or because you fail to ovulate and are infertile) or if you are obese or have diabetes or hypertension or if you reach menopause after age 52 (the average age in the United States) or if you take long-term estrogen replacement therapy after menopause. Women who use estrogen for long periods of time before menopause are also at higher risk, but oral contraceptives, which are combinations of estrogen and progestin, appear to reduce the risk of endometrial cancer.

As a result, there is now a greater likelihood that women who may benefit from post-menopausal estrogen therapy will be given smaller doses of estrogen in combination with progesterone, which causes shedding of the uterine lining similar to what happens when you are menstruating. The combination treatment prevents the build-up of endometrial tissues and may reduce the risk of endometrial cancer while still controlling such menopausal discomforts as hot flashes or the natural thinning of the vaginal lining that can make intercourse painful.

Some researchers have suggested that a high-fat diet may heighten the risk of endometrial cancer, but this remains to be proven.

Early detection. Seventy to 89% of all women whose endometrial cancer is diagnosed before it has spread beyond the lining of the uterus will be alive five years later. Overall, 63% of the women who develop endometrial cancer will be alive and disease-free five years after their cancer is diagnosed.

While you are still menstruating, the typical early warning sign of cancer of the endometrium is bleeding between your periods; after menopause, any vaginal bleeding is considered suspicious. A diagnosis of endometrial cancer can be confirmed by obtaining a sample of endometrial tissue either through dilation and curettage (D&C), which requires general anesthesia, or by suction curettage, a mechanical suctioning of the uterus. Suction curettage is a slightly less reliable diagnostic test than dilation and curettage, but it can be done in your doctor's office without anesthesia.

To lower your risk of endometrial cancer

See your doctor for regular examinations. A yearly gynecological examination is the best way to find uterine cancer while it is localized and highly curable.

The Pap (Papanicolaou) test, which is highly reliable in picking up cancer of the cervix, is less effective in detecting endometrial cancers. As many as 30% to 40% of these tests may be false-negative (negative even though there is cancer present).

The American Cancer Society recommends that women at high risk have an examination of endometrial tissue performed when menopause begins. Others suggest that women who are at high risk have yearly examinations of endometrial tissue.

ENDOMETRIOSIS

Known risk factors

Age:	Yes	Smoking:	No
Gender:	Yes	Drugs & medical procedures:	No
Race/ethnic group:	No	General health:	Yes
Family history:	No	Environment:	No
Diet:	No	Occupation:	No

Are you at risk?

Endometriosis is a term used to describe the presence of tissue from the endometrium (the lining of the uterus) in places other than the uterus. These implants, which are most often discovered during surgery for some other gynecological condition, usually occur in the abdomen, but they may also show up as far away as the bladder, the arm, the lungs and the head. The single irrefutable risk factor for endometriosis is being a woman of child-bearing age. Endometriosis is most common among women age 30 to 40; it rarely occurs after menopause.

It is chic but misleading to call endometriosis "the career woman's disease." Endometrial tissue implants also occur in women who choose to become home-makers. Postponing pregnancy does not cause endometriosis, but endometrial tissue blocking the fallopian tubes may make it difficult to become pregnant later in life. Twenty-five to 50% of all infertile women have endometriosis, which is also linked to a higher-than-normal risk of miscarriage, ectopic pregnancy, excessive menstrual flow and pain during intercourse or menstruation.

Early detection. Endometriosis is conclusively diagnosed by laparoscopy, a surgical procedure during which your doctor examines the tissue in the abdominal cavity with a flexible viewing tube inserted through an incision over the abdomen.

If you plan to have children, diagnosing endometriosis before it becomes extensive may make it possible for you to become pregnant before tissue implants begin to obstruct your fallopian tubes. Some gynecologists believe that becoming pregnant may slow the progress of the endometriosis, but this has never been scientifically proven. Whether or not surgical removal of the tissue implants will allow a woman whose infertility is due to endometriosis to become pregnant depends on how extensive the implants are. About 60% of the women whose infertility is caused by moderate endometriosis and 35% of the women whose infertility is caused by severe endometriosis may become pregnant after surgery.

To lower your risk of endometriosis

There is presently no way to reduce your initial risk of developing endometriosis.

EPILEPSY

Known risk factors

Age:	No	Smoking:	No
Gender:	No	Drugs & medical procedures:	?
Race/ethnic group:	No	General health:	Yes
Family history:	?	Environment:	Yes
Diet:	No	Occupation:	Yes

Are you at risk?

Epilepsy is a term used to describe any neurological disorder characterized by recurring episodes of altered patterns of electrical impulses in the brain that produce a physical effect known as *seizure*. The most common kind of seizure is the *convulsive seizure*, which starts with a loss of consciousness and is followed by jerking movements of the arms and legs. According to the Epilepsy Foundation of America, there are about 2 million people in this country with epilepsy, which makes it a relatively common condition.

Is epilepsy inherited? Only in the sense that all of us inherit some susceptibility to seizures. Whether or not we develop epilepsy seems to depend on whether or not we run into a triggering event such as a head injury or a high fever. Statistically, while the children of people with epilepsy do have a higher risk of developing the condition, the odds are still that they will never develop epilepsy themselves. In most cases, people who develop epilepsy have no family history of the illness.

The risk factors for epilepsy seem to vary with our age.

For babies, the greatest risks are a birth defect in the brain, a head injury during delivery or an uncontrolled high fever. Women who do not eat properly while pregnant may put their babies at risk because the deficient maternal diet starves the fetal brain. Babies born with phenylketonuria (PKU) or who develop hypercalcemia (a metabolic disorder that produces excess amounts of calcium in the blood) or a deficiency of pyridoxine (vitamin B6) may also be at higher risk for epilepsy, but the seizures usually end when the disorder is treated. (See PHENYLKETONURIA [PKU].)

Teen-agers and young adults are most at risk from an injury to the head; adults, from a brain tumor or an organic brain disease, and the effects of diabetes, kidney disease or withdrawal from alcohol or drugs. In old age, the most common causes of epileptic seizures are brain tumors, stroke and vascular disease.

At any age, your risk of epilepsy rises if you have a high fever or heat stroke or a brain infection (such as an abscess or encephalitis), or herpes, or syphilis or a central nervous system infection such as meningitis, rabies or tetanus. Children who swallow chips of lead paint and adults who are exposed to lead at work are at risk because seizures may be a consequence of lead poisoning. Other chemicals that affect brain function and may cause seizures are camphor and strychnine. Carbon monoxide, which cuts down the supply of oxygen to the brain, may also increase the chance of seizures.

Early detection. The basic diagnostic test for epilepsy is an electroencephalogram (EEG). An EEG records the pattern of the electrical impulses in your brain cells (a brain wave) through electrodes placed against your scalp.

Epilepsy produces a characteristic pattern of electrical abnormalities. If your brain waves are normal during the EEG but your doctor still suspects epilepsy, he may decide to leave the electrodes in place for 24 hours to detect changes that occur deep in the brain over a longer period of time. Or he may prescribe a CT-scan of the brain to detect any tumors, scars or other physical abnormalities that can trigger seizures.

To lower your risk of epilepsy

Wear your seat belt. Head injuries are the leading cause of epilepsy among people age 18 to 35 and the second leading cause among people age 12 to 18. The simplest way to reduce the number of these injuries is to buckle up every time you step into a car. To protect a young child, use a safety seat. Wear a protective helmet when you ride a motorcycle, bicycle or skateboard. And never dive into water unless you are absolutely certain it is deep enough.

If your baby has a fever, call the doctor. In most cases, babies who have seizures triggered by a high fever do not develop epilepsy, but the Epilepsy Foundation of America recommends the cautious but admittedly impractical course, which is to check with your doctor immediately if your child's fever goes to 101 degrees Fahrenheit or higher.

FETAL ALCOHOL SYNDROME (FAS)

Known risk factors

Age:	No	Smoking:	No
Gender:	No	Drugs & medical procedures:	No
Race/ethnic group:	?	General health:	Yes
Family history:	No	Environment:	No
Diet:	Yes	Occupation:	No

Are you at risk?

Fetal alcohol syndrome (FAS) is a pattern of birth defects that includes low birthweight, malformations of the heart and face, abnormal folds in the eyelid, unusual creases in the palm of the hands, small teeth with damaged enamel and mental retardation due to impaired development of the brain.

FAS was first identified in a study of alcoholic women who consumed six or more drinks a day. Since then, several studies have suggested a milder, but consistent, occurrence of lesser defects (a syndrome called fetal alcohol effects [FAE]) among babies born to women who reportedly have as few as three to four drinks every day or five drinks on any one occasion while pregnant. There has never been a measurable risk of FAS or FAE confirmed among babies born to women who have one drink a day or less while pregnant, but two early studies at Columbia University in New York did suggest the possibility of an increased risk of miscarriage among pregnant women who drink as seldom as twice a week. In studies on FAS, a drink is usually defined as a one-ounce serving of spirits (whiskey, bourbon, gin or vodka) or one four-ounce glass of wine or one 12-ounce glass of beer.

Early detection. Prenatally, ultrasonography may show some of the structural defects attributed to fetal alcohol syndrome.

To reduce your risk of fetal alcohol syndrome

Don't drink while pregnant. As of this writing, there is no conclusive evidence that moderate drinking, defined as consuming no more than one drink a day while pregnant, poses a serious risk of fetal alcohol syndrome or fetal alcohol effects, but avoiding alcohol entirely eliminates the risk of FAS.

FROSTBITE

Known risk factors

Age:	Yes	Smoking:	Yes
Gender:	No	Drugs & medical procedures:	Yes
Race/ethnic group:	No	General health:	Yes
Family history:	No	Environment:	Yes
Diet:	Yes	Occupation:	Yes

Are you at risk?

Anyone whose skin is exposed to sub-freezing temperatures for a sufficient length of time will eventually suffer from frostbite—whitened, hard patches on the skin that are insensitive to pain. If your resistance is low, you may end up with frostbite after a shorter-than-normal period of time outdoors; people who are tired or anemic or very young or very old have a harder time staying warm. You may also be at increased risk if you have heart disease or if you smoke or if you are an alcoholic or a drug abuser. Each of these conditions may interfere with your circulatory system's ability to deliver warming blood to the surface of your skin.

Early detection. Your body responds to cold in two ways. First, the small blood vessels just under the surface of your skin constrict so as to reduce the amount of heat lost when warm blood from the center of your body circulates to the skin. Second, you will begin to shiver to convert stored energy to heat to stay warm.

If you do not get to a warm place, your body will eventually become so cold that it stops shivering. At that point, you face major medical problems including accidental hypothermia, an internal body temperature lower than 95 degrees Fahrenheit. This may eventually be fatal if it is not brought back up to normal.

To reduce your risk of frostbite and cold-related injuries

Wear protective clothing. Never go out in the cold without protective clothing. When it is severely cold, with temperatures repeatedly far below freezing, or when a cold wind is blowing, add thermal underwear to hold a layer of warm air next to your skin. A warm hat is indispensable; one-third of the heat you lose from your body is lost through the top of your head. The best hats come with earlaps. A warm face mask will protect your forehead, nose and cheeks. Your boots and gloves should be waterproof and wind resistant, large enough to accommodate an extra pair of warm socks or glove liners. Boots and gloves that pinch can cut off circulation in your fingers and toes.

Keep moving. It's no old wives' tale: Jumping up and down when you are cold does keep you warm because, like shivering, it converts stored energy to body heat. If your hands are cold, put them under your armpits. Caution: *These are short-term measures. They will not protect you indefinitely.*

Do not drink or smoke before going out in the cold.

Do not ignore your body's warning signals. Head for shelter as soon as you start to shiver. If you develop frostbite, warm the affected skin slowly, without rubbing, to avoid damaging frozen cells.

GALLBLADDER DISEASE (GALLSTONES)

Known risk factors

Age:	Yes	Smoking:	No
Gender:	Yes	Drugs & medical procedures:	Yes
Race/ethnic group:	Yes	General health:	Yes
Family history:	Yes	Environment:	No
Diet:	Yes	Occupation:	No

Are you at risk?

Gallstones are common. More than 25 million Americans have them, and 1 million new cases are diagnosed every year. They occur most often among older people (one of every five Americans older than 65 has them), and a woman's risk of developing them is three times that of a man's, particularly if she is taking estrogen, either in oral contraceptives or as post-menopausal estrogen replacement.

Your family history counts. If one of your close relatives (mother, father, sister, brother) has gallstones, your risk of developing them is about twice that of a person who has no relatives with the disease. For as-yet-unexplained reasons, Americans of Scandinavian descent and Native Americans are at higher-than-normal risk, and black Americans are at lower-than-normal risk (but more than 33% of the people with sickle-cell disease also have gallstones).

According to data compiled at the University of Texas Health Science Center (San Antonio), moderate and heavy smokers are at higher risk than non-smokers. People with diabetes have a high risk of gallstones. So do people who are seriously overweight, particularly when they suddenly lose a lot of weight. When a person who is obese goes on a crash diet, his or her natural production of cholesterol increases, leading to the formation of cholesterol crystals that may become gallstones.

In America, about 80% of all gallstones are cholesterol stones. About 20% are pigment stones, formed from bile pigments. The people most likely to develop pigment gallstones are those of Oriental descent and those who have a medical condition such as liver disease or a disease such as sickle-cell anemia that causes continuing destruction of red blood cells.

Early detection. The early symptoms of gallbladder disease are heartburn, belching and a vague pain in the upper part of your body. Gallstones can cause nausea, vomiting and a steady pain in the upper right side of your body that gets worse when you move. The pain may last as long as three days, easing suddenly when the stone is dislodged. If the stone is in the bile duct, it may cause jaundice (yellowed skin).

A diagnosis of gallbladder disease or gallstones may be confirmed by ultrasonography.

To lower your risk of gallstones

Watch your diet, watch your weight, watch your lifestyle. The risk factors for gallbladder disease are similar to the risk factors for heart disease. So are the preventive measures: Keep your weight normal. Watch your cholesterol. Stop smoking. If you have diabetes, follow your doctor's advice scrupulously to control your disease.

GLAUCOMA

Known risk factors

Age:	Yes	Smoking:	No
Gender:	No	Drugs & medical procedures:	Yes
Race/ethnic group:	Yes	General health:	Yes
Family history:	Yes	Environment:	No
Diet:	No	Occupation:	No

Are you at risk?

Glaucoma produces a steady increase in the pressure inside the eye. This pressure can slowly cause the optic nerve to atrophy so that you first lose the ability to see to the side, then to the front. Eventually, untreated glaucoma will cause blindness.

Glaucoma seems to run in families, but because it is due to multiple genetic defects rather than a single defective gene, there is no clear pattern of genetic inheritance; your parents may be carriers who pass the glaucoma on to you without developing it themselves. Chronic open-angle glaucoma can occur at any age, but your risk is highest after age 30. If you injure your eye or develop cataracts, you may develop glaucoma earlier. Men and women are equally at risk. Race is a risk factor: glaucoma occurs earlier, more frequently and with more severe nerve damage among blacks.

Your risk of glaucoma goes up if you have diabetes or sickle cell disease or if you are taking steroids (which are sometimes used to treat asthma, arthritis, emphysema, kidney disease, the complications of a kidney transplant and some skin disorders). A small percentage of the babies with congenital cataracts are those born to women who had rubella while pregnant.

Early detection. Untreated chronic glaucoma that starts when you are 40 to 45 may leave you blind by the age 60 to 65, but early diagnosis and treatment can in most cases preserve useful vision throughout life.

Your ophthalmologist can detect early glaucoma by measuring the pressure inside the eye with an instrument called a tonometer. If your doctor is using an applanation tonometer, which measures the resistance of your eye to the slight pressure exerted by a small flat disc directly against your eye, examination with an applanation tonometer requires local anesthetic. An examination performed with an air tonometer, which measures the resistance of your eye to a jet of air, does not require anesthesia. In either case, increased resistance indicates increased pressure within the eye, leading to a diagnosis of early glaucoma.

To lower your risk of glaucoma

Schedule a yearly eye exam. Because there are no definite symptoms in the earliest stages of glaucoma, a yearly eye examination after age 35 to 40 is your best insurance. People age 20 to 25 with no family history of glaucoma, generally are advised to have the glaucoma exam every three to five years, but if one or more of your close relatives has glaucoma, your doctor may wish to examine your eyes more often, on a yearly schedule around age 30.

GOITER

Known risk factors

Age:	Yes	Smoking:	No
Gender:	No	Drugs & medical procedures:	Yes
Race/ethnic group:	No	General health:	Yes
Family history:	?	Environment:	No
Diet:	Yes	Occupation:	No

Are you at risk?

Your thyroid gland needs iodine in order to make thyroid hormones. If you don't get enough iodine, the gland will swell in its attempt to make the hormone. This swelling of the thyroid gland is called goiter.

Before the introduction of iodized salt and refrigerated food shipping, people who lived far from the seashore were at high risk of goiter because they rarely ate fish (a good source of iodine) and because the vegetables they ate lacked the iodine found in soil near the coast. Some researchers suggest that genetics may also play a part in goiter, perhaps an inherited enzyme defect that makes it hard for the body to use iodine.

Today, goiter caused by a diet low in iodine is virtually unknown, but the opposite problem—goiter caused by an excess of dietary iodine—has been reported in Japan where seaweed is an important part of the daily diet. Some Japanese may be get as much as 50,000 to 80,000 micrograms of iodine a day, 300 to 500 times the recommended amount. Eating this much inorganic iodine, the kind of iodine found in seaweed, makes it impossible for the thyroid to manufacture sufficient amounts of organic iodine, the kind of iodine used to make thyroid hormones. The thyroid then swells in an attempt to make more thyroid hormone, and the result is goiter.

Adolescents, pregnant women and women who are going through menopause have a slightly increased risk of goiter because puberty, pregnancy and menopause raise the body's demand for thyroid hormone. But giving these people additional iodine can create problems. Iodine may cause acne, a constant worry for adolescents; when a pregnant woman takes iodine, her fetus's own production of thyroid hormone decreases.

Taking lithium, the anti-tuberculosis drug aminosalicylic acid (PAS) or some sulfur compounds may increase your risk of goiter because they interfere with the metabolism of iodine and inhibit the synthesis of thyroid hormone.

Early detection. When the thyroid gland is swollen, your doctor may perform a tissue biopsy to find out whether the swelling is goiter (benign) or a thyroid cancer. Because thyroid cancer can occur in several spots in the gland, a negative biopsy of one spot may not mean there is no cancer present. If your doctor suspects a malignancy, he may order a thyroid scan. This test, performed after you are given an oral dose of radioactive material, measures the rate at which your thyroid absorbs the iodine. If there are "cold spots" (places where absorption is low), your doctor may request ultrasonography to rule out a cyst, or a biopsy to rule out thyroid cancer.

To lower your risk of goiter

Make sure your diet provides the iodine you need each day. The recommended dietary allowance (RDA) for iodine for a healthy adult is 150 micrograms, the amount of iodine in three ounces of fresh saltwater fish or one ounce of shellfish or two grams of iodized salt. The RDA for a pregnant woman is 175 micrograms; the RDA for a nursing mother is 200 micrograms. A microgram (mcg) is one one-thousandth of a milligram (mg), which is one-thousandth of a gram (g).

GONORRHEA

Known risk factors

Age:	Yes	Smoking:	No
Gender:	Yes	Drugs & medical procedures:	Yes
Race/ethnic group:	Yes	General health:	No
Family history:	No	Environment:	No
Diet:	No	Occupation:	No

Are you at risk?

Human beings are the only natural host for *Neisseria gonorrhoeae*, the organism that causes gonorrhea. According to the Federal Centers for Disease Control, about 1.4 million new cases of gonorrhea are reported each year in the United States. Your risk of contracting gonorrhea is directly related to your age, your sex, your sexual preference, your race, your economic and marital status, where you live and your educational level, all factors that generally influence your sexual behavior. Among people who are sexually active, the person most likely to have gonorrhea is young (most cases occur among people age 15 to 19), poor or poorly educated, non-white, unmarried and lives alone (at higher risk presumably because he or she has more sexual contacts) in a large city. Before the advent of AIDS, gonorrhea was most common among homosexual men, but the introduction of safer sex to reduce the spread of the AIDS virus, HIV, has also reduced the spread of gonorrhea among these men.

Menstruation increases the risk that a gonorrheal organism will migrate from the cervix up into the uterus and pelvis. So does using an intrauterine device (IUD).

A pregnant woman who has gonorrhea can pass it to her infant during delivery when the baby travels through the infected vaginal passage. Gonorrhea acquired in this fashion attacks the baby's eyes. To prevent blindness, all newborns in this country are routinely given a protective dose of silver nitrate solution or tetracycline or erythromycin ointment in each eye.

Early detection. Gonorrhea is diagnosed by the presence of *Neisseria gonorrhoeae* in a sample of the discharge from the urethra or the tissue of the urethra, the cervix, the rectum, the throat. This can be done by examining a sample of the urethral discharge under a microscope or by culturing a tissue sample (allowing bacteria to grow unimpeded) in a laboratory dish. If the organisms are present, the patient has the disease.

To lower your risk of gonorrhea

Choose protective contraception. Using a latex condom every time you have sex may reduce your risk of contracting gonorrhea. In countries such as Japan where the latex condom is the primary form of contraception the rate of gonorrhea and other sexually transmitted disease is much lower than it is in the United States.

The correct use of condoms begins with storing them properly in a cool, dry place to protect the latex from drying out. The condom should be put on gently to avoid tearing. Leave room at the tip to accommodate the ejaculate. After ejaculation, withdraw the penis with the condom still in place, holding it close against the base of the penis to avoid spilling any ejaculate. Discard all used condoms; never try to wash them out and use them again.

According to the American Social Health Association, you may increase the protective effect of a condom by using a spermicidal foam that contains nonoxynol-9. In laboratory studies, nonoxynol-9 appears to kill *Neisseria gonorrhoeae* on contact. But the two contraceptives must be used in tandem; on its own, the foam is not considered adequately protective.

If you have been exposed to gonorrhea, see your doctor. The incubation period for men is two to 14 days and seven to 14 days for women. But waiting for symptoms to show up is a bad way to decide whether or not to be tested; approximately 10% of all men and 20% to 30% of all women with gonorrhea have no symptoms at all for weeks, or even months, after infection.

In fact, asymptomatic gonorrhea is so common among American women that some doctors advocate routine culture of the tissue around the cervix for every sexually active woman who is younger than 30 or at high risk because of her sexual behavior.

Diagnosis is only the first step in the healing process. During the 1980s, there was a steady increase in the incidence of antibiotic-resistant gonorrhea. In the two years from 1986 to 1988 alone, cases of antibiotic-resistant gonorrhea in the United States more than doubled, from 16,450 to 35,000.

The incidence of penicillin-resistant gonorrhea is especially high in West Africa and Southeast Asia, but these strains have now arrived on our West Coast, as well as the port cities of Miami and New York. Some of the drugs now used to treat penicillin-resistant gonorrhea are cefoxitin (Mefoxin) with probenicid, ceftriaxone (Rocephin) and spectinomycin (Trobicin).

There is no guarantee that gonorrhea organisms will not become resistant to these antibiotics, as well. Indeed, the increase in antibiotic-resistant gonorrhea organisms is responsible for a growing number of relapses that require a new course of treatment. Anyone who has been treated for gonorrhea must have a second, and sometimes even a third, diagnostic test to be certain that the disease has truly been eradicated.

GOUT

Known risk factors

Age:	Yes	Smoking:	No
Gender:	Yes	Drugs & medical procedures:	Yes
Race/ethnic group:	Yes	General health:	Yes
Family history:	Yes	Environment:	No
Diet:	?	Occupation:	No

Are you at risk?

Gout is a form of arthritis triggered by an excess amount of uric acid in the blood. Uric acid is a natural by-product of nucleic acid metabolism. Ordinarily, it is extracted from blood as it circulates through your kidneys and eliminated from your body when you urinate. If for any reason your kidneys do not get rid of sufficient amounts of uric acid, the excess acid can form sharp, needle-like crystals that trigger pain and inflammation (gout) if they lodge in your joints and kidney stones if they collect in urine.

You might assume from this that people who eat a diet rich in high-protein foods such as meat and dried beans also have a higher risk of developing gout, but the best evidence is that nothing you eat has any real effect on whether or not you get gout or how your gout progresses once you have it. The one exception is alcohol. Excessive amounts of alcoholic beverages reduce your body's ability to get rid of uric acid and may precipitate an acute attack of gout.

Filipinos and some other Southeast Asians have an increased risk of gout. In America, gout seems to run in families. It is primarily a man's disease (94% of all gout patients are men) that occurs most frequently among people older than 40. Men consistently have higher levels of uric acid in their bodies, and post-menopausal women consistently have higher levels than women who have not yet gone through menopause, presumably because the kidneys' ability to extract uric acid from blood is influenced by male and female hormones and because just getting older brings a natural decline in kidney function.

Some drugs and medical conditions may also increase the amount of uric acid in your body. The diuretics used to treat high blood pressure may interfere with the kidneys' ability to take uric acid out of the blood. Diseases of the blood cells and/or blood-forming organs (spleen, liver, bone marrow) cause a rapid break-down of the cell nuclei that results in excess uric acid. High blood pressure, heart disease, advanced kidney disease, obesity or malfunctioning parathyroid glands may also lead to increased body levels of uric acid.

Early detection. Gout is diagnosed by a blood test that shows a higher-than-normal amount of uric acid or by a urinalysis that shows higher-than-normal amounts of uric acid and protein, as well as increased acidity. A microscopic examination of synovial fluid (the fluid around the affected joint) during an acute episode of gout will show crystals of uric acid. Later in the course of the disease, an X-ray examination of the affected joint may show characteristic bone loss.

To lower your risk of gout

At present, there is no known way to reduce your risk of gout, but controlling your diet may help reduce the number and severity of acute episodes. For specific dietary prescriptions, check with your doctor.

HAIR LOSS

Known risk factors

Age:	Yes	Smoking:	No
Gender:	Yes	Drugs & medical procedures:	Yes
Race/ethnic group:	No	General health:	Yes
Family history:	Yes	Environment:	No
Diet:	Yes	Occupation:	No

Are you at risk?

Will you end up bald? If you are a man, the best way to tell is to look at your male relatives on both sides of your family. Right now, as many as 55 million Americans are losing their hair, most of them because of male pattern baldness, an androgen (male hormone)-linked trait that runs in families and may be inherited either from your mother or your father. This kind of baldness, which starts either at the front of the head or in a circle on top, can begin as early as your mid-teens. The later it starts, the more hair you will retain as you get older.

Female pattern baldness is not as common as male hair loss, nor is it likely to be as drastic. A woman's hair may thin at the front and side, but she rarely becomes totally bald in any one area. Women may lose their hair if their level of male hormones increases, a condition known as virilism that can also cause excess hair on the face, an increase in muscle mass, a deepening voice and a decrease in the female secondary sexual characteristics.

Major surgery, a chronic illness, thyroid disease, an infection accompanied by a high fever, a fungal infection or the radiation treatments used for cancer therapy can cause temporary baldness or thinning hair due to an increase in the number of hairs in the resting (telogen) phase of the hair growth cycle rather than the growing (anogen) phase. This imbalance in the hair-growth cycle may also occur spontaneously, for no known reason.

Two or three months after she delivers a baby, a woman may shed large amounts of hair for as long as six months, but this condition is temporary.

Thinning hair may also be a side effect of treatment with the analgesic drug piroxicam (Feldene); the anti-acne drug isotretinoin (Accutane); the anti-depressant amitriptyline (Elavil, Endep); the anti-hypertensive clonidine (Catapres, Combipres); the mood stabilizer lithium (Eskalith, Lithane, Lithium, Lithobid), the psoriasis drug etretinate (Tegison); oral contraceptives; and the tranquilizer haloperidol (Haldol).

Baldness is a common side effect of many anti-cancer drugs including carmustine (BCNU), cyclophosphamide (Cytoxan), daunorubicin (Cerubidine), doxirubicin (Adriamycin), etoposide (VP-16), fluorouracil (5-FU, Adrucil), lomustine (CeeNu), vinblastine (Velban), and vincristine (Oncovin).

There is no such thing as an anti-baldness vitamin or mineral supplement, but crash dieting, excesses of vitamin A or deficiencies of iron or protein may increase the risk of hair loss.

Early detection. Because there are so many possible reasons why your hair may be thinning, it makes sense to ask your doctor to check out any unusual or sudden hair loss.

To lower your risk of hair loss

Consider minoxidil. You can't eliminate your genetic susceptibility to baldness, but if you are a man who is absolutely determined not to lose his hair, you may wish to investigate minoxidil (Rogaine), a drug originally used to treat hypertension.

Rubbing minoxidil into your scalp seems to promote new hair growth in areas where you still have hair. But you will have to use the drug for the rest of your life: When you stop using it, the new hair falls out. The long-term value and side effects of using minoxidil continuously on the scalp are not yet known, but some users have reported dry, itchy scalps, and some experts are concerned about its possible effects on people with diagnosed or suspected heart disease. As of this writing, the FDA has not yet approved minoxidil for use by women.

HAY FEVER

Known risk factors

Age:	Yes	Smoking:	No
Gender:	Yes	Drugs & medical procedures:	No
Race/ethnic group:	Yes	General health:	No
Family history:	Yes	Environment:	Yes
Diet:	No	Occupation:	Yes

Are you at risk?

Hay fever, also known as allergic rhinitis, is a seasonal allergy triggered by tree pollens in the spring and by grass and weed pollens in the summer.

We are all most sensitive to these allergens when we are young, particularly between the ages of 18 and 24, when as many as 33.3% of all men and 25% of all women may experience some kind of allergic reaction. Men are more sensitive than women to house dust, ragweed and grasses; black women are more sensitive than white women to ragweed.

According to the National Center for Health Statistics at the Department of Health and Human Services (HHS), where you live has a lot to do with whether or not you get hay fever. In the spring, summer and fall, the winds over the Northeast states carry pollen up from the South or across from the West, while the winds blowing over the Southern states come across the Gulf of Mexico or in from the Atlantic Ocean virtually free of pollen. As a result, as many as one-quarter of the people in the Northeast test positive for hay fever reactions; only 14% of the people in the South do. Hay fever is more common among people who live in urban areas where the air is polluted and among people who work outside or are exposed to pollens on the job.

Like other allergies, including sensitivity to animals, hayfever seems to run in families. If your mother or father has hay fever or sneezes when there's a cat or dog in the room, you are likely to inherit a sensitivity that can escalate into a full-blown allergic reaction when you are exposed to animals or to tree, weed or grass pollens. Your personal history counts, too. If you have had another allergic reaction such as dermatitis, hives or eczema, you have a higher-than-normal risk of hay fever.

Early detection. Hay fever is so common that most of us think of it as nothing more than a minor annoyance. But untreated, it may lead to asthma (which develops in as many as one-third of the people with hay fever); sinus infections; chronic nasal inflammation followed by nasal polyps, voice changes and a reduced sense of smell; and chronic otitis media, an infection of the middle ear that can cause hearing loss.

Hay fever is diagnosed by its symptoms. It is treated with antihistamines that lessen your body's reaction to the allergens in the air; decongestants that dry up secretions; and, sometimes, with desensitizing injections of gradually increasing doses of allergens to build up your resistance to the offending pollens.

To lower your risk of hay fever

Keep the air clean. You can't eliminate your inherited sensitivity to pollens, but you may be able to reduce the frequency and severity of your hay fever attacks by keeping the air you breathe as pollen-free as possible.

Use air-conditioning indoors during hay fever season. Your doctor may suggest a protective respirator mask to trap and filter the pollens out of the air you breathe, especially during periods of air pollution or in the fall when people are burning leaves. The respirator mask may also be considered standard equipment for hay fever sufferers whose job exposes them to pollens.

HEARING DISORDERS

Known risk factors

Age:	Yes	Smoking:	Yes
Gender:	Yes	Drugs & medical procedures:	Yes
Race/ethnic group:	No	General health:	Yes
Family history:	Yes	Environment:	Yes
Diet:	No	Occupation:	Yes

Are you at risk?

Hearing loss is increasingly common in the United States. Nearly 28 million of us have some loss of hearing; about 2 million have a hearing loss severe enough to interfere with normal communication.

Growing older is the most common risk factor. Presbycusis, the normal age-related loss of hearing, starts when you are about 20. At first, it reduces your ability to hear high-pitched sounds such as a child's voice; then, gradually it makes it hard for you to hear low-pitched sounds. The effects of presbycusis vary greatly from person to person. Some people have real trouble hearing by the time they are 60; others sail on into their late 80s perfectly able to hear the proverbial pin drop. Men seem to be at higher risk and to suffer more severe loss of hearing than women.

Another major risk factor is exposure to loud noise that can damage the nerve endings in the inner ear. The longer you are exposed to the noise and the louder it is, the greater the hearing loss is likely to be.

We measure the loudness of noise in terms of decibels (dB). A noise level of 0 dB represents the faintest sound the human ear can hear. A whisper is about 30 dB; a typewriter or normal conversation is 60 dB; a lawn mower or truck traffic is 90 dB; a chainsaw, pneumatic drill or snowmobile is 100 dB; a loud rock concert or an automobile horn is 115 dB; a jet engine or the noise from a gun muzzle is 149 dB. People who work with noisy equipment such as chain saws, engines or heavy machinery, or who are exposed to gunfire are at high risk for noise-related hearing loss, and anyone who is continuously exposed to noise in the range of 85 decibels will eventually suffer some loss of hearing.

Does smoking increase the risk of deafness? Maybe. A smoker has 300 to 400 parts per million (ppm) carbon monoxide in his lungs while smoking. At Johns Hopkins University, researchers exposed laboratory rats to slightly higher concentrations of carbon monoxide (500 ppm) for three and one-half hours. In the last two hours of the experiment, the researchers added loud noise in the range of 105 decibels, close to what you might experience when sandblasting or sitting in front-row seats at a rock and roll concert. A single such session caused the rats to suffer the kind of permanent hearing loss that in a human being would make it hard to hear normal conversation.

This confirmed earlier suggestions that people exposed to loud noise and high concentrations of carbon monoxide in tandem (as you might be in a smoky nightclub) have a higher risk of hearing loss than people exposed to either one alone. The explanation for this may be that carbon monoxide reduces the flow of oxygen to the nerve cells in the inner ear, which need more, not less, oxygen to function as the level of sound increases. Butyl nitrite (street name: Poppers) produces the same effect. People who use butyl nitrate while in loud places such as rock concerts are liable to suffer serious loss of hearing.

Several common infectious diseases including chicken pox, encephalitis, influenza, measles, meningitis, mononucleosis and mumps may cause a sudden, dramatic loss of hearing. In most cases hearing eventually returns.

If deafness runs in your family, it may be the result of otosclerosis, an inherited tendency to an overgrowth of bone in the ear that can interfere with the ability to get sound through the ear canal. Among Americans, about 10% of all adult caucasians have sites at which the bone may begin to grow this way, but only 10% of these people actually experience a hearing loss, beginning in their late teens or early 20s.

Many medicines are ototoxic (potentially damaging to the ear). The list includes the antibiotics amikacin (Amikin), gentamicin (Garamycin), kanamycin (Kantrex), neomycin (Colymycin S-Otic, Cortisporin Otic, Octicair), paromomycin (Humatin), streptomycin, tobramycin (Nebcin, Tobrex) and vancomycin (Vancocin); the anti-cancer drug cisplatin (Platinol); the antimalarials chloroquine (Aralen), quinine and quinidine; the diuretics ethacrynic acid (Edicrin) and furosemide (Lasix); and salicylates, including acetylsalicylic acid (aspirin).

Early detection. The simplest hearing test is one in which a person sitting about 20 feet away measures your ability to hear by whispering or speaking in a normal voice while you listen with ear covered. Or the person testing you may hold up a ticking stop watch and see how far away you can hear it.

A more precise and much preferred test is performed with an audiometer, a machine that produces pure tone sounds at various degrees of loudness. You wear earphones to test your air conduction, your ability to detect sounds coming to your ear drum and middle ear through your ear canal. An attachment from the audiometer pressed against the bone behind your ear tests your bone conduction, your ability to detect sound coming to the inner ear.

To lower your risk of hearing impairment

Wear protective equipment. According to the American Academy of Otolaryngology—Head and Neck Surgery, effective hearing protection devices such as specially made earmuffs and earplugs can reduce the noise of firearms, heavy machinery, power tools or noisy yard equipment 15 to 30 dB. Wearing the earmuffs and earplugs together adds another 10 to 15 dB protection. By contrast, stuffing your ears with home-made plugs of cotton will reduce noise only 7 dB. Protective devices do not block out all noise. A person with normal hearing should still be able to understand a regular conversation.

Use ototoxic drugs with caution. The safest course is to have a hearing test before you begin using a drug that may affect your hearing and then to repeat the test from time to time so as to catch any change before it becomes a serious hearing loss.

If you are pregnant, let your doctor know before any medication is prescribed. Some ototoxic drugs may cross the placental barrier and injure the fetus's auditory nerves. A woman who has not had rubella by the time she decides to start her family should have a rubella vaccination before she becomes pregnant to protect the fetus from congenital deafness. Babies whose mothers had rubella or took quinine while pregnant may be born permanently deaf.

HEART DISEASE

Known risk factors

Age:	Yes	Smoking:	Yes
Gender:	Yes	Drugs & medical procedures:	Yes
Race/ethnic group:	No	General health:	Yes
Family history:	Yes	Environment:	No
Diet:	Yes	Occupation:	?

Are you at risk?

In 1988, the American Heart Association (AHA) estimated that as many as 1.5 million Americans would suffer heart attack or angina (chest pain) and that more than 500,000 of them would die as a result.

Smoking raises the risk of a heart attack for men and women, perhaps because it makes it easier for blood to clot. These effects are so strong that smoking can actually wipe out a woman's apparent genetic advantage regarding heart disease. In 1987, researchers at the Harvard University School of Public Health released the results of a 10-year study of 120,000 married nurses between the ages of 30 and 55 that suggested smoking is responsible for nearly 50% of all cases of coronary artery disease among young and middle-aged American women.

An elevated level of serum cholesterol also appers to increase the risk of heart disease, but it's important to remember that your basic cholesterol reading is only a screening device. If you have a cholesterol reading that is "borderline high" (200 to 239 mg/dL) or "high" (240 mg/dL or higher) *and* two or more of the other major risk factors—high blood pressure, diabetes, smoking, obesity (more than 20% overweight) or a family history of heart disease—the AHA recommends that your doctor do further testing to measure the different kinds of cholesterol in your blood in order to assess your true risk.

As a rule, regardless of their total cholesterol readings, women are more likely than men to have high levels of high-density lipoproteins (HDLs), the protective fat-and-protein particles sometimes called "good cholesterol" that carry cholesterol out of your body, and relatively lower levels of the low-density lipoproteins (LDLs), the potentially hazardous fat-and-protein particles sometimes known as "bad cholesterol" that may carry cholesterol into the arteries. Regular exercise appears to raise the level of the protective HDLs and lower the risk of heart attack.

There are two kinds of LDLs, small particles that enter arteries and larger ones that do not. In 1985, researchers at the U.S. Department of Agriculture (USDA) Human Nutrition Research Center on Aging at Tufts University in Boston found that women are also more likely than men to have higher levels of the large LDLs. This may explain the observation that women live longer and have a life-long lower incidence of heart disease than men. Nonetheless, 250,000 (46%) of the 540,000 Americans who die each year of heart disease are women. Coronary heart disease is now the second leading killer of women younger than 40 and the leading cause of death in women older than 67.

Oral contraceptives appear to be another major risk factor for women. Several studies have suggested that when a woman is using oral contraceptives, the odds that she will have a heart attack rise, and some studies have shown that as long as 10 years after she stops using the pill, her risk may still be three times higher than that of a woman who never used oral contraceptives.

There is some question as to whether the new low-dose pills are as hazardous as the earlier high-dose ones. The pill's adverse effects on the heart seem to arise from the fact that their progestin raises serum cholesterol levels. In a recent study comparing the effects of four progestins commonly used in oral contraceptives, researchers at the Henry Ford Hospital in Detroit found that one progestin—ethynodiol diacetate—appeared to be less hazardous than the others because it raised the level of protective HDLs as well. All the women in this study used the older, high-dose oral contraceptives common in the 1960s and 1970s, not the newer, low-dose triphasic pills which now account for 97% of today's prescriptions for contraceptive pills.

In 1988, the Food and Drug Administration's Fertility and Maternal Health Drugs Advisory Committee recommended that contraceptive pills with more than 50 micrograms of estrogen be removed from the market, as has been the rule in Great Britain since 1969.

The risk posed by obesity may also be gender-related because where you carry your extra body fat seems to be more important than how fat you are. Data from the Framingham Heart Study that has been tracking the development of heart and blood vessel disease among residents of Framingham,

Massachusetts, since the 1940s show that being fat above your waist (a normal male body pattern) is a much stronger predictor of heart disease risk than being fat around the hips (a normal female body pattern.)

Early detection. One basic screening test for people at risk of heart disease is the blood test to measure your cholesterol level, but this is not an infallible guide to risk (see above).

Should a heart attack occur, prompt medical attention can make the difference between life and death. According to the AHA, studies show that at least half of all the people who suffer a heart attack wait more than two hours before getting help, and more than 300,000 people die of their heart attacks before they get to the hospital. About 60% of all deaths from heart attack occur in the first hour after the attack.

The AHA's warning signs of a heart attack are an uncomfortable pressure or pain in the center of the chest; pain that spreads out to the shoulders, neck or arms; shortness of breath, dizziness, sweating, fainting or severe chest pain. If these symptoms last longer than two minutes, seek medical help.

To lower your risk of heart disease

Stop smoking. Your risk of a heart attack goes down within days or even hours after you give up cigarettes because the nicotine's blood-clotting effect disappears as soon as you stop smoking. Smoking's effects on blood pressure and cholesterol should reverse over the next 12 months. Within one to five years, an ex-smoker who smoked less than a pack a day will have about the same risk of a heart attack as someone who never smoked. Even if you smoked more than a pack, your risk will drop substantially.

Simply smoking less won't do. Women who smoke as few as one to four cigarettes a day are two and one-half times more likely than non-smokers with normal blood pressure to have coronary artery disease.

Keep your blood pressure in check. Losing weight and watching your diet may control mild high blood pressure and reduce your risk of heart disease. If your hypertension does not respond to these simple measures, your doctor may prescribe anti-hypertensive medication. (See HIGH BLOOD PRESSURE.)

Exercise. A regular program of exercise several times a week appears to increase the level of protective HDLs and reduce the risk of heart disease.

Monitor your diet. To reduce serum cholesterol levels, the AHA recommends a diet that derives no more than 30% of its daily calories from fats and restricts daily cholesterol intake to 300 mg or less per day. For some people, this diet alone may reduce cholesterol levels by 10%.

Consider switching contraceptives. If you are using oral contraceptives and you are at high risk of heart disease, you may wish to consider switching to a different type of birth control such as a diaphragm or latex condom plus spermicide, which pose no known risk to your heart.

HEAT STROKE (SUNSTROKE)

Known risk factors

Age:	Yes	Smoking:	No
Gender:	No	Drugs & medical procedures:	Yes
Race/ethnic group:	No	General health:	Yes
Family history:	No	Environment:	Yes
Diet:	Yes	Occupation:	Yes

Are you at risk?

Heat stroke is a medical emergency that occurs when your body loses its ability to control its internal temperature. The most common victim of heat stroke is an athlete who neglects to replace the salt and water lost while working out in the sun. But you can also lose enough salts and water to trigger heat stroke when working in a very hot environment such as a steel mill, a railroad engine or a commercial bakery.

Old people, small children, people who have a chronic debilitating disease, alcoholics and people who are obese or tired or suffering from a respiratory infection are particularly susceptible to heat reactions, especially during a heat wave in a place where the climate is usually moderate.

Among the drugs that increase your risk of heat reaction are anti-spasmodics, muscle relaxants and some antihistamines and anti-depressants that interfere with your ability to perspire; caffeine, which constricts blood vessels and reduces the amount of blood flowing up to be cooled on the surface of your skin; and diuretics, which increase your loss of fluids.

Early detection. When you are overheated, your body automatically activates two systems designed to cool you down.

First, the surface blood vessels just under your skin dilate (widen) so that more blood can be cooled by circulating up from the warm center of your body to your skin. The cooled blood then returns to the center of your body, cooling your internal organs. Next, you begin to perspire. The moisture pools on your skin, cooling you as it evaporates.

But as you perspire, you lose water and salts that are essential to the normal operation of every cell in your body. If you do not replace them, you may begin to suffer from heat cramps, spasms of the muscles in your arms, legs and abdomen caused by salt depletion, which are the first sign of heat-related illness. Or you may develop the headache, nausea and mental disorientation that signal heat exhaustion.

Heat cramps and heat exhaustion are defense mechanisms designed to get you to slow down. If you ignore them, your temperature may rise as high as 106 degrees Fahrenheit, your skin may turn hot, red and dry, and you may lose consciousness—all the signs of heat stroke.

To lower your risk of heat related illness

Get out of the heat. Stay in the shade, not the sun, and use an air-conditioner to keep indoor temperatures in a safe range.

Drink more liquids. Cold water is the best hot weather thirst quencher. As long as you don't have any gastrointestinal problem that would bar you from eating iced food and beverages, the very cold liquid can only do you good: It tastes better and it lowers your internal temperature faster.

Avoid high-calorie beverages such as milk shakes; the extra calories only provide extra heat. It is better to avoid alcoholic or caffeine beverages, but if you prefer them, mix the alcohol with lots of ice and water or soda and the coffee or tea with plenty of ice to offset their natural diuretic effect. If you are not on a salt-restricted diet, you can use a glass of iced bouillon to slake your thirst and replace salts lost in perspiring.

Pick a proper diet. When the temperature rises, your appetite usually falls. But it takes energy to perspire, and people who exercise more in the summer months actually need more calories. The trick is to pick the foods that are easiest to digest.

Fruits and vegetables, which are low in fat and protein, but rich in the sodium and potassium we lose in perspiring, are natural hot weather foods. If you still crave a steak, eat it in the evening when the air has cooled and the food won't make you uncomfortably warm. Hot spicy foods such as curries and chilies can help cool you down because they contain hot peppers, which stimulate nerves that trigger perspiration.

HEMOPHILIA

Known risk factors

Age:	No	Smoking:	No
Gender:	Yes	Drugs & medical procedures:	No
Race/ethnic group:	No	General health:	No
Family history:	Yes	Environment:	No
Diet:	No	Occupation:	No

Are you at risk?

Hemophilia is a genetic defect transmitted on the X chromosome. A woman has two X chromosomes, one from her mother and one from her father. If one of her X chromosomes has the gene for hemophilia, she is a carrier who can pass the hemophilia along to her children, but her other, normal X chromosome will nearly always protect her from having hemophilia herself. In rare cases, a female carrier may bleed heavily during surgery or during her menstrual period. Even more rarely, a woman will inherit an X chromosome with the hemophilia gene from her father and from her mother, making her a true hemophiliac, but this situation is highly unlikely.

A man, on the other hand, has one X chromosome (from his mother) and one Y chromosome (from his father), so if he inherits an X chromosome with the hemophilia gene, he will have the disease. This situation occurs about once in every 3,500 to 5,000 boys born in this country.

If you are the son of a man who has hemophilia and a woman who is not a carrier, you do not have a significantly increased risk of hemophilia because you inherited your father's Y chromosome and one of your mother's X chromosomes without the hemophilia gene. If you are this couple's daughter, you will be a carrier because you inherited the X chromosome with the hemophilia gene from your father and a second X chromosome, without the gene, from your mother. Every son of a woman who carries the gene for hemophilia and a man who does not has a 50% chance of being a hemophiliac; every daughter has a 50% chance of being a carrier.

Early detection. In families with a history of hemophilia, it is possible to tell before the baby is born whether or not it has hemophilia by comparing a sample of DNA from any relative who has hemophilia or is a known carrier with a sample of the fetus' DNA obtained either by amniocentesis or chorionic villus biopsy, an examination of a sample of tissue from the outermost membrane surrounding the fetus.

After a baby is born, hemophilia may be diagnosed either by a test that measures prothrombin time (the time it takes for blood to clot; an increased prothrombin time indicates hemophilia) or a blood test to measure the level of clotting Factor VIII or, less commonly, one of the other natural substances that make it possible for blood to clot (deficiencies of any of these indicates hemophilia).

In America, where circumcision is common, baby boys with severe hemophilia are typically diagnosed within days after birth because they bleed heavily when circumcised. Moderate hemophilia may not be discovered until the baby is old enough to crawl around and bump into things. Mild hemophilia may remain undetected until the teen-age years or even into the early 20s. Both moderate and mild hemophilia are generally discovered after an injury that causes bleeding into a joint such as the knee or ankle.

To lower your risk of hemophilia

If you have a family history of hemophilia, seek genetic counseling before you begin your own family. Today, women who carry the hemophilia gene (but do not have hemophilia) can be identified by DNA testing performed on a small sample of blood.

HEMORRHOIDS

Known risk factors

Age:	Yes	Smoking:	No
Gender:	No	Drugs & medical procedures:	No
Race/ethnic group:	No	General health:	Yes
Family history:	?	Environment:	No
Diet:	Yes	Occupation:	Yes

Are you at risk?

Hemorrhoids are the price we pay for standing up on two legs, a posture that increases the pressure inside the blood vessels in the anal area, sometimes enough to make them varicose (swell). If you are going to get hemorrhoids, you are most likely to develop them between the ages of 20 and 50. Hemorrhoids often seem to run in families, perhaps because we inherit our body structure from our parents. Any work that requires you to sit or stand still for long periods of time increases the risk of your developing hemorrhoids.

With hemorrhoids, what you eat is, to put it bluntly, what you get. A low-fiber diet that is also low in fluids may produce hard, stiff, constipating stool that forces you to strain when defecating, increasing the pressure on your anal blood vessels. A fiber-rich diet can have the opposite effect, producing bulky stool that is easier to eliminate.

Medical conditions that increase pressure and raise the risk of hemorrhoids or make existing hemorrhoids worse include diarrhea, an anal infection, cancer of the rectum, a pelvic tumor, heart failure, liver disease and prolonged coughing, sneezing or vomiting.

Being pregnant is a common aggravator of hemorrhoids in young women. During pregnancy, the growing uterus presses against blood vessels in the abdomen. Labor contractions may worsen existing hemorrhoids.

Early detection. External hemorrhoids, which are varicose veins outside the anal sphincter (the ring of muscle surrounding the opening to the rectum), can be diagnosed by simple observation. Internal hemorrhoids, which are varicose veins underneath the mucous membrane lining of the anus, can be found by digital examination. However, because rectal cancers may cause bleeding mistakenly attributed to hemorrhoids, before your doctor begins to treat your hemorrhoids, he may wish to rule out the possibility of rectal polyps or colorectal cancer by sigmoidoscopy (an examination of the rectum and colon with a flexible lighted instrument).

To lower your risk of hemorrhoids

Watch your diet. To reduce the risk of certain types of cancer, the National Cancer Institute (NCI) recommends that Americans consume 20 to 30 grams of fiber a day. There is no such precise recommendation on the amount of fiber that will best prevent constipation and reduce the risk of hemorrhoids. The following servings, however, will give you 10 grams of fiber each:

- Two one-cup servings of fresh or lightly cooked fruit and vegetables. If the skin is edible, serve the fruit/vegetable unpeeled.
- Four to six servings of whole wheat bread or whole wheat pasta or a whole wheat grain such as kasha or brown rice. (One serving equals one slice of bread or one-half cup of pasta or grain.)
- Four tablespoons of plain wheat bran or one-half cup of a high bran cereal such as Kellogg's All-Bran. (Note: The fiber in oat bran is not as effective as wheat bran in producing large soft stools.)

Whenever you increase the fiber content of your diet, be sure to increase the amount of fluids you drink. Without sufficient fluids, fiber can clump together and, in rare cases, actually obstruct the intestines.

HEPATITIS

Known risk factors

Age:	No	Smoking:	No
Gender:	No	Drugs & medical procedures:	Yes
Race/ethnic group:	No	General health:	Yes
Family history:	No	Environment:	Yes
Diet:	No	Occupation:	Yes

Are you at risk?

Hepatitis A virus (HAV) is spread by oral contact with fecal material. It is less commonly spread by sharing intravenous needles or through transfusion of blood from a person who has the infection. Your risk is greatest if you are exposed to food prepared by an infected person who did not wash his hands after defecating or if you live in an undeveloped country where the water is contaminated with feces. Raw shellfish taken from such waters also carry the viruses (which are killed by thorough cooking).

Hepatitis B virus (HBV), which is itself a risk factor for liver cancer, is transmitted by contact with infected blood or through intimate sexual contact, particularly anal intercourse. Worldwide, there are believed to be about 200 million people carrying the virus for hepatitis B. In the United States, where there are believed to be about 1 million carriers, more than 300,000 new cases are diagnosed each year.

The people at highest risk for hepatitis B are male homosexuals, people who are sexually promiscuous with multiple partners, intravenous drug users who share needles, people who have hemophilia and others who receive frequent blood transfusions, kidney disease patients at hemodialysis centers and health workers exposed to blood and body fluids. Pregnant women who are infected with hepatitis B can transmit the virus to the baby through the umbilical cord.

Hepatitis C virus (HCV), which was once known as non-A, non-B virus, is responsible for 80% to 95% of the hepatitis caused by contaminated blood transfusions. People who are at high risk of hepatitis B are also at high risk of hepatitis C.

Early detection. The three forms of hepatitis are diagnosed by blood tests that show the presence of the virus or antibodies to the viruses. The blood test for hepatitis C was developed and put into clinical trials in 1989.

To lower your risk of hepatitis

Wash your hands. Hepatitis A, which is passed through fecal/oral contact, can be avoided simply by washing your hands after defecating and insisting that anyone who handles food do the same.

Practice safer sex. Using condoms every time you have sex may reduce the risk of acquiring hepatitis B, which can be transmitted through intimate contact.

The correct use of condoms begins with storing them properly in a cool, dry place to protect the latex from drying out. The condom should be put on gently to avoid tearing. Leave room at the tip to accommodate the ejaculate. After ejaculation, withdraw the penis with the condom still in place, holding it close against the base of the penis to avoid spilling any ejaculate. Discard all used condoms; never try to wash them out and use them again.

If you are exposed, get prophylactic treatment. If you have had close contact with a person who has infectious hepatitis, your doctor will routinely prescribed a prophylactic dose of gamma globulin. Prior to exposure, vaccination against hepatitis B has been shown to reduce the incidence of that form of hepatitis by as much 92% among people who are considered to be at high risk, so the vaccine is now recommended for newborns whose mothers had hepatitis and people who are traveling to areas such as China and Southeast Asia where hepatitis is endemic.

Because the introduction of the vaccine for hepatitis B coincided with the rise of AIDS, many people mistakenly associate the two and refuse to use the vaccine. There is no known connection between being vaccinated for Hepatitis B and contracting the AIDS virus (HIV).

HERPES

Known risk factors

Age:	Yes	Smoking:	No
Gender:	No	Drugs & medical procedures:	Yes
Race/ethnic group:	No	General health:	Yes
Family history:	No	Environment:	Yes
Diet:	No	Occupation:	No

Are you at risk?

We are all at risk for herpes. In fact, 90% of us have acquired the herpes virus before the age of four. Most of us have picked up herpes simplex type 1 (HSV-1), the virus primarily responsible for herpes infections on the lips. Herpes simplex type 2 (HSV-2), the virus primarily responsible for genital herpes infections, is less common, but still affects about one in every six American adults.

You are at risk of acquiring the virus if you come in close contact with a person who has an active herpes infection. Herpes is passed from one person to another (or from one part of the body to another) by direct skin-to-skin contact with the infected area. Transmission is most likely when there are visible sores, but the virus may sometimes be spread even when there are no obvious symptoms.

Babies born to women who have an active genital herpes infection at delivery are at risk of picking up the virus as they pass through the vaginal canal. In rare cases, the virus may cross the placenta to attack the fetus in the uterus, leading to complications of pregnancy or premature delivery. While they are pregnant, some women develop *herpes gestationis* (herpes of pregnancy), skin eruptions that occur during pregnancy, disappear when the baby is delivered, and may appear again during subsequent pregnancies or at menstruation or when using estrogen or oral contraceptives. Despite its name, *herpes gestationis* is not a herpes infection.

Once you have the herpes virus, it is yours for as long as you live. According to the American Social Health Association (ASHA), many people carry the herpes virus without even knowing that they have it.

The more common pattern, however, is a series of active infections interspersed with periods during which the virus lies dormant in nerve endings at the site of the original infection until activated by some form of stress. An injury (from dental treatment, for example), a fever, a cold, fatigue or exposure to an environmental irritant such as cold weather, warm weather, sun or wind can bring it to life again.

Anyone who harbors the herpes virus is at increased risk for flare-ups when using the anti-acne drug isotretoin (Accutane), the anti-psoriasis drug etretinate (Tegison) and the anti-hypoglycemia drug diazoxide (Proglycem). Women are at risk of recurrence every month, right before menstruation begins.

Early detection. Examining cells from a blistery sore under a microscope can provide clues that there are herpes viruses present, but only a tissue culture can confirm the diagnosis and identify the virus as either HSV-1 or HSV-2. New blood tests currently being developed can identify herpes viruses in the absence of symptoms, but these tests are not yet widely available.

To lower your risk of herpes

Practice safer sex. You can reduce your risk of getting herpes by having sex only with a person who does not have herpes and who has sex only with you (mutual monogamy).

The herpes virus can be transmitted from person to person even when there are no visible sores. Using a latex condom every time you have sex may also reduce your risk of acquiring the herpes virus from a person who has an inactive infection, but the American Social Health Association stresses the fact that no method of contraception is considered reliably protective during an active infection when ASHA advises abstinence as the only sure way to avoid transmitting or acquiring the virus.

The correct use of condoms begins with storing them properly in a cool, dry place to protect the latex from drying out. The condom should be put on gently to avoid tearing. Leave room at the tip to accommodate the ejaculate. After ejaculation, your partner should withdraw the penis with the condom still in place, holding it close against the base of the penis to avoid spilling any ejaculate. Discard all used condoms; never try to wash them out and use them again.

According to the American Social Health Association, you may increase the protective effect of a condom by using a spermicidal foam that contains nonoxynol-9. In laboratory studies, nonoxynol-9 appears to kill the herpes virus on contact. But the two contraceptives must be used in tandem; on its own, the foam is not considered adequately protective.

Never touch an active sore. If you have an active herpes infection, wash your hands every time you touch the sore to avoid spreading the virus to another part of your body.

HIGH BLOOD PRESSURE
(HYPERTENSION)

Known risk factors

Age:	Yes	Smoking:	No
Gender:	Yes	Drugs & medical procedures:	Yes
Race/ethnic group:	Yes	Environment:	No
Family history:	Yes	Occupation:	No
Diet:	?		

Are you at risk?

There are approximately 37 million Americans with high blood pressure defined as sustained blood pressure readings above 140/90. Ninety percent of them have essential hypertension, high blood pressure for which there is no obvious medical reason. If you are black, your risk of developing essential hypertension is about two times higher than it would be if you were white, and you are four times more likely to die of its effects.

Essential hypertension, which usually shows up first between the ages of 25 and 55, often runs in families. Regardless of race, if your relatives have high blood pressure, you have a higher-than-normal chance of developing it; children of people with hypertension often develop the condition at an earlier age than other people.

Old wives' tales to the contrary, neither stress nor smoking causes high blood pressure, although both can make existing cases worse. Not everyone who has high blood pressure is sensitive to salt, but if you are one of the 60% of all hypertensives who do react to this condiment, consuming it may worsen your hypertension. Being overweight raises your risk. So does a steadily rising level of serum cholesterol.

Ten percent of all Americans with high blood pressure have secondary hypertension, high blood pressure caused by another medical condition such as kidney disease; a brain tumor; or a narrowed aorta (the large artery leading away from the heart). In pregnant women, high blood pressure may be a result of pre-eclampsia or eclampsia.

You are also at increased risk for high blood pressure if you are using oral contraceptives, or allergy medication, cold remedies, decongestants or weight control products that contain drugs such as ephedrine, norpinephrine and pseudephedrine that mimic the effects of the sympathetic nervous system and constrict blood vessels. If you are using an MAO inhibitor, a class of drugs used to treat depression or hypertension, and you consume a food that is high in the amino acid tyramine, the result may be a hypertensive crisis (sustained high blood pressure). Foods high in tyramine include aged meat such as liver paté, aged cheese, and red wines.

Early detection. Hypertension is a silent disease that may develop without any obvious symptoms. If left untreated, however, it may eventually lead to heart damage, heart failure and stroke.

Traditionally, blood pressure readings are expressed in two numbers, such as 130/80. The first, higher number is your systolic pressure, the pressure measured in millimeters of mercury during the time when your heart is contracting to pump blood out into your arteries. The second, lower number is your diastolic pressure, the pressure when your heart is relaxed between beats.

Although experts disagree over exactly what constitutes high blood pressure, most believe that a diastolic pressure higher than 90 in a person younger than 50 or higher than 100 in a person older than 60 is a serious warning sign.

To lower your risk of high blood pressure

Control your cholesterol. In 1988, three independent scientific studies—two from the Kaiser Permanente health maintenance organization in California and one from the University of North Carolina—were able to show that men who were given drugs that reduce the levels of low density lipoproteins (LDLs), the "bad cholesterol" fat-and-protein particles that carry cholesterol into your arteries, had a lower incidence of high blood pressure. Nobody has identified the real link between cholesterol levels and hypertension, but a good guess is that the cholesterol deposits narrow your blood vessels, forcing your heart to work harder to push blood through.

Control your weight. Sometimes an overweight person with high blood pressure can bring the pressure down into a normal range just by losing weight. One extra benefit of a diet to control cholesterol is that it often reduces weight, as well.

HODGKIN'S DISEASE

Known risk factors

Age:	Yes	Smoking:	No
Gender:	?	Drugs & medical procedures:	No
Race/ethnic group:	No	General health:	No
Family history:	?	Environment:	No
Diet:	No	Occupation:	No

Are you at risk?

Hodgkin's disease is a cancer of the lymphatic system. Approximately 7,400 new cases are diagnosed each year in the United States. The disease, which is rare before age 10 and occurs most frequently among people between age 15 and 34 or after 60, is slightly more common among men than among women. Your risk of Hodgkin's is higher if you or a close relative have an inherited immunological deficiency. Your risk is also higher if you have a brother or sister with Hodgkin's, particularly if you are the same sex, but simple propinquity does not seem to be the precipitating factor. Although there is some suspicion that Hodgkin's disease is linked to a virus, health workers who specialize in the care of patients with lymphatic cancer do not seem to be at higher-than-normal risk.

Early detection. The symptoms of Hodgkin's disease—swollen liver, increasing numbers of white blood cells, intense itching, fever, weight loss and heavy perspiration during sleep—may resemble those of leukemia, mononucleosis, non-Hodgkin's lymphatic cancer or toxoplasmosis. Hodgkin's is conclusively diagnosed by a biopsy of the lymph node that shows cells characteristic of the disease.

Today, more than than seven out of every 10 people who develop Hodgkin's disease can be cured with chemotherapy or radiation or a combination of the two. The earlier the disease is found, the more likely it is that it can be treated with radiation or chemotherapy alone, thus reducing the side effects of treatment.

To lower your risk of Hodgkin's disease

There is currently no medically certain way to reduce your risk of developing Hodgkin's disease.

HUNTINGTON'S DISEASE

Known risk factors

Age:	No	Smoking:	No
Gender:	No	Drugs & medical procedures:	No
Race/ethnic group:	No	General health:	No
Family history:	Yes	Environment:	No
Diet:	No	Occupation:	No

Are you at risk?

Huntington's disease is an ultimately fatal inherited neurological disorder that kills nerve cells in the brain, causing psychological problems (usually angry rages), muscle spasms and loss of coordination, and a steady, progressive loss of memory. At present, there are approximately 25,000 Americans with the disease; 500 to 1,000 new cases are diagnosed each year.

The people at risk are those with a family history of Huntington's disease (HD). People with no family history of HD are not considered at risk. Huntington's affects men and women alike, and it appears in all ethnic and racial groups. It rarely shows up before age 30; most cases are diagnosed between the ages of 35 and 50. If your mother or father had Huntington's, you have a 50% chance of inheriting the defective gene that causes the disease. The gene for Huntington's is a dominant one; if you inherit it from either parent, you will inherit the disease. However, there is some evidence to suggest that people who inherit the gene from their father are likely to have a more severe form of the disease.

Early detection. Huntington's has traditionally been diagnosed by its symptoms and by the presence of a family history of the disease. Newly developed analyses of DNA patterns now make it possible to identify most victims in families affected by Huntington's years before the disease becomes evident, if they choose to be identified.

To lower your risk of Huntington's disease:

There is no way to alter a person's genetic make-up so as to eliminate the risk of Huntington's disease. If you have close relatives with Huntington's disease, you may wish to seek genetic counseling or testing before you choose to have a family of your own.

INFERTILITY

Known risk factors

Age:	Yes	Smoking:	?
Gender:	No	Drugs & medical procedures:	Yes
Race/ethnic group:	Yes	General health:	Yes
Family history:	No	Environment:	No
Diet:	Yes	Occupation:	Yes

Are you at risk?

The woman most likely to be infertile is older than 35, has a history of pelvic infections or endometriosis, and may have used oral contraceptives or an intrauterine device (IUD).

The most frequent cause of infertility in women is a blockage of the fallopian tubes that keeps the egg and sperm from meeting. Gonorrhea, pelvic inflammatory disease (PID) or vaginitis may cause scarring that blocks the fallopian tubes, but the most common cause is endometriosis, implants of tissue that has migrated from the lining of the uterus. Indeed, as many as 50% of all infertile women have endometriosis. Other medical conditions that increase the chance of female infertility are polycystic ovarian disease, pituitary failure and thyroid disease, all of which may interfere with the production or release of reproductive hormones.

A woman's choice of contraception may also affect her risk of infertility. Women who use oral contraceptives have sometimes failed to ovulate for as long as four to five years after they stop taking the pill. IUDs may contribute to pelvic infections that scar and block the fallopian tubes. In a roundabout way, diet may affect the ability to conceive: women who gain or lose excessive amounts of weight may cease to ovulate and menstruate.

The most important cause of infertility in men is failing to produce enough healthy sperm. A man may also be infertile because his epididymides, the tiny tubes through which the sperm move from the testes, are blocked by scars from a sexually transmitted infection such as gonorrhea. Occupational exposure to lead is known to interfere with sperm production. The same goes for exposure to the kind of high heat that occurs in a commercial bakery or a foundry. In fact, sperm production is so sensitive to heat that even a hot bath can temporarily slow it down.

Men with an un-descended testes, varicocele (a varicose vein in the testes), an injury to the testes, a testicular infection, chronic infections of the prostate, childhood mumps or a disorder of the pituitary gland that interferes with the production of male reproductive hormones are also at risk. So are men with cystic fibrosis, who often have structural defects in the reproductive system that interfere with sperm production and/or delivery, although desire and potency remain completely normal.

Among the medications known to lower sperm production are the anti-cancer drugs bisulfan (Myleran), chlorambucil (Leukeran), cyclophosphamide (Cytoxan, Neospar), methotrexate (Mexate), and mechloramine (Mustargen); the anti-inflammatory drug sulfathiazine (Azasulfadine); the anti-gout drug colchicine; the urinary antiseptics nitrofuradantoin (Furadantin, Microdantin) and trimethoprim-sulfamethoxazole (Bactrim, Septra). Men who abuse alcohol or marijuana may also produce fewer sperm.

Early detection. The first step in detecting infertility is defining it. Infertility is the failure to conceive after a full year of intercourse without contraceptives.

The test for male fertility is a semen analysis. A man needs a minimum of 20 million sperm per ml of semen for fertilization. Semen samples from fertile men normally contain 60 million to 120 million sperm per ml. The person who examines the semen sample will also look for sperm that move about actively. If they aren't sufficently mobile, sperm cannot make their way through the vaginal canal to the uterus and up to the fallopian tubes.

The simplest tests for female fertility are those that tell whether or not a woman is ovulating. First, she must keep a record of her temperature every day for one month. If she is ovulating, her temperature should go up a degree or so halfway through the menstrual cycle and remain elevated until right before she begins to menstruate. If she doesn't show this kind of pattern every month, she may be ovulating only occasionally or not at all.

The second simple test for ovulation requires a woman to observe the texture of her vaginal mucus. At mid-cycle, right before ovulation, the mucus is sticky and clear. At ovulation, a small plug of mucus may escape or there may be slight bleeding. After ovulation, the mucus is thin and opaque.

Once a woman's doctor determines that she is ovulating, he or she will next want to find out if the egg she produces can get through the fallopian tube to meet her partner's sperm. The simplest way to find out is to perform a Rubin test, introducing a small amount of carbon dioxide into the uterus. If the fallopian tubes are open, the gas will rise through them into the abdomen. The doctor can hear it moving by pressing a stethoscope against the abdomen.

To identify a partial blockage or blockage of a single tube, the doctor may order an hysterosalpingogram, an X-ray taken after dye is injected into the uterus. If the fallopian tubes are open, the X-ray will show the dye flowing out into the abdomen.

If neither the Rubin test or the X-ray are conclusive, the doctor may opt for laparoscopy, the introduction of a small lighted viewing device through an abdominal incision. Laparoscopy, which allows the doctor to see the surface of the internal reproductive organs, is performed under general anesthetic.

To lower your risk of infertility

Keep your weight normal. A healthy woman's body is ordinarily 25% fatty tissue. Having much more (or much less) interferes with the body's ability to make the female reproductive hormones that enable a woman to ovulate. As a result, infertility is most common among seriously obese women and their opposites, female athletes who reduce the amount of body fat to less than 20%.

Start your family early. Changing lifestyles have changed our ideas about when to start a family. The result is an increased number of couples who put off having a baby until they are into their 30s and 40s. Unfortunately, the older you are, the greater your risk of being infertile, and some experts estimate that as many as 2.5 million married American couples may now be infertile.

Be patient, check your timing—and don't try too hard. When you are trying to conceive, it is important to have intercourse on a regular basis at the right time, around mid-cycle when ovulation occurs and conception is most likely. It is also important not be too eager. In general, it takes 24 to 48 hours after ejaculation for a man to build up a maximum sperm count. If you have intercourse more frequently than that, the ejaculate may not contain a sufficient number of sperm.

INFLAMMATORY BOWEL DISEASE

Known risk factors

Age:	Yes	Smoking:	No
Gender:	No	Drugs & medical procedures:	No
Race/ethnic group:	Yes	General health:	No
Family history:	Yes	Environment:	No
Diet:	No	Occupation:	No

Are you at risk?

Chronic inflammatory bowel disease may follow one of two patterns. The first, ulcerative colitis, causes inflammation in the colon. The second, Crohn's disease, can cause inflammation any place along the entire length of the gastrointestinal tract. A third, acute, form of inflammatory bowel disease, antibiotic-associated colitis, is an inflammation that may occur when you are using antibiotics that destroy organisms that live naturally in the gut, allowing the growth of pathogenic organisms that produce toxins damaging to the lining of your intestinal tract. Among the antibiotics most often blamed for this condition are ampicillin, cephalosporins, clindamycin (Cleocin), erythromycin, lincomycin (Lincocin), sulfamethoxazole-trimethoprim (Bactrim, Septra) and tetracycline.

Chronic inflammatory bowel disease occurs most frequently among people age 15 to 30 or 50 to 70. The older you are when you develop the disease, the more serious it is likely to be. The illness is more common among whites than among people of other races; the people at highest risk are those of Jewish and/or northern European ancestry. A family history of inflammatory bowel disease slightly increases your risk; 2 to 5% of all people with ulcerative colitis have one or more relatives with the same problem.

Although people with inflammatory bowel disease often suffer from psychological stress, the stress appears to be a symptom of the illness rather than its cause. The role of diet is still an open question, with some experts saying that a low-fiber diet increases the risk of ulcerative colitis while others suggest that a high fiber diet makes existing disease worse.

Early detection. Because people with long-standing, extensive ulcerative colitis are at increased risk of colon cancer, early detection and follow-up are extremely important.

If you have symptoms of inflammatory bowel disease such as chronic diarrhea, abdominal pain, fever, loss of appetite and unexplained weight loss, your doctor's first step may be to order stool tests to rule out a bacterial or parasitical infection. If you are a woman, you doctor will want to make sure you are not suffering from pelvic inflammatory disease (PID), ectopic pregnancy, ovarian cysts and tumors or an inflammation of the colon caused by a reaction to oral contraceptives.

The diagnostic test for ulcerative colitis is sigmoidoscopy, an examination of your colon with a flexible lighted tube that allows your doctor to see the surface of the mucous membrane lining of the gut. The diagnostic test for Crohn's disease is an X-ray taken after you have been given a barium enema, which will show the outlines of your colon on the X-ray film.

To lower your risk of inflammatory bowel disease

Because the cause of chronic inflammatory bowel disease remains a mystery, there is presently no known way to reduce your risk of the disease.

INFLUENZA

Major risk factors

Age:	No	Smoking:	?
Gender:	No	Drugs & medical procedures:	No
Race/ethnic group:	No	General health:	No
Family history:	No	Environment:	No
Diet:	No	Occupation:	No

Are you at risk?

Influenza, which is also known as grippe or flu, is an acute viral infection of the upper respiratory tract. Everyone who has not been immunized to the virus is considered to be at risk for influenza. According to the Federal Centers for Diseases Control, even people who have been immunized may catch the flu, but if they do, their symptoms are likely to be less severe than they would have been otherwise.

Early detection. Influenza is diagnosed by its symptoms: a sudden high fever, sore throat, headache, muscle aches and a hacking cough, that can linger for several days during which the flu victim may hardly be able to muster the energy for ordinary, everyday tasks.

To lower your risk of influenza

Vaccination. The true risk of influenza lies in the possibility of the patient's developing viral or bacterial pneumonia. The Food and Drug Administration recommends vaccinating people in groups considered at high risk for these complications.

This high-risk group includes people who are very young or older than 65, and those with asthma, diabetes, heart disease or a chronic lung disease such as emphysema. Children age six months to 18 years who are on long-term aspirin therapy are also considered at risk because giving aspirin to a child who has a viral infection such as chicken pox or the flu has been linked to the onset of Reye's syndrome, a rare and potentially fatal condition.

Warning: The flu vaccine is grown in an egg medium. The Food and Drug Administration warns that people who are allergic to eggs should not be vaccinated. If you have any questions regarding your sensitivity to the flu vaccine, discuss them fully with your own doctor before being vaccinated.

INSOMNIA

Known risk factors

Age:	Yes	Smoking:	No
Gender:	No	Drugs & medical procedures:	Yes
Race/ethnic group:	No	General health:	Yes
Family history:	No	Environment:	No
Diet:	Yes	Occupation:	No

Are you at risk?

Insomnia is a symptom, not a disease, but when you can't sleep, it is hard to care about the difference. About 50% of all Americans go through a bout of insomnia at some point in their lives; one-third of us have it more often or on a regular basis.

Any time you are suffering from physical pain and discomfort, your risk of insomnia goes up. Diseases of the heart, lungs, liver, kidneys, pancreas and digestive organs often keep us awake at night. People who have emotional problems such as anxiety, phobia or depression, are at risk for the type of insomnia that makes it hard to fall asleep.

Others fall asleep easily but wake up very early and are unable to get back to sleep. This form of insomnia occurs most often among older people, but may be associated with depression as well. One important benefit of tricyclic anti-depressant drugs is their ability to smooth out disturbances in the sleep cycle.

What you eat can affect your risk of insomnia. Large amounts of caffeine keep some people awake, and we all become more sensitive to caffeine as we get older. But this effect is very variable. Some people stay awake after one cup of decaffeinated coffee; others find a cup of strong brew relaxing. Withdrawing from alcohol or sedatives can interfere with your natural sleep/wake cycle, but the disruption is likely to be temporary. People who travel across time zones are at risk of temporary insomnia, as are people who work different shifts that can disrupt normal sleep patterns. (See JET LAG, page 86.)

Early detection. One night without sleep, especially if there is a good reason for your having stayed awake, does not qualify as insomnia. But if you find yourself consistently unable to get to sleep or stay asleep throughout the night, check with your doctor. Ignoring insomnia is a mistake. Sleep deprivation not only makes you less alert and capable, it can interfere with personal relationships because lack of sleep also makes most people irritable and short-tempered.

To lower your risk of insomnia

Tailor your diet to your sleep schedule. Caffeine's stimulating effects may last for as long as seven hours after you drink a cup of tea or coffee. If you are sensitive to caffeine but hate to give up your favorite beverage, compromise by having it early in the day, never later than three o'clock in the afternoon. If you eat late at night, keep the meals small; large amounts of food can keep you awake. Avoid drinking large amounts of alcohol late in the evening. Drinking late at night can shorten your night's sleep because you run into a mini-withdrawal effect early in the morning and awake restless.

Adjust your lifestyle to your sleeping habits. Exercise regularly, if you like, but not late in the day or right before bedtime, when it can be stimulating rather than relaxing. Sex is a maybe. Some people find it relaxing, others say it keeps them awake. The same can be said of the proverbial warm bath, which is nice if it makes you drowsy, but not if it sets you up for another six hours' activity.

If your insomnia is not responding to self-treatment, seek help. Insomnia caused by an illness, stress or overindulgence in food and drink often disappears when the situation changes. If your insomnia is hanging on, you may wish to seek help from a professional specializing in sleep disorders.

IRON DEFICIENCY ANEMIA

Known risk factors

Age:	Yes	Smoking:	No
Gender:	Yes	Drugs & medical procedures:	Yes
Race/ethnic group:	No	General health:	Yes
Family history:	No	Environment:	No
Diet:	Yes	Occupation:	No

Are you at risk?

Iron is an essential nutrient, a constituent of hemoglobin, the red pigment in the blood that carries oxygen to every cell in your body. People who are iron deficient have less hemoglobin than normal in their red blood cells, a condition known as iron deficiency anemia.

The person at highest risk of iron deficiency anemia is a woman of childbearing age who loses blood each month when she menstruates and doesn't get a sufficient amount of iron in her diet. Women who are using oral contraceptives are less likely to be iron-deficient. Being pregnant increases the risk because it increases the amount of iron needed to sustain both mother and child; so does breast-feeding a baby.

Reducing diets put you at risk because they cut down the amount of food you eat. Vegetarian diets may be risky because they omit meat, fish and poultry—the best sources of dietary iron. Adolescent girls, who are growing quickly but are often on reducing diets, are at high risk. In fact, many nutritionists believe that iron deficiency anemia is the most common nutritional deficiency among teen-agers.

Occult (hidden) internal bleeding, particularly from the gastrointestinal tract, is the leading cause of iron deficiency among men. You are at risk for this kind of bleeding if you are using a drug that irritates the lining of the intestinal tract or have a medical condition that causes internal bleeding.

Among the drugs known to trigger intestinal bleeding are aspirin and other salicylates; non-steroidal anti-inflammatory drugs (NSAIDs) such as ibuprofen (Advil, Motrin), indomethacin (Indocin) and naproxen (Naprosyn); anti-cancer drugs such as cyclophosphamide (Cytoxan), dactinomycin (Cosmegen), fluorouracil (5–FU, Adrucil), methotrexate (Mexate) and plicamycin (Mithracin, Mithramycin); reserpine (found in many diuretics) and steroid drugs.

Among the illnesses known to cause internal bleeding are peptic ulcers, colon cancer, diverticulitis, swollen blood vessels in the esophagus, hiatus hernia, inflammatory bowel disease and intestinal parasites such as hookworm.

Donating blood too frequently will also raise the risk of iron deficiency anemia, which is why all reputable blood banks place limits on how often you can give blood.

Early detection. The screening test for iron deficiency anemia is a complete blood count (CBC) to measure hemoglobin levels. For men, a hemoglobin count of 14 to 18 g/dL is considered normal; for women, 12 to 16 g/dL. Hemoglobin counts lower than these indicate anemia. If your doctor suspects another cause for the anemia, she may request tests to rule out internal bleeding.

To lower your risk of iron deficiency anemia

Eat enough food. In general, Americans consume a diet that provides an average 5 mg to 7 mg iron for each 1,000 calories. The recommended dietary allowance (RDA) for healthy men and women who are past menopause is 10 mg. The RDA for a woman of childbearing age who is not pregnant is 15 mg. The RDA for a pregnant woman is 30 mg. The RDA for a nursing mother is 15 mg.

Increase your absorption of iron from food. Heme iron, the form of iron that accounts for 40% of all the iron found in meat, poultry, fish, eggs and milk, is five times easier for your body to absorb than non-heme iron, which accounts for 60% of the iron in animal tissues and 100% of the iron found in vegetables, fruits and grains. That is why vegetarians are at increased risk for iron deficiency anemia.

Iron is absorbed more easily when the environment in your stomach is acid, so you can increase the amount of iron you get from plant food by eating fruits and vegetables with meat or milk, which increase the acidity in your stomach.

To increase the amount of iron you get from any dish, serve it with a food rich in vitamin C, which changes the iron in food from hard-to-absorb ferric iron to easy-to-absorb ferrous iron. Serve pasta with tomato (or tomato and beef) sauce; baste beef or chicken with an orange sauce.

If you are at risk for iron deficiency, ask your doctor about the need for iron supplements. Then ask about supplements most easily absorbed by your body. As a general rule, iron supplements with the word "ferrous" in their name are absorbed better than supplements with the word "ferric."

Ferrous sulfate is the best known; ferrous succinate, ferrous lactate, ferrous fumarate, ferrous gluconate and ferrous glutamate are absorbed approximately as well as ferrous sulfate.

Keep all iron supplements out of the reach of small children and pets. Every year, there are more than 2,000 cases of iron poisoning in the United States, most of them among young children who swallow quantities of iron supplements. As few as 16 tablets of a 300 mg ferrous sulfate supplement may prove lethal for a two-year-old.

JET LAG

Known risk factors

Age:	No	Smoking:	No
Gender:	No	Drugs & medical procedures:	Yes
Race/ethnic group:	No	General health:	No
Family history:	No	Environment:	Yes
Diet:	Yes	Occupation:	Yes

Are you at risk?

Jet lag, which is also known as circadian dysrhythmia (*circadian* = daily; *dysrhythmia* = irregular rhythm), is an environmental condition that occurs when we are exposed to situations that defy our natural sleep/wake cycle.

The symptoms of jet lag are disruptions in sleep and eating patterns accompanied by fatigue and irritability that gradually disappear as our bodies readjust to a new schedule. You are most likely to suffer from jet lag when you travel east or west across time zones. The more time zones you cross, the greater your discomfort is likely to be. According to a 1989 study of fliers conducted by the Upjohn Company, 94% of the people who cross three or more time zones end up with jet lag. Flying west to east seemed to provoke more problems than flying east to west.

Jet lag may also be an occupational hazard. People in industrial plants, transportation workers, health-care professionals, security or police officers, firefighters, entertainers, and airline personnel who work rotating shifts, daytime hours one week, nighttime hours the next, or who constantly cross time zones are all at risk.

Early detection. Jet lag is a self-evident condition.

To lower your risk of jet lag

Adjust your sleep schedules.

When traveling across time zones, if you are going to be at your destination only for a day or two, researchers at the Stanford University Center for Insomnia Research suggest that you try to stick to your own sleep/wake times. If you are going to be there longer, try to work yourself into the new time schedule right away. Go to sleep at the "right" time in the new place on the very first night; get up for breakfast at the "right" time the very first morning.

Use the sun to re-set your biological clock. According to the Stanford scientists, exposure to sunlight at your destination may help reschedule your sleep-wake cycle. After flying east, get up early in the morning for a walk in the sunshine to move your biological clock ahead. After flying west, re-verse the process with exposure to the late afternoon sun or sunset.

Reduce the disruption of rotating shift work. The longer you work on one shift, the less disrupting it will be. Studies have shown that shifting from days to nights every other week is far more disturbing to your body than working each shift for three weeks at a time. The order of the shifting is also important. For example, a series of shifts from day to evening to night work is less disruptive than shifting from day to night to evening.

KIDNEY CANCER

Known risk factors

Age:	Yes	Smoking:	Yes
Gender:	Yes	Drugs & medical procedures:	No
Race/ethnic group:	No	General health:	No
Family history:	No	Environment:	Yes
Diet:	No	Occupation:	Yes

Are you at risk?

Approximately one of every 50 cancers diagnosed among American adults is a tumor of the kidneys. In 1990, the American Cancer Society estimated 24,000 new cases of kidney cancer and 10,300 deaths.

In general, the risk of kidney cancer rises with your age. The exception is Wilms's tumor, a highly malignant cancer of the kidney, which occurs almost exclusively in children younger than six. A man's risk of kidney cancer is twice as high as a woman's, and smokers are at higher risk than non-smokers. Statistically, the person most likely to develop kidney cancer is a male smoker age 55 to 60, a gender difference that may be explained simply by the fact that in America more men have smoked for longer periods of time.

People who are exposed to cadmium, a poisonous metal that is used in foundries and in making storage batteries, may also be at higher risk.

Early detection. As many as 84% of the people whose kidney cancer is detected when it is still confined within the kidney will be alive five years after diagnosis. The five-year survival rate for people whose tumor has spread to major blood vessels around the kidney is 52%. If the tumor has invaded nearby lymph nodes before being found, the five-year survival rate is 5% to 15%. Seven percent of the people whose tumors have metastasized to distant organs before diagnosis will survive five years.

The basic diagnostic test for kidney cancer is an X-ray taken after you have been given an intravenous injection of a dye that circulates through the kidneys to provide a contrast that will outline any abnormality. If a mass is found, ultrasonography may be used to distinguish between non-malignant cysts and kidney cancers, but the most conclusive test is a biopsy performed by drawing fluid from the mass and examining it for cancer cells.

To lower your risk of kidney cancer.

If you smoke, stop. Although the link between smoking and kidney cancer remains to be proven conclusively, it is well known that tobacco smoke contains benzo[a]pyrene and other carcinogens that are eliminated through the kidneys and bladder.

KIDNEY STONES

Known risk factors

Age:	Yes	Smoking:	No
Gender:	Yes	Drugs & medical procedures:	Yes
Race/ethnic group:	No	General health:	Yes
Family history:	Yes	Environment:	No
Diet:	Yes	Occupation:	No

Are you at risk?

The person most likely to develop kidney stones is a man past 30 who has relatives with kidney stones, but there are some interesting wrinkles in the picture.

Kidney stones are formed around crystals of solid material in urine. Seventy-five to 80% of all kidney stones are calcium-based. Men are two or three times more likely than women to develop calcium stones. Once you have had one calcium stone, you are likely to have more, and the time between stones may get shorter as you get older.

What you eat may affect your risk of calcium stones. In the United States, kidney stones are most common in an area centered around the Carolinas where the weather is warm year round, people sweat a lot and become dehydrated, concentrating their urine and precipitating solid crystals. Combine that with a diet that includes greens such as collards that are high in calcium oxalate and you can see why they call this "the kidney stone belt." Some other foods that are high in oxalates and may contribute to the formation of calcium oxalate stones are cocoa, nuts, pepper, rhubarb and tea.

Five to 8% of all kidney stones are uric acid stones. Your risk of uric acid kidney stones is higher if you are a man, or if you have gout (which is nine times more common among men than among women), or if uric acid kidney stones run in your family.

A third kind of kidney stone, struvite stones, are commonly known as infection stones because they only occur in the presence of bacteria that split urea apart into crystals of magnesium ammonium phosphate, the chemical compound known as struvite. Struvite stones are considered a sign of urinary infection. Because women are more likely than men to develop urinary infections, they are also at higher risk for struvite stones.

Early detection. Undetected kidney stones can cause infection that destroys kidney tissue. The first indication of kidney stones, even when there are no symptoms, may come from a urinalysis that shows an increased amounts of solid crystals in your urine. Urinalysis is also useful in identifying the kind of crystals in stones that have already formed and may cause pain or fever.

An X-ray of your abdomen may show a stone that has formed but is not yet causing discomfort, or it may be used to show the position of a troublesome stone. Finally, your doctor may use ultrasonography to differentiate between a kidney stone, a kidney tumor and a kidney infection.

To lower your risk of kidney stones

Drink enough water. It is impossible for you to control your gender and your family history, two important risk factors for kidney stones, but you may be able to lower your risk of a recurrence of uric acid or calcium stones by following your doctor's diet advice to the letter. It is certainly to your advantage to keep your urine copious and dilute so as to reduce the precipitation of solid crystals. It may also lower the risk of a urinary infection leading to struvite stones (see URINARY TRACT INFECTIONS).

The old wives' tale that tells you to drink eight glasses of water a day is intelligent medical folklore. Eighty ounces (2,400 ml) of water is just about what an average healthy adult loses each day through urination, perspiration and metabolism, about 600 ml less than the three liters of water a day often suggested for people who repeatedly form uric acid kidney stones. Check this out with your doctor.

LEGIONNAIRES' DISEASE

Known risk factors

Age:	No	Smoking:	No
Gender:	No	Drugs & medical procedures:	No
Race/ethnic group:	No	General health:	Yes
Family history:	No	Environment:	Yes
Diet:	No	Occupation:	Yes

Are you at risk?

Since 1943, there seem to have been several mini-epidemics of the form of pneumonia known as Legionnaires' disease. The first known cluster occurred in 1957 among workers in a meat packing plant in Austin, Minnesota. The most famous outbreak, however, occurred in 1976, when there were 220 cases among members of the American Legion meeting in Philadelphia, and the causative bacteria, *Legionella pneumonium*, was identified and named.

The organism that causes Legionnaires' disease lives naturally in water. The illness—which accounts for about 3% of all cases of pneumonia—is most likely to occur in late summer and early fall, and you are most at risk if you live near a body of water or work or live in a building whose air-conditioners have evaporative condensers or a water system with contaminated shower heads or faucets.

Although there is no evidence that the illness can spread directly from one person to another through breathing, coughing, touching or intimate contact, health workers in hospitals and people who work in medical laboratories are considered to be at higher risk.

Early detection. The diagnostic test for Legionnaires' disease is a culture of the bacteria from the sick person's respiratory tract to confirm the presence of the Legionnaires' organism.

To lower your risk of Legionnaires' disease

Stay fit. As an individual, you have very little control over your own exposure to Legionnaires' disease. In order to prevent the illness, it is necessary to eradicate the organism that causes it. In theory, this means inspecting and cleaning every single source of standing water where the Legionnaires' bacterium can grow, but there are so many of these sites that most experts settle for periodic testing of places where illness has occurred or where there are groups of sick people, such as hospitals, as well as laboratories where scientists are working with infectious material.

But if you can't completely control your environmental exposure, you can keep yourself fit so as to increase your resistance to this disease, as well as many other infectious diseases. The healthier you are, the more likely your chance of fighting off infection or reducing the severity of symptoms if you do get sick.

LEPROSY (HANSEN'S DISEASE)

Known risk factors

Age:	Yes	Smoking:	No
Gender:	Yes	Drugs & medical procedures:	No
Race/ethnic group:	No	General health:	No
Family history:	Yes	Environment:	Yes
Diet:	No	Occupation:	No

Are you at risk?

Around the world, there are an estimated 10 to 20 million people with leprosy. You are at highest risk in Asia and Africa, where the illness is endemic and where there are areas in which as many as one or two people in every 100 is infected. Leprosy is also found in Central and South America. It is rare in the United States, but the number of cases is increasing due to immigration from Asia and Latin America.

There are presently pockets of leprosy in Texas, Louisiana and Hawaii, as well as areas such as California, Florida and New York City, which are centers for immigration from Central America, South America, Asia and the Philippines. Most Americans with leprosy acquired the illness abroad.

Exactly how leprosy spreads from person to person remains a mystery, but if you have close relatives who have the disease, your risk is significantly higher. Leprosy has an incubation period that may run anywhere from six months to 30 years. Most adults who get leprosy seem to have had long-term exposure as a child to someone with the disease. Leprosy rarely occurs in a child younger than a year, but in developing countries as many as 20% of all cases occur in children younger than 10. Among children, boys and girls are at equal risk; among adults, the ratio of male to female patients is approximately two to one.

Among adults, leprosy may be spread via tattooing needles.

Early detection. Leprosy attacks nerve tissues, causing a loss of sensation and deformity, particularly in the hands and feet. Untreated leprosy is the world's most common cause of crippling destruction of the hand. It also destroys cartilage, which is why leprosy patients may lose their ears and nose.

Leprosy is commonly diagnosed by its symptoms and by the presence of the leprosy bacterium, *Mycobacterium leprae*, in tissue samples from the skin or secretions from the nose. Researchers are now working on a new test that will diagnose the disease by the presence of antibodies to the leprosy organism in your blood.

To lower your risk of Hansen's disease

Avoiding areas where the disease is endemic and practicing scrupulous personal sanitation in the presence of persons with Hansen's disease reduces your risk of acquiring it.

LEUKEMIA

Known risk factors

Age:	Yes	Smoking:	Yes
Gender:	?	Drugs & medical procedures:	Yes
Race/ethnic group:	No	General health:	No
Family history:	?	Environment:	Yes
Diet:	No	Occupation:	Yes

Are you at risk?

Leukemia is a form of cancer that affects the tissues that form blood cells. Your risk goes up as you get older. Only one form of leukemia, acute lymphoblastic leukemia (ALL), is more common among children, appearing most frequently among youngsters age three to seven. All other acute and chronic forms of leukemia are more common among adults, and all occur more frequently among men than among women.

Most cases of leukemia arise from unknown origins. One known risk factor is exposure to ionizing radiation, the kind of radiation that damages the internal structure of body cells. Uranium miners, radiologists and other health workers exposed to radiation, people who are given radiation treatments to cure other forms of cancer and babies born to women who have had diagnostic X-rays while pregnant all have a higher-than-normal chance of developing leukemia. The risk is dose-related: The higher the exposure, the higher the risk.

Another well-known risk factor is exposure to benzene, a substance that occurs naturally in petrochemicals and is found in solvents, rubber, gasoline, inks, paints and tobacco smoke. Because this risk factor was identified by studying groups of people who worked in industries where they were exposed to benzene, the major source of benzene exposure has been assumed to be in working or living near chemical plants, oil refining operations or gasoline stations.

In 1989, however, the Environmental Protection Agency (EPA) found that only a relatively small number of people are still exposed to benzene at work. Today, our single most important source of benzene exposure is smoking or being exposed to tobacco smoke. According to EPA, a smoker's risk of developing leukemia is half again as high as a non-smoker's.

Driving in a car or bus or living in a house with an attached garage accounts for 20% of our exposure; breathing in automobile exhaust fumes or the emissions from chemical plants or oil refineries, another 20%. The amount of exposure due to benzene's leaking from building materials, adhesives and coatings is uncertain.

Does leukemia run in families? Maybe. If you have a brother or sister with leukemia, your own risk may be as much as five times greater than it would be if you had no affected siblings, and if one identical twin develops leukemia, the other is likely to, as well. Leukemia is also more common among people born with certain congenital disorders such as Down's syndrome; Fanconi's syndrome, an inherited kidney disorder; Klinefelter's syndrome, a disorder characterized by a missing chromosome; and the Wiskott-Aldrich syndrome, an inherited deficiency of the immune system.

As a general rule, leukemia is not considered a communicable disease. Feline leukemia, a viral disease, can be passed from one cat to another, but repeated epidemiological studies of men and women whose husbands and wives have leukemia and children born to women who developed leukemia while pregnant have shown no evidence that people with leukemia can pass the disease to others.

The single known exception to this general rule is adult T-cell leukemia (ATL), a form of leukemia endemic in southwest Japan and parts of the Caribbean and Central America. In the United States, ATL occurs most frequently among people of black African ancestry. Like feline leukemia, ATL is caused by a virus, in this case the human T-cell leukemia virus (HTLV). The HTLV virus can be spread through sexual contact with infected people, sharing of contaminated needles, or use of contaminated blood products.

Early detection. The screening test for leukemia is a blood test to detect a proliferation of immature blood cells. A diagnosis of leukemia is confirmed by analysis of a sample of bone marrow to measure the quantities of specific kinds of white blood cells.

To lower your risk of leukemia

If you smoke, stop. In 1989, the Environmental Protection Agency estimated that smoking may be responsible for 500 cases of leukemia every year. Passive smoking, inhaling the smoke from someone else's cigarette, cigar or pipe, may add another 50.

LUNG CANCER

Known risk factors

Age:	Yes	Smoking:	Yes
Gender:	No	Drugs & medical procedures:	Yes
Race/ethnic group:	?	General health:	No
Family history:	?	Environment:	Yes
Diet:	No	Occupation:	Yes

Are you at risk?

In 1990, the American Cancer Society (ACS) estimated that there would be 157,000 new cases of lung cancer and 142,000 deaths from the disease. Having passed breast cancer as the leading cause of cancer deaths among women, lung cancer is now the number-one cancer killer of both men and women.

If you smoke, you are unquestionably at risk. True, not everyone who smokes will get lung cancer, but the overwhelming majority of lung cancer patients are (or have been) smokers. In fact, smoking is considered a factor in 85 to 90% of all lung cancers among men and 75% of all lung cancers among women, a gender difference that is expected to even out as women pile up more years as smokers. Black Americans, who are more likely than white Americans to smoke, have a higher incidence of lung cancer and are more likely to die of the disease.

A number of studies over the past 10 years have strongly suggested that the effects of tobacco smoke, which contains several carcinogens, including benzo[a]pyrene, are not limited to smokers. People who have never smoked may increase their risk of lung cancer by about one-third if they live or work in close proximity to a smoker; the risk is doubled by exposure to a heavy smoker.

A small proportion of lung cancers (15% in men, 5% in women) are believed to be caused by exposure to radiation and chemicals such as arsenic, asbestos, chloromethyl ethers, chromates and nickel, raising the risk for asbestos workers, painters and paint-makers, radiologists and foundry workers. In every case, the risk is compounded by smoking.

Lung cancer isn't contagious and you can't inherit the disease itself, but close blood relatives (sons, daughters, sisters, brothers) of people with lung cancer seem to be about three times more likely than other people to develop lung cancer, even if they don't smoke.

Recent research at the National Institutes for Health (NIH) suggests that what you inherit is a chromosomal weakness that makes you susceptible to the disease. In 1988, NIH researchers identified a region on chromosome 3 that is almost always missing in cells taken from people with small cell lung cancer and sometimes missing from cells taken from people with other kinds of lung cancer.

We all have two versions of each chromosome, one from our mother, one from our father. Both versions of chromosome 3 must be damaged before we develop lung cancer. It may be that people who develop lung cancer inherit a defective chromosome 3 from one parent and then lose the pertinent section of the other chromosome 3 at some time through exposure to tobacco smoke or another carcinogen associated with lung cancer.

Early detection. Fifty percent of the people whose lung cancer is found while it can still be completely removed by surgery will be alive five years later. That number drops steadily as the cancer grows and spreads. As of 1989, the overall five-year survival rate for people with lung cancer was estimated to be 13%.

The simplest test most likely to detect lung cancer is a chest X-ray. If it shows a suspicious mass, your doctor may request bronchoscopy, an examination of the air passages to the lung with a flexible lighted tube, and/or a needle biopsy, the removal of tissue for microscopic examination.

To lower your risk of lung cancer

Stop smoking. You may never be as safe as you would have been if you had never smoked at all, but your chances of developing lung cancer do go down dramatically when you stop smoking.

If you are at risk, discuss the value of periodic screening with your doctor. Although the research is contradictory, some studies in which men older than 45 who smoked two packs of cigarettes a day or more were screened with chest X-rays and microscopic analysis of cells in their sputum every four months have found four to eight cases of lung cancer among every 1,000 patients.

With follow-up screening, another four cases per 1,000 persons may be found each year. Ninety percent of these cancers had not yet caused any symptoms, so there would have been no reason for the person to visit his doctor. Without screening programs, only 5 to 15% of lung cancers are diagnosed before they cause any symptoms.

Increase your consumption of deep green and yellow fruits and vegetables. According to the American Cancer Society, a diet that includes plenty of yellow, red, orange and deep green fruits and vegetables rich in carotenes may offer some protection against certain cancers, including lung cancer. Exactly what the protective ingredient in these foods is remains a mystery.

Although some carotenes are converted to vitamin A in your body, there is no evidence that increasing your consumption of vitamin A itself confers the same benefits as eating these fruits and vegetables. In fact, large doses of vitamin A may be toxic.

LYME DISEASE

Known risk factors

Age:	No	Smoking:	No
Gender:	No	Drugs & medical procedures:	No
Race/ethnic group:	No	General health:	No
Family history:	No	Environment:	Yes
Diet:	No	Occupation:	Yes

Are you at risk?

Lyme disease, named for Old Lyme, Connecticut, the place where it was first identified in 1962, is now the second fastest-growing illness in the United States, right behind AIDS. By 1989, data compiled by the Federal Centers for Disease Control (CDC) showed that it had spread to 43 states. More than 5,000 new cases were reported in 1988, twice as many as during the year before.

Lyme disease is caused by a spirochete *Borrelia burgdorferi* carried by species of ticks that prey on mice, deer, people and household pets (cats may acquire the disease by eating infected mice). The main carrier in the Northeast and Midwest is *Ixodes dammini;* in the West, it is *Ixodes pacificus*. Neither tick discriminates among human beings by age or sex or race. Everyone who is exposed to an infected tick is equally at risk, but not everyone who is bitten by a tick gets sick, since the tick must bite for as long as 12 to 24 hours in order to transmit the disease.

Lyme disease may also be spread by contact with the urine of infected animals such as horses, cows, dogs or laboratory rabbits, so veterinarians, animal breeders, farmers, laboratory researchers and pet owners in infected areas are at higher-than-normal risk.

Where you live affects your risk. The ticks that carry Lyme disease flourish where there is dense foliage, a warm climate and plenty of animals and human beings to support them. Lyme disease is seasonal, following the life cycle of the tick. Infection is most likely from May through September, with the highest number of cases occurring in June and July.

Early detection. Untreated Lyme disease causes severe headaches, problems with memory, lightheadedness, numbness or paralysis of the facial muscles, overwhelming fatigue, an irregular heartbeat, shortness of breath and recurring attacks of arthritic pain. These symptoms may not appear for months or even years after infection. For most people, the first symptom is a characteristic rash at the site of the tick bite.

The screening test for Lyme disease is a blood test to detect the presence of antibodies to the infection, but the test is not always reliable in the earliest stages of the disease.

To lower the risk of Lyme disease

Wear protective clothing. The proper gear for a walk in the woods where ticks may be resident is a long-sleeved shirt tucked into long pants tucked into socks or boots. Light-colored clothes are a good idea, since the tiny, dark ticks show up better on them. The Federal Centers for Disease Control recommends spraying an insect repellent that contains DEET or permethrin on your long pants, socks and shoes. Use sparingly as directed on the container.

Walk a cleared path or trail. Avoid the dense foliage where ticks may be hiding.

When you get home, conduct a serious search-and-destroy mission. Check your clothes and body thoroughly for ticks. Don't forget to check your scalp: ticks can hide under hair. If you find a tick, grasp it with a pair of tweezers as close to the head and mouth as possible. Then pull straight up without squeezing the tick's body so as to remove the complete tick. You may wish to save the tick in a closed container for identification. After removing the tick, contact your doctor to determine if you need further treatment. The Animal Medical Center in New York recommends your wearing protective plastic or rubber gloves while removing ticks and cautions against using petroleum jelly, lighter fluid or matches to remove the ticks.

Check your pets. The ticks that carry Lyme disease can attach themselves to household pets who can pass the tick along to you and are susceptible to Lyme disease themselves. In general, you should bathe your pet regularly during the summer. Use a tick dip only as directed by your veterinarian. According to the Animal Medical Center, tick repellents containing DEET have been known to harm or even kill pets. Repellents should be used only as directed by your vet.

MALARIA

Known risk factors

Age:	No	Smoking:	No
Gender:	No	Drugs & medical procedures:	No
Race/ethnic group:	No	General health:	No
Family history:	No	Environment:	Yes
Diet:	No	Occupation:	No

Are you at risk?

Malaria is caused by a protozoa transmitted from person to person by the bite of an infected female mosquito. The most important risk factor for malaria is exposure to infected mosquitoes. You are at risk if you live or travel in a part of the world where malaria is endemic. This includes Africa, the Middle East, Haiti, Central and South America, Southeast Asia, the Indian subcontinent, China, Turkey and Malaysia.

Malaria has not been widespread in the United States since 1950, but it continues to show up among people who bring it in from abroad. Until the mid-'60s, the number of imported cases never went above about 200 a year, but that changed during the Vietnam war, when the number of cases among infected service personnel returning home reached 4,000 in 1970. After the war ended, the number of cases dropped, only to rise again as travel to endemic areas increased during the late 1970s and 1980s. In 1985, about 1,000 cases of malaria were reported in this country.

Early detection. Malaria is diagnosed by a test that confirms the presence of malaria protozoa in the blood.

To lower the risk of malaria

Ask your doctor about preventive medication. The anti-malarial drugs quinine, chloroquine and amodiaquine (which is only available abroad) destroy protozoa circulating in your blood or prevent infection. When traveling to an area where malaria is endemic and your doctor recommends your taking anti-malarial drugs, you will have to start before you leave and continue after you return, perhaps for as long as six weeks. For more information about preventive medicine for malaria, contact your doctor or the Parasitic Disease Division, Centers for Infectious Disease, Centers for Disease Control (CDC), Atlanta, Georgia 30333.

Wear protective clothing. When traveling through an area where malaria is endemic, you should wear protective clothing, especially between dusk and dawn, when the mosquitoes are most likely to bite. That means long-sleeved shirts and long pants tucked into socks, plus closed shoes. You may also wish to use insect repellent on your clothes.

Protect your living quarters. Make sure all window screens, door screens and mosquito netting are intact. You can also spray the room with an insect repellent designed to kill mosquitoes.

MEASLES (RUBEOLA)

Known risk factors

Age:	Yes	Smoking:	No
Gender:	No	Drugs & medical procedures:	No
Race/ethnic group:	No	General health:	No
Family history:	No	Environment:	No
Diet:	No	Occupation:	No

Are you at risk?

Measles is a contagious disease caused by the rubeola virus. More than 90% of the susceptible people living in a house with a measles patient catch the disease. Once you've had measles, though, you have life-long immunity. Before the widespread use of measles vaccine, the disease was most common among young children who had not been exposed to the virus and thus had not acquired immunity. Today, the people most likely to catch measles are young adults who were vaccinated before 1980 when a stabilizing agent was added to protect the potency of the measles vaccine while it was being stored. Half of the 14,714 cases of measles reported by The Federal Centers for Disease Control for 1989 occurred among people who had been vaccinated.

Early detection. At the start, a case of measles may resemble any one of a number of illnesses, including rubella ("German measles"), roseola, scarlet fever, a drug reaction, infectious mononucleosis and various other viral infections.

Measles is identified by its rash and by the presence of Koplik's spots, small red spots with white centers that show up on the inside of your mouth even before the measles rash appears.

To lower the risk of measles

Ask your doctor about immunization. The Federal Centers for Disease Control (CDC) recommends an immunization with live virus vaccine at the age of 15 months old, and the American Academy of Pediatrics recommends a second immunization for all adults younger than 32. In 1989, New York State passed a law requiring all full-time college freshmen and sophomores at New York schools to have the second innoculation. The measles vaccine is often combined with mumps and rubella vaccine in an immunization known as MMR.

Children who live in an area where there has been a reported outbreak of measles in the prior five years should be vaccinated earlier, around the age of nine months.

People who are not immunized against measles may be protected with a dose of gamma globulin given within five days of their being exposed to someone who has measles. During a measles outbreak, all susceptible people should consider gamma globulin, but the protection is most important for pregnant women, people who have had tuberculosis and people whose immune system has been impaired (for example, by cancer chemotherapy).

A pregnant woman who has not had measles cannot be vaccinated lest the live virus cross the placental barrier and damage the developing fetus. A woman who has already had measles can pass antibodies along to her fetus in the womb, conferring an immunity that lasts for most of the first year of life.

MIGRAINE HEADACHE

Known risk factors

Age:	Yes	Smoking:	No
Gender:	Yes	Drugs & medical procedures:	Yes
Race/ethnic group:	No	General health:	Yes
Family history:	Yes	Environment:	No
Diet:	?	Occupation:	No

Are you at risk?

Migraine headaches are most likely to appear first in adolescence, and they tend to go away in middle age. The classic migraine, which starts with nausea and vomiting or visual disturbances such as flashing zig zag lights, is three times more common among women than among men.

Among women, the risk of developing this kind of headache is higher right before menstruation and when using oral contraceptives. It is lower during pregnancy. For everyone, the risk of developing migraine is slightly higher if you have close relatives with migraine.

Cluster headaches, so-named because they occur in bunches from time to time, are believed by some experts to be migraine headaches. They occur four times more often among men, predominantly middle-aged men who often have no family history of severe headache.

If you have had migraine or cluster headaches in the past, exposure to certain environmental stresses, such as bright sunshine, flickering fluorescent lights, changes in weather or high altitudes, may also raise the likelihood of a new attack.

Does what you eat affect your risk? Nobody knows for sure. People who are sensitive to specific foods such as milk and wheat may experience a headache after eating them, but there is no guarantee that avoiding the foods will eliminate the chance of a headache. Among the foods and food additives most often cited as causes of migraine headaches are very cold foods such as ice cream and ices; nitrates and nitrites in smoked fish and meats and cured meats; monosodium glutamate (MSG) in Asian foods, instant soups and gravies, some seasoning mixes and TV dinners; caffeine; tyramine, a naturally occurring substance in aged cheese, avocados and liver pates; and overripe bananas, pickled herring and red wine.

Early detection. Migraine or cluster headaches are characteristically diagnosed by their distinctive symptoms.

To lower your risk of migraine headaches

If your head hurts, consulting the professionals at a headache clinic may provide relief. Because the original cause of migraines remains a mystery, there is presently no certain way to reduce your susceptibility. But once you have developed migraines, you may be able to reduce their incidence either with medication or changes in diet or behavior. Because each case is different, your best guide to a program that works for you is a doctor specializing in headache.

MISCARRIAGE

Known risk factors

Age:	No	Smoking:	Yes
Gender:	Yes	Drugs & medical procedures:	Yes
Race/ethnic group:	No	General health:	Yes
Family history:	?	Environment:	Yes
Diet:	No	Occupation:	Yes

Are you at risk?

Miscarriage, which is also known as spontaneous abortion, is defined as the delivery of an embryo or fetus during the first 20 weeks of pregnancy; delivery after the 20th week is called premature birth, or stillbirth if the fetus is not born alive.* Nearly 85% of all miscarriages occur in the first trimester of pregnancy. In many cases, the embryo or fetus aborted is so grossly malformed or has such serious chromosomal abnormalities that it would not have survived if carried to term.

Although researchers have identified a growing list of drugs, illnesses and environmental conditions that cause birth defects, very little is known for sure about exactly what raises the risk of embryonic or fetal devastation so complete as to cause a miscarriage. In the main, these are considered reproductive accidents that nature eliminates via spontaneous abortion.

It's a different story for miscarriage in the second trimester, when the loss of the fetus may often be triggered by a pregnant woman's own health problems or behavior. Among the things known to increase the risk of a second trimester miscarriage are a damaged cervix or an abnormal uterus (two known effects of a female baby's being exposed to DES while still in her mother's womb), diabetes, kidney disease, a viral infection such as cytomegalovirus, herpes, rubella, smoking and, rarely, a severe emotional shock.

Another risk factor is using an intrauterine device (IUD). If a woman becomes pregnant with the IUD in place, there is a 50/50 chance that she will miscarry.

Does your work put you at risk? Perhaps.

---

*Until eight weeks after conception, the developing organism is known as an embryo; after that, it is called a fetus.

Although the exact mechanism remains to be demonstrated, numerous studies have suggested that the rate of spontaneous abortion is higher among women exposed to a host of environmental situations, including medical workers who are exposed to anesthetic gases, textile workers and paint manufacturers exposed to carbon disulfide, rubber workers exposed to chloroprene and firing range attendants, welders, solderers and others exposed to lead. Women whose male partners are exposed to lead also have a higher risk of miscarriage.

Finally, a surprising word about the relationship between morning sickness and miscarriage. In 1989, researchers at the National Institutes of Health (NIH) who examined the medical records of 9,000 pregnant women found that the women who went through bouts of nausea and vomiting early in pregnancy also had a lower rate of stillbirth and premature delivery than women who sailed easily through the first trimester. For now, the researchers theorize that women who experience morning sickness may have higher levels of hormones needed to sustain pregnancy.

Early detection. The warning signs of miscarriage are uterine bleeding and cramping. Miscarriage is confirmed by examining the uterus with ultrasound to be certain that the embryo or fetus has been expelled.

An incomplete miscarriage in which the membranes have ruptured but the embryo or the fetus has not yet been completely expelled or a missed abortion in which the embryo or fetus has died but has not been expelled from the uterus must be completed by removing the fetus via dilation and curettage (D & C) or suction curettage to protect the mother from subsequent complications such as hemorrhage.

In 1990, researchers at the Rosie Maternity Hospital and University College Medical School in Cambridge, England, published a report in the British medical journal *Lancet* describing a simple blood test which may be able to predict a woman's risk of miscarriage even before she becomes pregnant. The test measures the level of luteinizing hormone (LH) in the blood. LH is the hormone that controls ovulation, the release of a mature egg each month. Women with abnormally high blood levels of LH are less likely to conceive and more likely to miscarry if they do become pregnant. As of this writing, the efficacy of this test remains to be proven.

To lower your risk of miscarriage:

Seek prenatal care. Careful medical management can often reduce the risk of miscarriage. Because every case is individual, your doctor must tailor her advice to your specific situation, but the fact that good prenatal care helps to protect both mother and child is indisputable.

MONONUCLEOSIS, INFECTIOUS

Known risk factors

Age:	Yes	Smoking:	No
Gender:	No	Drugs & medical procedures:	No
Race/ethnic group:	No	General health:	No
Family history:	No	Environment:	Yes
Diet:	No	Occupation:	No

Are you at risk?

Infectious mononucleosis (popularly known as mono) is sometimes called The Kissing Disease because the Epstein-Barr virus that causes it may be spread through an exchange of saliva. The likeliest candidate for mono is a teen-ager, 14 to 18 years old. Adolescent girls—who ordinarily begin to date earlier than adolescent boys—often develop mono at a younger age than boys do. Paradoxically, the risk as a teen-ager is higher among those who live in areas where sanitation is good, because the cleaner your environment as a child, the less likely you were to be exposed to the E-B virus early on as a "silent" infection or one too mild to be diagnosed as mono. Even this mild encounter allows you to develop the antibodies that give you lifelong protection against a second infection. Without these antibodies, if you are exposed to the virus when you are in your teens or early 20s, you are more likely to experience the flu-like symptoms and swollen glands we associate with infectious mononucleosis.

The risk of acquiring mono goes down dramatically after age 20.

Early detection. Mononucleosis is diagnosed via blood tests that show increased numbers of atypical white blood cells, antibodies to the Epstein-Barr virus and increased amounts of the blood pigment bilirubin, and the enzyme alkaline phosphatase suggestive of decreased liver function, which is likely to occur when you have mono.

To lower your risk of infectious mononucleosis

At present, there is no known way to reduce the risk of infectious mononucleosis for people who have not developed protective antibodies.

MULTIPLE SCLEROSIS

Known risk factors

Age:	Yes	Smoking:	No
Gender:	Yes	Drugs & medical procedures:	No
Race/ethnic group:	Yes	General health:	No
Family history:	Yes	Environment:	Yes
Diet:	No	Occupation:	No

Are you at risk?

There are approximately 500,000 Americans with multiple sclerosis (MS), a progressive disease of the brain and spinal cord that destroys the myelin (fatty tissue) sheath surrounding the nerve fibers. As the myelin is destroyed, scar tissue forms and hardens (scleroses), reducing the nerve's ability to send messages to the muscles that move the body. The result is pain and loss of movement.

Multiple sclerosis is more common among women (60%) than among men (40%). It appears most often among people age 25 and 40. There are some tantalizing clues to suggest that it may be an environmental disease. MS is more common in the temperate zones than in the tropic zone. The number of cases in northern Europe, Canada and the northern U.S. is approximately 10 times that in tropical regions. MS is rare in Japan, the rest of the Orient and Africa. People who live in the temperate zone until their 15th birthday and then move to the tropic zone have the same risk as people who remain in the temperate zone all their lives. People who move from the temperate to tropic zone before their 15th birthday have the lower risk of the tropic zone.

Because there are variations in the incidence of MS from place to place even in the same zone, it is impossible to say that MS is caused or influenced by temperature or climate. Some suggest, therefore, that it may be linked to a slow-acting virus native to the temperate zones. It is also possible that MS may turn out to be an inherited disorder of the immune system. If your parents have MS, your risk may be as high as eight times that of people whose parents do not have MS. If you have a sister or brother with MS, your risk may be 20 times that of people with no MS relatives. MS is more common among American whites than among American Indians and blacks who live in the same area.

How this risk is transmitted remains a mystery, but researchers at the National Institute of Communicative Disorders and Stroke have identified two genes that, when inherited in tandem, appear to triple the chance of developing MS. In 1989, scientists at Massachusetts General Hospital in Boston discovered a specific gene that may play a role in the function of immune cells linked to the development of MS. People who have this gene appear to have a risk of MS three times higher than the risk of people without the gene.

Early detection. Multiple sclerosis is diagnosed by the presence of demyelinated areas (plaques) on nerves as seen via magnetic resonance imaging (MRI) or CT-scans.

To lower your risk of multiple sclerosis

At present, there is no known way to reduce your risk of multiple sclerosis.

MUMPS

Known risk factors

Age:	Yes	Smoking:	No
Gender:	No	Drugs & medical procedures:	No
Race/ethnic group:	No	General health:	No
Family history:	No	Environment:	No
Diet:	No	Occupation:	No

Are you at risk?

Anyone not protected by prior vaccination or by having had mumps (one bout gives life-long immunity) can get mumps, but the likeliest candidate is a child age five to 15.

Mumps is unusual in a child younger than two because infants are usually protected by immunity acquired in utero. About one-third of all cases occur among people older than 15. The likeliest victim in this older group is a person who was not immunized in the 10 years between 1967 (when the mumps vaccine was first introduced) and 1979 (when it became standard preventive treatment for children).

Although mumps occurs throughout the year, it is most common in the late winter and early spring, especially in April and May.

Early detection. Mumps is diagnosed by its symptoms: chills, headache, loss of appetite, fever that rises as the salivary glands swell and a general feeling of discomfort. The disease is easy to identify when there is an epidemic, but can be confusing when it occurs one case at a time because the characteristic swelling of the salivary glands may resemble a bacterial infection, a tumor, a swollen lymph gland characteristic of leukemia or a symptom of poor oral hygiene, typhoid or typhus.

If there is any doubt, a diagnosis of mumps can be confirmed with a blood test that shows the presence of mumps virus or antibodies to the mumps virus.

To lower your risk of mumps

Vaccination. From 1967 to 1988, the number of mumps cases in the United States declined steadily each year except for the atypical years 1986 and 1987. According to statistics compiled by the Federal Centers for Disease Control (CDC), the lowest incidence of mumps is in the District of Columbia and the 17 states that require full proof of vaccination for children from kindergarten to the 12th grade. By contrast, Tennessee and Illinois, which had not required such proof, together accounted for 88% of all the cases of mumps reported in the United States. Both states now require children to be vaccinated for mumps before they go to school.

The mumps vaccine is usually given together with the vaccines for measles and rubella in a combination known as MMR.

MUSCULAR DYSTROPHY

Known risk factors

Age:	Yes	Smoking:	No
Gender:	Yes	Drugs & medical procedures:	No
Race/ethnic group:	No	General health:	No
Family history:	Yes	Environment:	No
Diet:	No	Occupation:	No

Are you at risk?

Muscular dystrophy is a term used to describe a group of inherited disorders that lead to progressive weakening and wasting of the muscles that control body movement. These disorders include Duchenne muscular dystrophy, which affects the large muscles of the lower trunk and upper legs; Becker muscular dystrophy, a less severe form of Duchenne; facio-scapulo-humoral (Landouzy-Dejerine) dystrophy, which affects the muscles of the face, shoulder and upper arms; limb-girdle dystrophy, which may start in the shoulder muscles or the muscles of the lower trunk and legs; and myotonic dystrophy (Steinert's Disease), which starts within the fingers, hands, arms, lower legs or feet.

The most common form of muscular dystrophy is Duchenne muscular dystrophy. It occurs only among males and appears early in childhood, between age three and seven. Duchenne muscular dystrophy is caused by a gene carried on the X chromosome, but at least one-third of all boys born with it have no relatives with Duchenne. Their illness may be caused by a spontaneous mutation rather than inherited defect.

Becker's muscular dystrophy is also caused by a gene on the X chromosome and also occurs only in males. It is less severe than Duchenne, occurs only one-tenth as often, and shows up slightly later in life, between the ages of five and 15. Boys with Duchenne muscular dystrophy are unlikely to live long enough to have children; they cannot pass the condition along. Boys with Becker's muscular dystrophy may live into adulthood and can have families of their own.

Will their children have muscular dystrophy? Probably not, but their grandchildren may. Here is why. All men have one X chromosome and one Y chromosome; all women have two X chromosomes. Unless a man with Becker's muscular dystrophy marries a woman who is a carrier, none of his sons will have the condition because their single X chromosome comes from a healthy mother. But every daughter of a man with Becker's carries the gene for muscular dystrophy because she inherits one of her two X chromosomes from her father. If a woman who carries the Becker's gene has a son, there is a 50% chance that he will have muscular dystrophy.

Facio-scapulo-humeral dystrophy and myotonic dystrophy are caused by a dominant gene that affects both sexes. Limb-girdle dystrophy is caused by a recessive gene; it also affects both sexes.

Early detection. One screening test for muscular dystrophy is a biopsy of muscle tissue to determine whether there are increased amounts of connective tissue and fatty deposits, a sign of the illness.

Your doctor may also request electromyography (EMG), an examination during which a needle is inserted through the skin into muscle tissue to measure the strength of the electrical discharge in the muscle when you move. People with muscular dystrophy show less electrical activity in their muscles.

A third test measures the level of the enzyme creatine kinase (CK) in your blood. CK is released by damaged muscle; people with muscular dystrophy may have CK levels 100 times higher than normal.

To lower your risk of muscular dystrophy

Genetic counseling. At present, there is no known way to reduce the chance that a male child of a woman who carries the gene for Duchenne or Becker muscular dystrophy will inherit the disease. A woman who has male relatives with these dystrophies and wishes to become pregnant may choose to have a blood test to measure the levels of creatine kinase in her blood, but this test is not infallible. As many as 30% of all women carrying the muscular dystrophy gene have normal CK levels; women with a family history of muscular dystrophy may wish to seek genetic counseling regarding their risk of passing on the disease.

MYASTHENIA GRAVIS

Known risk factors

Age:	Yes	Smoking:	No
Gender:	Yes	Drugs & medical procedures:	No
Race/ethnic group:	No	General health:	No
Family history:	?	Environment:	No
Diet:	No	Occupation:	No

Are you at risk?

Myasthenia gravis is a disorder of the immune system that causes episodes of weakness in muscles controlled by cranial nerves, such as the muscles of the eyes. The disorder is thought to be caused by antibodies to the receptors for the neurotransmitter acetylcholine, a natural chemical in the body that makes it possible to transmit impulses from one nerve to another, but this remains to be proven.

Between 400 to 1,100 new cases of myasthenia are diagnosed each year. Women are at slightly higher risk. There are approximately three women with myasthenia gravis for every two men. Women are also likely to develop it earlier than men do, in their 20s rather than in their 50s and 60s, as is more common with men.

There is no evidence to suggest that myasthenia gravis is an inherited disease that can be passed from parent to child, but babies whose mothers have myasthenia gravis while pregnant are born with antibodies to acetylcholine receptors circulating in their bloodstream. One in eight of these infants may develop transient neonatal myasthenia gravis, an immune response that shows up during the first few hours of life and usually disappears within three weeks after birth.

Early detection. To confirm a diagnosis your doctor may perform a tensilon test. Tensilon (edrophonium chloride) is a chemical used as an antidote for drugs that paralyze muscles. If you have muscle weakness due to myasthenia gravis, an intravenous injection of edrophonium chloride will produce improved muscle function within a minute.

To lower your risk of myasthenia gravis

At present, there is no known way to reduce the risk of developing myasthenia gravis.

OBESITY

Known risk factors

Age:	Yes	Smoking:	No
Gender:	No	Drugs & medical procedures:	No
Race/ethnic group:	Yes	General health:	Yes
Family history:	Yes	Environment:	No
Diet:	Yes	Occupation:	No

Are you at risk?

Among all people of all ages and races, the ones most likely to be obese are middle-aged black women. According to statistics published by the U.S. Department of Health and Human Services in 1984, approximately 60% of all American black women 45 to 64 years of age were overweight. The comparable figure for white women in this age group is 30%; for black men, 33%; for white men, 28%.

Obesity runs in families. If both your mother and your father are obese, you have an 80% chance of being overweight yourself. If only one of your parents is obese, you have a 40% risk. If neither of your parents is obese, there is only one chance in 10 that you will be obese. In 1989, a research study at the University of Iowa suggested that for a small number of people, about 5% of all who are obese, these risks are explained not by nurture (what your parents fed you) but by nature—an "obesity gene." The gene appears to be recessive; you have to get one from each parent in order to be obese.

That doesn't mean nurture is irrelevant. Social class (your parents' as well as your own) is an important risk factor in determining whether or not you are fat, especially for women. People who are poor and badly educated are more likely than people who are well off and well educated to be overweight. (For women, the risk is six times as high.) Your ethnic heritage and your religious affiliation may also be risk factors either because you inherit a body type common in one part of the world or another or because you follow eating patterns that encourage overweight.

Do your glands make you fat? Probably not. Endocrine and metabolic factors that encourage weight gain are far more likely to be the result of your being overweight than to have caused the problem in the first place. The same may be true of psychological problems. On the other hand, there are some physical problems that can make you gain weight. For example, everyone's risk of obesity rises as we get older, either because our metabolism slows down and we burn fewer calories or because we are less active (with the same result).

Finally, there is one case in which doing the right thing can be counterproductive, at least temporarily. Everyone who stops smoking can expect to gain some weight. Some will gain a lot of weight. The reason is simple. Since you metabolize about 200 calories for every 24 cigarettes you smoke, smoking raises the amount of calories you can consume without gaining weight. When you stop smoking, you will have to cut your food intake by the same 200 calories a day to stay the same weight.

But most of us eat more, not less, when we are withdrawing from cigarettes, and we gain a pound for every 3,500 calories we consume but don't use up. Eventually, our bodies stabilize, and we begin to lose some of the weight we gained, but if we eat normally, we may never again be as thin as we were when we were smoking. That's the bad news. The well-publicized good news trade-off is a healthier heart and lungs.

Early detection. Doctors who specialize in treating obesity gauge overweight the same way we do: by looking. To a trained observer, that is a more reliable guide than tables that describe "normal" and "desirable" weights. Although obesity is commonly defined as weighing 20% or more in excess of what the standard height/weight tables compiled by the Metropolitan Life Company say you should weigh, there is some disagreement as to whether their estimates of differing body builds accurately reflect the reality.

Nor do most tables reflect age differences. After age 20 almost everyone who starts out normally lean and eats a normal diet will gain about five to 10 pounds every 10 years. Women continue to gain weight into their 70s; men appear to level off in their 60s. As a result, the National Institute on Aging (NIA) has suggested that the weights in the Metropolitan tables are too high for 20-year-olds and too low for 50-year-olds.

If you have high blood pressure or an abnormally high cholesterol level or come from a family with a tendency to diabetes, however, you should ignore all weight tables and follow your doctor's advice on weight maintenance.

To lower the risk of obesity

At present, there are no medically certain ways in which to make fat people thin for life, but there is one promising pathway to explore in lowering the risk of obesity by preventing it early in life.

When a child becomes obese, his growing body may produce five times more fat cells than it would have if he had remained at normal weight. As a result, for the rest of his life, he will be unable to lose weight or even hold a lower weight without true deprivation because even normal amounts of food will fill up these excess fat cells and make him overweight.

It is important not to interpret this as meaning that you should put a growing child on an adult's reducing diet. A child's nutritional needs are different from an adult's. For example, early in the 1980s, doctors at North Shore University Hospital in Manhasset, New York, were faced with a mini-epidemic of babies who did not grow. What they eventually discovered was that the parents were giving their babies skim milk in an attempt to keep them from developing high levels of serum cholesterol. Because skim milk lacks essential fatty acids that babies need, the infants could not thrive. The same principle applies to calories. A young child's growing body needs more calories per pound than an adult's simply to run its various organs and systems (respiration, heartbeat, brain activity, digestion and the like).

According to formulas established by the National Research Council, which sets the recommended dietary allowances (RDA) for nutrient consumption in this country, an average three-year-old, 30-pound boy needs 25 calories per pound of body weight to run his various body systems while he is completely at rest; an average 30-year-old, 150-pound man needs only 11 calories per pound when completely at rest. (Activity requires extra calories.)

ORAL CANCER

Known risk factors

Age:	Yes	Smoking:	Yes
Gender:	Yes	Drugs & medical procedures:	Yes
Race/ethnic group:	No	General health:	No
Family history:	No	Environment:	Yes
Diet:	No	Occupation:	No

Are you at risk?

In 1990, the American Cancer Society estimated that 21,200 Americans would be newly diagnosed with an oral cancer (cancer of the lip, tongue, soft palate and cheek). A man's risk is about twice as high as a woman's; in both sexes, these cancers are most frequent after the age of 40.

The most important risk factors for oral cancer are exposure to sunlight (cancer of the lip) and exposure to tobacco (cancers inside the mouth). The people at highest risk are those who smoke more than one pack of cigarettes a day and drink alcoholic beverages on a regular basis. In 1989, scientists at the University of California, San Francisco, released a study showing that baseball players who use smokeless (chewing) tobacco have a risk of developing pre-cancerous oral lesions that is 25 times higher than the risk for players who do not use chewing tobacco. A recent National Cancer Institute survey of more than 250 North Carolina women with oral cancer suggested that women who habitually smoked and used smokeless tobacco had a risk of cancers of the gum and cheek nearly 50 times higher than women who used neither form of tobacco. The risk for women who use only smokeless tobacco alone is four times higher than normal. All smokers, including those who smoke pipes or cigars, have a higher risk of cancers of the lip.

Early detection. Routine screening of smokers and others at risk may dramatically increase the rate of early discovery and prolong survival time. Overall, slightly more than half of all people diagnosed with an oral cancer can expect to survive five years or longer, but survival rates do vary according to the site of the cancer. For example, 91% of all patients with cancer of the lip are still alive five years or more after diagnosis, while the five-year survival rate for advanced cancers inside the mouth is about 30%.

To lower the risk of oral cancer

Smoking and sunlight: Avoid them both. If you smoke or use chewing tobacco, stop. When you spend time in the sun, protect your lips as well as your skin. You may use a lipstick that contains a sunscreen or a sunscreen product made specifically for lips. Don't use your regular sunscreen on your lips; the product may contain chemicals not considered safe for over-the-counter drugs used on the mouth.

Have regular dental check-ups. Your yearly visit to the dentist isn't just to check for cavities. Your dentist should also do a thorough job of checking for lesions on the inside of your mouth, and suspicious red or white spots should be biopsied. When they are, anywhere from one-third to two-thirds of these lesions turn out to be malignant.

Between trips to the dentist, self-examination is a worthy goal, but it is virtually impossible for you to do a complete examination of the inside of your own mouth. If you do discover a white or red patch that does not heal in ten days or that recurs after apparently healing, see the doctor. The fact that the spot or sore isn't painful doesn't guarantee that it's benign. Some benign spots may be intensely painful; some malignancies begin painlessly. Smokers should be particularly careful to watch for "smoker's patch," a firm, brown potentially pre-cancerous spot on the lip (usually the lower lip) that may develop in the place where you usually rest your cigarette, cigar or pipe.

OSTEOPOROSIS

Known risk factors

Age:	Yes	Smoking:	Yes
Gender:	Yes	Drugs & medical procedures:	Yes
Race/ethnic group:	Yes	General health:	No
Family history:	Yes	Environment:	No
Diet:	Yes	Occupation:	No

Are you at risk?

Osteoporosis is a loss of bone mass severe enough to cause repeated crippling fractures. It affects nearly 20 million Americans, causing approximately 1.5 million fractures each year in people older than 45. Among people who live to be older than 90, 32% of the women and 17% of the men will suffer a broken hip due to osteoporosis.

The person most likely to develop osteoporosis is a woman with a family history of the disease. She is white or Oriental; black women consistently have bone mass about 10% higher than white women. She smokes. She doesn't exercise regularly (exercise builds muscle that protects bones). She is underweight, not simply small, but fragile. As a teen-ager, when her bones were accumulating mass, she didn't get enough calcium to make her bones dense enough to offer a margin of safety after age 30 to 35, when everyone—men and women alike—begins to lose bone density.

The pattern of a woman's menstrual cycles may also predict her risk. In 1987, a team of researchers at Yale University Medical School reported a link between osteoporosis, endometriosis and irregular menstrual cycles longer than 35 days apart. Why? Women with long cycles are likely to have lower levels of estrogen, a hormone that protects bones. Women with endometriosis have a different problem. Endometriosis is characterized by the presence of endometrial tissue outside the uterus. This tissue appears to trigger the secretion of a hormone (interleukin-1) that activates osteoclasts, cells that break down bone.

Other medical conditions that raise the risk of osteoporosis for men as well as women include diabetes, hyperthyroidism (an overactive thyroid gland) or hyperparathyroidism (overactive parathyroid glands), which may reduce bone density early in life, or are taking cortisone, a medication that interferes with the bones' ability to absorb calcium.

Early detection. Although standard X-rays of the spine are the most widely available radiographic tests, they are not sensitive enough to show bone loss until bone density has decreased by 20 to 30%. The preferred procedure is dual photon absorptiometry.

During this examination, which exposes you to less than one-tenth the radiation you get from an ordinary chest X-ray, you lie on a table while radioactive isotopes pass underneath you and a detector passes over your body. The detector measures how much radiation from the isotopes goes through your body to the detector. The more porous your bones, the more radiation will get through to register on the detector.

Unless you have a condition known to reduce bone density, your doctor is likely to advise you to wait until you are in your 40s or are beginning menopause before you schedule osteoporosis screening.

To lower the risk of osteoporosis

Get enough calcium. In 1989, the National Research Council issued new Recommended Dietary Allowances (RDA), raising RDAs for people younger than 25 to 1,200 mg calcium, approximately the amount found in four eight-ounce glasses of milk. For people older than 25, the RDA is 800 mg a day. In 1984, however, a National Institutes of Health Conference had suggested that 800 mg is too low. The NIH conference report advised raising the RDA to 1,500 mg for women older than 65 who were not taking estrogen supplements. The suggested RDA for women on estrogen therapy: 1,000 mg.

Because most Americans, especially women, usually do not get even 800 mg of calcium a day, many experts recommend the insurance of calcium supplements for high-risk individuals, but the value of supplements in preventing or arresting osteoporosis in adults remains to be proven.

Also awaiting confirmation: The idea that boron, an element found in many fruits and vegetables, may be what's needed to get calcium into adult bones and keep it there.

Boron research is so new that as late as 1983 standard nutrition textbooks described it as an element required by plants but not people. Now, scientists at the USDA Human Nutrition Research Center in Grand Forks, North

Dakota, have studies to suggest that boron may play a role in regulating the body's use of both calcium and the female hormone estrogen, which seems to slow a woman's natural loss of bone after menopause.

In these studies, older men (who also lose bone as they age) and post-menopausal women on estrogen therapy had increased bone loss when the boron level in their bodies was low. The researchers also found that giving estrogen and boron together kept estrogen in the women's blood longer.

The amount of boron that may be toxic has not yet been identified. To avoid overdosing, the researchers suggest that you pass up supplements in favor of real food. You can get the boron you need (about 1 mg a day) from two apples or two or three ounces of raisins or a glass of grape juice.

Exercise—but maintain a normal weight. Regular, moderate exercise protects your bones in two ways. Under normal circumstances, we all lose muscle mass as well as bone mass as we age. Exercise may strengthen bones; it definitely strengthens and maintains the muscle tissue that supports bones.

Avoiding unnecessary reducing diets and maintaining a normal body weight with a normal proportion of fatty tissue may also be protective. Women store and convert estrogen, the female hormone that protects bones, in fatty tissues. For women, maintaining an adequate supply of the fatty tissue that continues to produce estrogen even after menopause may be crucial to controlling osteoporosis.

Post-menopausal estrogen supplements will protect against bone loss, but they are also known to raise the risk of uterine cancer and recent studies have suggested that they may also raise the risk of breast cancer.

If you smoke, stop. Like long menstrual cycles, smoking has been linked to reduced levels of estrogen and may be implicated in bone loss.

OVARIAN CANCER

Known risk factors

Age:	Yes	Smoking:	No
Gender:	Yes	Drugs & medical procedures:	No
Race/ethnic group:	Yes	General health:	Yes
Family history:	Yes	Environment:	No
Diet:	?	Occupation:	No

Are you at risk?

Cancer of the ovary is the fifth leading cause of cancer death among American women. According to the American Cancer Society (ACS), there were an estimated 20,500 new cases of ovarian cancer diagnosed in this country in 1990 and 12,400 deaths from the disease. ACS also estimates that one in every 70 newborn baby girls in this country will develop this cancer at some time in her life.

Your risk of ovarian cancer rises as you get older; most cases occur among women older than 65. There seems to be a family link. If you have close relatives (mother, sister, daughter) with the disease, you are presumed to be at higher risk. As with breast cancer, there is a lack of precise data to show whether this higher risk is due to genetic factors such as an "ovarian cancer gene" or inherited metabolic anomalies or to environmental factors such as diet.

In America, ovarian cancer is about 50% more common among white and native Hawaiian women than among black, Hispanic and Chinese women. The lowest rates are among native Americans, whose risk is only one-quarter that of white and native Hawaiian women. This may suggest genetic factors at work. On the other hand, Japanese women, who ordinarily have a lower risk of ovarian cancer (and breast cancer) while they are living in Japan, have an increased risk when they move to this country, which suggests that there are environmental factors at work. Ovarian cancer occurs less frequently in Asia and Africa than in northern Europe and North America.

Your own reproductive history may affect your risk. According to a 1989 study at Stanford University, women who ovulate but fail to become pregnant after 10 years of unprotected intercourse have a risk double that of women who became pregnant after two years of unprotected intercourse. Women who have never had children are at higher risk; women who had their first child when they were younger than 20 are at lower risk, as are women who have had several children.

Using oral contraceptives appears to lower the risk of ovarian cancer. One study at the Boston University School of Medicine has shown that women who use the pill had a risk of ovarian cancer 50% lower than women who use other forms of contraception. This protective effect, which became stronger the longer the women in the study stayed on the pill, appeared to last as long as 10 years after the women stopped using oral contraceptives. The results of this study are supported by six other similar investigations, including one from the Federal Centers for Disease Control.

Women who have had breast cancer and endometrial cancer are two times more likely than other women to develop cancer of the ovary. Having cancer of the colon also seems to increase the risk of ovarian cancer, but the risk decreases the longer you survive after the colon cancer is diagnosed.

Early detection. Eighty-five percent of the women whose ovarian cancers are diagnosed and treated while the tumors are still small and confined to the ovary will be alive five years later. When the cancer is diagnosed after it has spread, the five-year survival rate may drop as low as 23%.

Because cancer of the ovary may grow without producing any obvious symptoms other than a general feeling of pelvic discomfort, it is difficult to detect in its early stages. The primary screening test for this cancer is a pelvic examination that allows the doctor to detect a change in the size of the ovary or the presence of a tumor on the surface.

If the ovary is enlarged or a tumor is discovered, but your doctor suspects a benign ovarian cyst rather than ovarian cancer, she may recommend a second examination one month later to see if the tumor has disappeared spontaneously. This course is most likely in young women, who have a higher risk of ovarian cysts and a lower risk of ovarian cancer. In older women, specifically in women past menopause, the more likely diagnostic course is laparoscopy (examination of your internal pelvic organs with a light, flexible tube inserted through an incision in your abdomen) or pelvic surgery to remove the tumor and confirm a diagnosis with a biopsy. Three-quarters of all ovarian tumors removed by surgery are benign.

In 1989, researchers at King's College School of Medicine and Dentistry in London announced the development of a new test to detect early ovarian cancers. The test, known as transvaginal color flow imaging, creates an ultrasound image of the ovaries that shows blood vessel growth and a color picture of the blood flow through the vessels. Both benign and malignant tumors produce new blood vessels, but malignant growths produce more and the blood vessels for a malignant tumor are more resistant to blood flow. The new test will have to be evaluated on large numbers of patients before it can be reliably used to replace diagnostic surgery for suspicious tumors.

To lower your risk of ovarian cancer

Because the exact causes of ovarian cancer are still unknown, there is presently no medically certain way to reduce your risk. However, some doctors recommend that women who have two or more close relatives with ovarian cancer have both ovaries surgically removed by age 35 or as soon as they have completed their families.

PANCREATIC CANCER

Known risk factors

Age:	Yes	Smoking:	Yes
Gender:	Yes	Drugs & medical procedures:	No
Race/ethnic group:	Yes	General health:	Yes
Family history:	No	Environment:	No
Diet:	?	Occupation:	Yes

Are you at risk?

Cancer of the pancreas accounts for about 3% of all cancers and 5% of all cancer deaths in this country. According to the American Cancer Society

(ACS), there were an estimated 28,100 new cases of pancreatic cancer and 25,000 deaths in 1990, making this the fifth most common cause of cancer death, right behind lung cancer, colon cancer, breast cancer and cancer of the prostate.

Your risk of developing pancreatic cancer rises as you get older. The disease occurs most frequently among people age 65 to 79. A man's risk is about 30% higher than a woman's. A black person's risk is about 50% higher than a white person's. A smoker's risk is more than twice as high as a non-smoker's. Having diabetes appears to double your risk, and there are unconfirmed studies suggesting that your risk is also higher if you have a chronic pancreatitis (inflammation of the pancreas) or cirrhosis of the liver.

The as-yet-unconfirmed suspicion that a high-fat diet may raise your risk of pancreatic cancer is based largely on the fact that this cancer is more common in countries where people eat more fatty foods. Early studies suggesting that drinking coffee might increase the chance of developing pancreatic cancer have not been borne out by subsequent investigation. It is a curious but unexplained fact that the highest incidence of pancreatic cancer among men occurs in the California Bay Area; the highest incidence among women, among American Indians living in New Mexico.

Early detection. Because pancreatic cancer is a silent disease that develops without apparent symptoms until it is far advanced, overall only 3% of all patients live more than five years after diagnosis. The figure is much higher, 30%, for people whose cancers occur in the pancreas' insulin-producing cells rather than in the cells of the duct leading out from the gland.

Your doctor can confirm the presence of a tumor in the pancreas via ultrasound examination and/or a CT-scan; a diagnosis of malignancy is confirmed by a needle biopsy of the mass.

To lower your risk of cancer of the pancreas

If you smoke, stop. Because so little is known for sure about the causes of cancer of the pancreas, there is presently no certain way to reduce your risk. However, people who smoke are at higher risk of pancreatic cancer, and smoking appears to be a risk factor you can control.

PANIC DISORDER

Known risk factors

Age:	Yes	Smoking:	No
Gender:	?	Drugs & medical procedures:	No
Race/ethnic group:	No	General health:	No
Family history:	Yes	Environment:	Yes
Diet:	No	Occupation:	No

Are you at risk?

Panic disorder is an emotional illness characterized by attacks of paralyzing fear along with intense symptoms of emotional and physical discomfort.

One to 2% of all Americans—approximately 3 million people—suffer from an episode of panic disorder at one point in their lives. The disorder is most likely to occur for the first time during the late teens or early twenties. Statistics compiled by the National Institute for Mental Health show two female patients for every male patient with panic disorder. Many experts believe, however, that this reflects a sex bias towards illness (with men being more reluctant than women to admit to feelings of fear or weakness and to seek treatment for emotional disorders) rather than the true incidence of the disease.

People who have relatives with panic disorder seem to be more likely than other people to develop it themselves, which suggests a genetic component at work. Positron emission tomography (PET), a sophisticated but still experimental test that measures body functions by observing the action of injected radioactive substances, has shown biological differences between brain function in people with panic disorder and those without it.

Early detection. The symptoms of a panic attack may include a feeling that one is "out of control" or "going crazy," as well as chest pain, quickened or pounding heartbeat, shortness of breath, choking, nausea and upset stomach, chills or flushing, numbness or tingling in the skin, dizziness, trembling, or sweating. In general, anyone who experiences four attacks of unprovoked panic within four months or fewer attacks followed by at least a month of persistent fear of another attack may be diagnosed as suffering from panic disorder.

Precise diagnosis is very important because panic disorder can mimic many different illnesses, most commonly heart disease. In 1987, a study of patients at University Hospital, University of Missouri, who had symptoms suggestive of a heart attack showed that 59% of them did not have heart disease and that in many cases their symptoms were caused by a panic attack.

To lower your risk of panic disorder

The cause of panic disorder remains a mystery, so there is presently no sure way to reduce your risk of an initial attack. However, 85% of panic attack victims find that their symptoms disappear or diminish in intensity in response to treatment. In 1990, the Food and Drug Administration approved the use of the anti-anxiety tranquilizer alprazolam (Xanax) for the treatment of panic disorder.

PELVIC INFLAMMATORY DISEASE (PID)

Known risk factors

Age:	Yes	Smoking:	No
Gender:	Yes	Drugs & medical procedures:	Yes
Race/ethnic group:	No	General health:	No
Family history:	No	Environment:	No
Diet:	No	Occupation:	No

Are you at risk?

Pelvic inflammatory disease (PID) is a term used to describe an infection in one or more of a woman's reproductive pelvic organs: the cervix (cervicitis), the fallopian tubes (salpingitis), the ovaries (oophoritis) and the uterus (endometritis). It is estimated that there may be as many as 1 million cases of PID every year among American women.

The most important risk factor for PID is sexual intercourse. The infection occurs most frequently among sexually active teen-agers and young women who have sex with more than one partner. It is rare among women who are not sexually active, but it may, infrequently, occur after childbirth or an abortion. The risk is lowest before the first menstrual period (menarche) and after menopause.

A woman who uses an intrauterine device (IUD) has a risk about twice that of women who use other forms of contraception because the bacteria that cause PID may ascend into the uterus on the "tail" of the IUD that hangs out through the cervical opening as a check to let an IUD wearer know the device is in place.

Early detection. A painful pelvic inflammation can mimic the symptoms of ectopic pregnancy, the implanting of a fertilized egg in one of the fallopian tubes. Your doctor tells them apart by administering a pregnancy test, which, of course, comes up negative when the pain is caused by PID.

Your doctor may also want to rule out appendicitis, and if your condition does not respond to antibiotics, she may perform laparoscopy, an examination that involves the insertion of a flexible viewing tube through an incision in your abdomen. Looking through the tube, your doctor may pinpoint the source of your problem by direct observation of the pelvic organs.

To lower your risk of PID

Use protective forms of contraceptives: Although no contraceptive offers guaranteed protection against sexually transmitted diseases, some may reduce your risk. For example, using a barrier contraceptive such as a condom may prevent infectious organisms from reaching the cervix and uterus.

The correct use of condoms begins with storing them properly in a cool, dry place to protect the latex from drying out. The condom should be put on gently to avoid tearing. Leave room at the tip to accommodate the ejaculate. After ejaculation, your partner should withdraw the penis with the condom still in place, holding it close against the base of the penis to avoid spilling any ejaculate. Discard all used condoms; never try to wash them out and use them again.

According to the American Social Health Association, you may increase the protective effect of a condom by using a spermicidal foam that contains nonoxynol-9. In laboratory studies, nonoxynol-9 appears to kill a number of the organisms that cause sexually transmitted diseases on contact. But the two contraceptives must be used in tandem; on its own, the foam is not considered adequately protective.

Oral contraceptives may alter the pH of the vagina so as to make it inhospitable for disease-carrying micro-organisms. As noted above, IUDs are believed to increase the risk of PID. If you are currently using one, you may wish to discuss with your doctor whether or not it would be beneficial for you to switch to another kind of contraception.

PENILE CANCER

Known risk factors

Age:	Yes	Smoking:	No
Gender:	Yes	Drugs & medical procedures:	No
Race/ethnic group:	No	General health:	No
Family history:	No	Environment:	No
Diet:	No	Occupation:	No

Are you at risk?

The most important risk factor for cancer of the penis is lack of personal cleanliness. Cancer of the penis is most common in parts of the world where circumcision is unusual and personal hygiene is ordinarily poor. In the United States, where circumcision is common and standards of personal hygiene are high, cancer of the penis is rare, with fewer than 1,000 new cases diagnosed each year.

There is some research to suggest that a second risk factor may be exposure to the human papilloma virus already linked to cancer of the cervix. Some studies imply that this virus, which is transmitted during sexual intercourse, may also be implicated in the development of cancer of the penis. The case remains to be proven.

Early detection. The early symptoms of cancer of the penis include painless bumps, warty growths or an ulcer on the skin. Later symptoms include pain and bleeding. The earlier the cancer is diagnosed by tissue biopsy, the less radical the surgery to treat it may be. Advanced cancers may require extensive surgery, up to removal of the penis itself.

To lower your risk of cancer of the penis

Consider the benefits of circumcision. The circumcision of newborn baby boys appears to provide a real life-long reduction in the risk of cancer of the penis. Since 1930, it is estimated that there have been about 35,000 to 50,000 cases of cancer of the penis in this country. Only nine of them are known to have been diagnosed in circumcised men. Circumcision also appears to reduce the risk of urinary tract infections for men and reproductive cancers for their female sexual partners.

Practice safer sex. Although the link between human papilloma virus and cancer of the penis remains to be proven, plain good sense dictates the virtue of practicing safer sex: avoiding multiple sex partners and using protective contraception such as a condom.

The correct use of condoms begins with storing them properly in a cool, dry place to protect the latex from drying out. The condom should be put on gently to avoid tearing. Leave room at the tip to accommodate the ejaculate. After ejaculation, your partner should withdraw the penis with the condom still in place, holding it close against the base of the penis to avoid spilling any ejaculate. Discard all used condoms; never try to wash them out and use them again.

According to the American Social Health Association, you may increase the protective effect of a condom by using a spermicidal foam that contains nonoxynol-9. In laboratory studies, nonoxynol-9 appears to kill many organisms that cause sexually transmitted diseases on contact. But the two contraceptives must be used in tandem; on its own, the foam is not considered adequately protective.

PERIODONTAL DISEASE

Known risk factors

Age:	Yes	Smoking:	Yes
Gender:	No	Drugs & medical procedures:	Yes
Race/ethnic group:	No	General health:	Yes
Family history:	Yes	Environment:	No
Diet:	No	Occupation:	No

Are you at risk?

Periodontal disease is a term used to describe any disorder of the tissues surrounding the teeth. As many as three-quarters of all American adults have periodontal disease, ranging from gingivitis (inflamed gum tissue) to periodontitis, the chronic destructive form of periodontal disease that erodes the bone in which teeth are anchored and is the most common cause of tooth loss in people older than 35.

Whether or not you develop gingivitis depends to a large extent on how clean you keep your mouth, but recent research suggests that your risk of developing periodontitis is clearly linked to genetic factors beyond your control. Because periodontitis is about three times more common among women than among men and may worsen during pregnancy or flare up right before menstruation begins, some suspect a hormonal trigger as well.

If your mother or father have periodontitis, consider yourself at risk. Periodontal disease that runs in families may develop even if you keep your teeth scrupulously clean and free of plaque and tartar. It is most likely to show up before you get to be 25.

You may also be at risk for periodontal disease if you have uncontrolled diabetes, leukemia, pellagra (the vitamin B1 deficiency disease), or scurvy (the vitamin C deficiency disease) or if you are using the anti-seizure drug phenytoin (Dilantin).

Early detection. According to the American Dental Association, seven out of every 10 teeth lost in this country are lost to periodontal disease. The value of early detection and vigorous treatment is that it can reduce the damage done by periodontal disease and may allow you to keep your own teeth as long as you live.

To lower your risk of periodontal disease

Keep your teeth clean. Floss, brush and rinse as directed by your periodontist or dentist. Scrupulous attention to oral hygiene will reduce your risk of gingivitis. Get regular check-ups. No matter how clean you keep your teeth, you still need regular check-ups and a professional "scaling" (cleaning under the gum around the root of the tooth).

If you smoke, stop. Smoking heats the tissues around your teeth and makes them more vulnerable to infection, thus increasing your risk of both gingivitis and periodontitis.

PHENYLKETONURIA (PKU)

Known risk factors

Age:	Yes	Smoking:	No
Gender:	No	Drugs & medical procedures:	No
Race/ethnic group:	No	General health:	No
Family history:	Yes	Environment:	No
Diet:	Yes	Occupation:	No

Are you at risk?

People with PKU lack sufficient amounts of the enzyme needed to metabolize the amino acid phenylalanine. As a result, phenylalanine accumulates in their body tissues. In newborns, the accumulation of phenylalanine caused by untreated PKU may lead to mental retardation.

On average, PKU occurs once in every 16,000 live births in this country. Although people of almost every ethnic group carry the PKU gene, infants of Irish and Scottish descent are at highest risk. Among these babies, one in every 5,000 has PKU. PKU is least common among babies born to blacks and people of Jewish or Finnish descent; only one in every 300,000 in these groups has the condition.

Early detection. The screening test for PKU is a blood test to detect higher-than-normal blood levels of phenylalanine. The blood test is standard treatment for American newborns. An infant who tests positive for PKU is immediately put on a phenylalanine-restricted diet.

The blood sample taken to test for PKU may also be used to screen for several other metabolic disorders, such as inherited galactosemia (an inability to metabolize galactose) and congenital hypothyroidism, as well.

To lower the risk of PKU

PKU testing for older children and adults. If you have close relatives with PKU, you can be tested for PKU before you decide to start a family.

Unfortunately, the test is not a fool-proof guide as to whether or not you are carrying the PKU gene. The gene is recessive; you need to inherit one from each parent in order to develop PKU or its symptoms. It is possible to have a PKU gene without showing symptoms or testing positive for PKU.

However, if you have two PKU genes, your test will be positive. Knowing that you have the PKU genes can be very important if you are a woman who plans to have a family. As many as 90% of the babies born to women who have PKU but do not follow a low-phenylalanine diet during pregnancy are likely to be mentally or physically retarded because they are exposed to elevated levels of phenylalanine in their mothers' blood.

Several recent studies have suggested that controlling a mother's phenylalanine levels before and during pregnancy may protect her infant. If you have PKU, ask your doctor about a protective diet before you become pregnant.

PLAGUE

Known risk factors

Age:	No	Smoking:	No
Gender:	No	Drugs & medical procedures:	No
Race/ethnic group:	No	General health:	No
Family history:	No	Environment:	Yes
Diet:	No	Occupation:	Yes

Are you at risk?

Bubonic plague, once known as The Black Death, is an infectious disease spread by the bite of fleas carrying the plague bacteria, *Yersinia pestis*, and characterized by painful swollen lymph nodes (buboes). Bubonic plague that spreads to the lungs is known as pneumonic plague, a contagious illness that can be transmitted from person to person or, rarely, from a sick animal to a human being by droplets sprayed into the air while coughing.

Although modern air travel makes it possible for plague to cross international borders, where you live or travel still plays an important role in determining whether you are at risk. Plague is endemic in the southern Soviet Union, India, Indochina and South Africa. In the last 30 years, there have been increasing numbers of cases in the southwestern United States where infection is endemic among wild squirrels, mice, chipmunks and prairie dogs. Hikers, campers, hunters and young children (who may attempt to play with these animals) are at risk, as are park rangers and medical researchers and technicians who work with plague bacteria in research laboratories.

Early detection. Untreated, bubonic plague will kill 60% of those who get it; untreated pneumonic plague is nearly 100% fatal. Prompt treatment with anti-microbials (streptomycin, tetracyclines) can reduce the death rate from plague to under 5%.

Plague is diagnosed by culturing (growing) the plague bacterium in a sample of the patient's blood or sputum or liquid from an enlarged lymph node.

To lower your risk of plague

Protect yourself from fleas. Where plague is endemic, insecticidal sprays for people and pets are the first line of defense whenever you go into wooded areas or places where wild rodents are present. Never handle a sick wild animal; avoid carcasses; seek professional help if necessary to control the wild rodent population on your own grounds.

Immunization. When you travel to an area such as Southeast Asia where plague is endemic or if your work puts you at risk, you will want to ask your doctor about plague vaccine. For continuing protection, you must be re-vaccinated every six months. During a brief visit to a plague area, preventive anti-microbials may suffice.

PNEUMONIA

Known risk factors

Age:	Yes	Smoking:	No
Gender:	No	Drugs & medical procedures:	No
Race/ethnic group:	No	General health:	Yes
Family history:	No	Environment:	No
Diet:	No	Occupation:	No

Are you at risk?

Because the widespread use of anti-microbials has reduced the death rate from pneumonia over the last 30 years, most of us now think of pneumonia as a toothless relic from the past. Unfortunately, this is an inaccurate picture. Every year, nearly 2 million Americans will still develop pneumonia, and as many as 70,000 die of it.

Getting older raises the risk of pneumonia because aging reduces the efficiency of the immune system. So does having an immune disorder such as AIDS or taking medication such as anti-cancer or immunosuppressant drugs. People with chronic respiratory conditions such as bronchitis and emphysema are at higher risk because of reduced lung function. So are people with flu or heart disease, as well as alcoholics. Having to spend time in a hospital raises your risk. Pneumonia is one of the most common hospital-acquired infections.

Early detection. Pneumonia is diagnosed by its symptoms: acute fever, chills, chest pain, cough and fluid in the lungs. Pneumonia may be caused by any one of a variety of micro-organisms: bacteria, viruses, fungi. The cause is identified by cultures or studies of the patient's sputum or blood.

To lower your risk of pneumonia

Ask your doctor about pneumonia immunization. The Federal Centers for Disease Control now strongly recommends immunization against *pneumonococcus*, the most common causes of bacterial pneumonia for people who are older than 65 or have an immune deficiency or chronic illness.

POLIOMYELITIS

Known risk factors

Age:	Yes	Smoking:	No
Gender:	No	Drugs & medical procedures:	Yes
Race/ethnic group:	No	General health:	No
Family history:	No	Environment:	Yes
Diet:	No	Occupation:	Yes

Are you at risk?

Polio is a viral infection that spreads by transmission of a virus from one person to another by fecal-oral contact. Anyone who has not acquired immunity to the virus either by having had polio or by taking polio vaccine is at risk if exposed to someone who is carrying the virus or to the virus itself, for example, while working in a medical laboratory.

Did you grow up in an area where cleanliness and preventive medicine are highly valued? Believe it or not, these conditions actually increase your risk of paralytic polio.

In places where sanitation is poor, people are exposed to the polio virus early in life and acquire immunity through a childhood infection so slight that it may not affect the central nervous system and or even cause any recognizable symptoms. In developed countries, by contrast, exposure is delayed and people who are not immunized remain susceptible into their teens, their early 20s, or even later when infectious disease is more severe and more likely to be paralytic.

Early detection. Non-paralytic polio may look like several other illnesses including the flu, a herpes infection, mumps or even a brain abscess. The disease can only be conclusively diagnosed by culturing polio virus from the patient's throat or feces.

Paralytic polio may be diagnosed by its symptoms (paralysis of the respiratory muscles or the skeletal muscles controlled by spinal nerves), but it, too, is conclusively identified by culturing the virus from the patient's feces or throat.

To lower your risk of poliomyelitis

Vaccination. Immunization with polio vaccine virtually eliminates your risk of paralysis by eliminating your risk of polio.

There are two forms of polio vaccine. The Salk vaccine, introduced in 1955 and administered by injection, is composed of killed virus. The Sabin vaccine, introduced in 1963 and administered orally, is composed of live virus. Both vaccines are effective, but the Sabin vaccine, which is easy to give, has become the standard preventive for healthy children in the United States, making polio so rare here that immunization is not recommended for healthy adults unless they are exposed to polio or plan to travel to areas where the disease is endemic.

There is a small but measurable risk of contracting paralytic polio if you get the live vaccine or are in close contact with someone who gets it. Experts estimate that this kind of infection may occur once for every 3.7 million doses of the vaccine. As a result, the Federal Centers for Disease Control recommends that pregnant women, who might pass the live virus to their fetuses, receive the killed virus Salk vaccine. The Salk vaccine is also considered safer for people who are immune deficient or who live in a household with someone who has a disease such as AIDS or who are taking any medication such as corticosteroids or anti-cancer drugs that impair the responses of the immune system.

PREMENSTRUAL SYNDROME (PMS)

Known risk factors

Age:	Yes	Smoking:	No
Gender:	Yes	Drugs & medical procedures:	No
Race/ethnic group:	No	General health:	No
Family history:	No	Environment:	No
Diet:	?	Occupation:	No

Are you at risk?

PMS is a group of symptoms that may include acne, bloating, breast pain, headaches, irritability and mood swings. These symptoms ordinarily occur mid-way through the menstrual cycle, after ovulation, in the week to 10 days before a woman's period begins. Most women find that these symptoms go away as soon as the menstrual flow starts, but women who are going through menopause may feel miserable right through menstruation.

In theory, every woman who menstruates is at risk for PMS, but anywhere from one-half to two-thirds of all American women will never develop any symptoms. The others will have at least one episode at some point in their reproductive years.

Whether or not what you eat affects your risk is still an open question. Some women have specific food cravings (most commonly for sweet or salty foods), but there is no scientific evidence that these certain foods will cause PMS or that avoiding them will cure it even though some women do experience relief of PMS symptoms when they change their diet.

It has been suggested that women who suffer from serious PMS are deficient in vitamin B_6 (pyridoxine) or magnesium or have too much calcium or are the victims of a complicated mix of vitamin and mineral imbalances. There is, as yet, no scientific proof that this is so, and self-treatment with large doses of these nutrients may be hazardous. For example, in amounts of 500 mg a day or more, vitamin B_6 is known to cause neurological symptoms such as numbness and tingling in the hands and feet as well as difficulty in walking, while large doses of magnesium may interfere with calcium absorption or act as a strong laxative. In fact, magnesium salts are the active ingredients in some over-the-counter laxative products.

By the way, eating more than usual in the second half of the menstrual cycle (after ovulation) now seems to be natural. According to a 1987 report in the *American Journal of Clinical Nutrition*, a woman's energy needs may rise as much as 8% to 16% in the 10 days to two weeks between ovulation and menstruation, an extra 150 to 200 calories a day. The authors of the study suggest that the increase in appetite may be due to the natural cyclical increase in the female hormone progesterone (an appetite stimulant).

Early detection. What makes PMS so difficult to treat is the fact that it is entirely subjective. At present, there are no objective diagnostic tests to tell your doctor what you have or how serious it is. In short, how you feel is how you are.

To lower your risk of PMS

There are no scientifically certain ways to reduce your risk of PMS. On the other hand, there are innumerable folk cures and word-of-mouth remedies and preventives for premenstrual symptoms.

Some women find that avoiding salty or spicy foods in the second half of the menstrual cycle reduces bloating because it reduces fluid retention. Others use regular exercise as a way to maintain mental, as well as physical, fitness. Still others report success with low-dose oral contraceptives, perhaps because they smooth out hormonal fluctuations. Unfortunately, the lack of confirming scientific studies makes it impossible to predict whether or not these remedies and preventives will work for you.

PROSTATE CANCER

Known risk factors

Age:	Yes	Smoking:	No
Gender:	Yes	Drugs & medical procedures:	No
Race/ethnic group:	Yes	General health:	No
Family history:	?	Environment:	No
Diet:	?	Occupation:	No

Are you at risk?

Prostate cancer is rare in the Near East, Africa and Central and South America. It is more common in northwestern Europe and the United States, where it is the third leading cause of cancer deaths among American men, the second most common malignancy among those older than 55 and the third most common cause of cancer deaths in this age group.

According to the American Cancer Society, there are about 100,000 new cases diagnosed each year in this country and 20,000 deaths. For reasons no one yet understands, it is most common among American black men who have the highest rate of prostate cancer in the world.

A man's risk of prostate cancer rises as he gets older. Nearly 80% of all cases occur in men older than 65. The risk may also be higher among men who have relatives with prostate cancer, but this remains to be proven.

Some experts suggest a link between a high-fat diet and an increased risk of prostate cancer, but this is speculation based largely on the fact that men born in Japan who move to the United States begin to develop the disease at the same rate as native-born Americans. Men who are exposed to cadmium at work in manufacturing alloys, electrical coatings or electrical batteries are known to be at higher risk.

Early detection. The overall five-year survival rate for cancer of the prostate is 71%. Eighty-four percent of all men whose prostate cancers are diagnosed when they are still localized in the general region of the prostate gland are expected to be alive five years later.

The screening test for cancer of the prostate is a rectal examination that allows the doctor to feel an enlarged or hardened prostate gland. A diagnosis of prostate cancer may be confirmed by a needle biopsy of the prostate gland.

To lower your risk of prostate cancer

At present, there is no known way to reduce the risk of cancer of the prostate.

PSITTACOSIS

Known risk factors

Age:	No	Smoking:	No
Gender:	No	Drugs & medical procedures:	No
Race/ethnic group:	No	General health:	No
Family history:	No	Environment:	Yes
Diet:	No	Occupation:	Yes

Are you at risk?

Psittacosis, which is popularly known as parrot fever, is a form of pneumonia caused by *Chlamydia psittaci*, a micro-organism carried by a wide variety of birds including budgies, cockatiels, canaries, love birds, parakeets, pigeons, poultry and snowy egrets. You can be infected with psittacosis if you are exposed to an infected bird's respiratory discharges or feces (which may fly into the air when a bird kicks or blows up with his wings the dust at the bottom of his cage).

Adding antibiotics to poultry feed and imposing quarantine restrictions on imported birds have steadily reduced the incidence of psittacosis in this country. Today the people at highest risk are those who work with birds in breeding aviaries, poultry processing plants, pet stores, zoos and so forth. You are also at risk if you are exposed to someone with the disease.

Early detection. As many as 30% of all people with severe untreated psittacosis die of the disease.

If you have a history of exposure to birds and you develop respiratory symptoms suggestive of psittacosis, your doctor can confirm a diagnosis with an X-ray film that shows pneumonia and a blood test that shows the presence of antibodies to the psittacosis micro-organism.

To lower the risk of psittacosis

Be discriminating when you shop for pet birds. Like other pets, birds should be purchased only from a reputable shop that allows you to return the animal (or will pay for treatment) if it is sick. Any new pet should be examined by your veterinarian within a day or two of purchase.

Handle sick birds with care. If your pet bird becomes depressed, refuses to eat, begins to lose weight, passes greenish or mustard colored urine and shows signs of respiratory problems, take him right to the veterinarian. Waiting may prove to be hazardous for owner and pet.

PSORIASIS

Known risk factors

Age:	Yes	Smoking:	No
Gender:	No	Drugs & medical procedures:	No
Race/ethnic group:	Yes	General health:	No
Family history:	Yes	Environment:	No
Diet:	No	Occupation:	No

Are you at risk?

Psoriasis is a defect in the production of the outer layer of skin cells. Normally the process takes 26 to 28 days; for people with psoriasis, it takes three to four. The result is an abnormal build-up of cells that look like silvery scales covering red patches of skin.

Psoriasis is fairly common. It is the third most common cause of visits to the dermatologist, right behind acne and warts. Psoriasis occurs most frequently in people age 10 to 40. It is more common among whites than among blacks, but men and women are equally at risk. (In women, psoriasis may improve during pregnancy and worsen after delivery.) Psoriasis is not contagious, but there is a strong hereditary link, and if you have relatives with psoriasis, your risk is higher than normal.

Environmental factors, such as a change in weather, do not cause psoriasis, but they may affect its progress. Warm weather and moderate sun exposure seem to make the condition less bothersome for many people with psoriasis; cold weather seems to make it worse.

Some unrelated health conditions may affect the course of psoriasis. For example, people with psoriasis may experience an acute episode if the skin is sunburned or injured. The HIV infection that precedes full-blown AIDS can cause an intense flare-up of existing psoriasis. Streptococcal infections may trigger flare-ups, especially in children. Taking *beta* blockers (drugs used to treat high blood pressure) or the anti-malaria drug chloroquine or withdrawing from corticosteroids may also exacerbate existing psoriasis.

Early detection. Psoriasis is most commonly diagnosed by its appearance. Your doctor may wish to confirm the diagnosis with a biopsy of the affected skin tissue. The biopsy can differentiate psoriasis from other dermatologic disorders such as allergy, eczema, a fungal infection, lupus erythematosus (SLE), seborrhea, skin cancer and syphilis.

To lower your risk of psoriasis

At present, there is no known way to reduce your initial risk of psoriasis, but you may be able to lower the risk of episodes by avoiding controllable trigger factors such as sunburn.

RAYNAUD'S DISEASE

Known risk factors

Age:	Yes	Smoking:	No
Gender:	Yes	Drugs & medical procedures:	No
Race/ethnic group:	No	General health:	Yes
Family history:	Yes	Environment:	Yes
Diet:	No	Occupation:	Yes

Are you at risk?

People with Raynaud's disease suffer from spasms of the tiny blood vessels in the tips of their fingers and toes, or the tips of their nose and tongue, that interrupt the circulation of blood, turning the skin pale and cold.

Sixty to 90% of all cases of Raynaud's occur among women between the age of puberty and 40 who have relatives suffering from Raynaud's. People with circulatory problems, rheumatoid arthritis, systemic lupus erythematosus (SLE) or an underactive thyroid gland may develop Raynaud's phenomenon, which looks like Raynaud's disease but occurs only in one hand or foot. (Raynaud's disease almost always affects both sides of the body.)

Raynaud's disease is not caused by exposure to cold air, but its symptoms may be triggered or exacerbated by plunging your hands into cold water or reaching into the freezer compartment of your refrigerator or going outside without warm gloves and boots. The same thing goes for smoking, which does not cause the disease but can make its symptoms worse because nicotine is a vasoconstrictor, a chemical that causes blood vessels to constrict temporarily.

Raynaud's disease sometimes occurs in people who work with constantly vibrating machines like grinders in foundries or lumberjacks working with chainsaws or who are constantly moving their fingers like typists and pianists or who continually work in the cold and damp like butchers in cold storage lockers. It is unclear whether these conditions precipitate Raynaud's or simply make its symptoms worse.

Early detection. Raynaud's is diagnosed by characteristic changes in the color of the skin. During an attack, the skin first turns pale as circulation slows, then bluish, then red as the blood begins to flow again. This sequence is known formally as the tricolor phasic response.

To lower your risk of Raynaud's disease

Protect the vulnerable parts of your body from cold. Right now, there is no known way to reduce your risk of developing Raynaud's disease, but you may be able to reduce the incidence and severity of symptoms by keeping your hands, feet and face warm when you are exposed to cold and by using biofeedback to increase blood flow to sensitive areas. If you work with vibrating machinery, it is important to keep your tools working as smoothly as possible and to take regular breaks. If you smoke, stop.

REYE'S SYNDROME

Known risk factors

Age:	Yes	Smoking:	No
Gender:	No	Drugs & medical procedures:	Yes
Race/ethnic group:	No	General health:	Yes
Family history:	No	Environment:	No
Diet:	No	Occupation:	No

Are you at risk?

Reye's syndrome is a rare but potentially serious illness that occurs primarily in children younger than 18 who are recovering from a viral infectious disease, most commonly influenza or chicken pox. The exact cause of Reye's syndrome is unknown, but there appears to be a link with aspirin therapy. In 1986, the Food and Drug Administration issued a regulation requiring the following statement on all products containing aspirin: "WARNING: Children and teenagers should not use this medicine for chicken pox or flu symptoms before a doctor is consulted about Reye's syndrome, a rare but serious illness reported to be associated with aspirin."

Early detection. The death rate for Reye's syndrome ranges from a low of 2% percent among patients whose illness is caught early to a high of perhaps 80% among patients whose untreated illness reaches the most serious stage: seizures and respiratory failure. The early symptoms of Reye's syndrome may include lethargy, persistent vomiting, and confused, agitated or angry behavior. Notify your child's doctor immediately if these symptoms occur.

To lower your child's risk of Reye's syndrome

Warning: *When your child is ill, check with your doctor before administering aspirin or any other medication.*

RHEUMATIC FEVER

Known risk factors

Age:	Yes	Smoking:	No
Gender:	Yes	Drugs & medical procedures:	No
Race/ethnic group:	No	General health:	Yes
Family history:	?	Environment:	Yes
Diet:	No	Occupation:	No

Are you at risk?

Rheumatic fever is a potential complication of any streptococcus infections such as tonsillitis or otitis (an infection of the ear). Untreated rheumatic fever can lead to rheumatic heart disease, which damages the valves of the heart.

Although it is still common in undeveloped countries, rheumatic fever is now increasingly less common in countries such as the United States where anti-microbials are routinely used to treat the streptococcus infections that still affect more than 2 million Americans every year. Nonetheless, American Heart Association statistics estimate that 6,520 people died of rheumatic fever and rheumatic heart disease in 1988.

Anyone can get rheumatic fever, but the likeliest candidate is a young child, age five to 15, who may develop it a week or so after an untreated strep infection. Many experts believe that rheumatic heart disease is the most common heart problem among school children and may also be responsible for nearly half of all rejections from the armed services for cardiac abnormalities. For unknown reasons, some families seem to be more susceptible than others.

Having rheumatic fever does not confer any immunity. In fact, according to the American Heart Association, people who have already had one bout of rheumatic fever may actually be more susceptible to the condition and more likely to suffer heart damage if they get it again.

Where you live may raise (or lower) your risk of rheumatic fever. Environmental factors such as climate and crowding can affect the incidence of streptococcus infections. These infections are more common in cold, damp climates, in crowded places such as cities and military barracks, among large families and, most specifically, in the Third World countries where the effects of over-crowding are complicated by widespread malnutrition and a lack of adequate treatment.

Early detection. Diagnosing and treating streptococcus infections early on may prevent rheumatic fever and rheumatic heart disease.

Rheumatic fever is diagnosed by its symptoms: high fever and arthritic joint pains following a streptococcus infection. Chest pains, pallor and shortness of breath may suggest that the infection has moved to the heart.

These symptoms may resemble those of several other illnesses, including an allergic reaction, arthritis, a joint injury, a nerve injury, polio, a heart infection, sickle cell anemia, systemic lupus erythematosus (SLE) or tuberculosis.

Blood tests and/or a culture of tissue from the throat will allow your doctor to conclusively diagnose the streptococcus infection that triggers rheumatic fever. A chest X-ray and an electrocardiogram are commonly used to detect symptoms of heart damage and diagnose rheumatic heart disease.

To lower your risk of rheumatic fever

Never ignore a possible streptococcus infection. Prompt treatment with the appropriate anti-microbial can significantly reduce the possibility of rheumatic fever.

RICKETS

Known risk factors

Age:	Yes	Smoking:	No
Gender:	No	Drugs & medical procedures:	No
Race/ethnic group:	Yes	General health:	Yes
Family history:	No	Environment:	Yes
Diet:	Yes	Occupation:	No

Are you at risk?

Rickets is a condition caused by a deficiency of vitamin D, a nutrient essential to our body's ability to absorb calcium. We get vitamin D from food or we can synthesize it in the fatty layer just under the skin when we are exposed to sunlight.

If we do not get enough vitamin D, we cannot absorb sufficient amounts of calcium. Children who do not get enough vitamin D are likely to develop the characteristic deformed bones and demineralized teeth known as rickets. Adults who do not get enough vitamin D will begin to lose calcium and other minerals, a condition known as osteomalacia. Some experts suggest that the lack of sufficient amounts of vitamin D may be one part of the complex bone loss process that leads to osteoporosis in older people.

Fortifying milk with vitamin D has drastically reduced the incidence of rickets and osteomalacia in the United States. Breast-fed infants who do not get supplemental vitamin D and are not exposed to sunlight are still at risk. The same goes for people with very dark skin.

How much vitamin D we form naturally when we are exposed to the sun depends on how long we are in the sun and how heavily pigmented our skin is. The heavier the pigmentation, the less vitamin D we produce. Skin that is very dark may block as much as 95% of the ultraviolet radiation to which it is exposed from penetrating to the fatty layers under the skin where the vitamin is actually synthesized.

In parts of the world where there is limited sunlight, as in the Arctic where the winter "night" lasts for months, or where there is heavy atmospheric pollution, people may also lack enough exposure to ultraviolet light to form the vitamin D they need.

Some medical conditions may also reduce our ability to synthesize, absorb or use vitamin D. These include kidney failure, a disorder of the parathyroid glands, an inability to absorb fat (which carries vitamin D) and any intestinal disease that interferes with the normal cycling of vitamin D through the liver.

Early detection. Because rickets and osteomalacia are preventable and potentially curable, it is important to diagnose and treat them early on. Their symptoms may resemble those of other conditions such as arthritis, osteoporosis and metabolic bone disorders such as *osteogenesis imperfecta*. Each of these is ruled out in confirming a diagnosis of vitamin D deficiency disease.

To lower your risk of rickets

Consume a diet that includes a sufficient amount of vitamin D. But don't overdose: Large doses of vitamin D are toxic.

Vitamin D RDAs

	Age	RDA
Infants		
	0.0–0.5	300 IU
	0.5–1.0	400
Children		
	1–3	400
	4–6	400
	7–10	400
Adult men & women		
	11–14	400
	15–18	400
	19–24	400
	25–50	200
	51+	200
Pregnant women		400
Lactating women		400

Source: National Research Council, *Recommended Dietary Allowances* (Washington D.C.: National Academy Press, 1989)

RINGWORM

Known risk factors

Age:	Yes	Smoking:	No
Gender:	No	Drugs & medical procedures:	No
Race/ethnic group:	No	General health:	Yes
Family history:	No	Environment:	Yes
Diet:	No	Occupation:	Yes

Are you at risk?

Ringworm is a fungal infection that has different names depending on where it occurs. Ringworm of the body is *tinea corporis*. Ringworm of the nails is *tinea unguium*. Ringworm of the scalp is *tinea capitis*. Ringworm of the genital area, familiarly known as jock itch, is *tinea cruris*.

The people most susceptible to ringworm infection are very young children and anyone who has a nutritional deficiency or a medical condition that weakens the immune system. Ringworm of the scalp is most common among children. Ringworm of the genital area is most common in warm weather among people who wear tight-fitting undergarments and perspire a lot, for example, athletes and people who are obese.

You can catch ringworm from an infected animal. Owning a dog or cat increases your risk of acquiring *Microsporum canis*, the organism that causes most cases of ringworm in these small animals. Being around horses increases your risk of acquiring *Trichophyton equinum*, which causes most ringworm in horses. Cattle farming increases your risk of acquiring *Trichophyton verrucosum*, which causes most ringworm in cattle. Pet store workers, farm workers, veterinarians and others who handle infected animals or infected grooming tools are all at higher risk.

Early detection. Ringworm's symptoms may resemble those of an allergic reaction to drugs, a candida (yeast) infection, contact dermatitis, psoriasis or secondary syphilis, among others.

Ringworm fungi glow when exposed to specific frequencies of light, so a diagnosis of ringworm can be confirmed by examining the skin eruptions under an ultraviolet light. A second way to identify a ringworm infection is to find the fungi in hair or skin by examining a hair or a skin scraping under a microscope.

To lower your risk of ringworm

Practice intelligent hygiene. Because fungi flourish on damp skin, the first line of defense against ringworm is to keep your skin and clothes clean and dry. In very warm weather, stick to loose-fitting clothes that allow air to circulate to your skin. Always dry your skin thoroughly after bathing. Don't share unlaundered clothes or towels. To avoid ringworm of the scalp, don't share hats, combs and brushes.

Protect yourself by protecting your animals. Don't use the same grooming tools on two animals without sterilizing the tools between uses. Otherwise you may spread an unsuspected infection from one to the other. Wash your pet's towels and bedding with chlorine bleach in a load separate from your own clothes. See your veterinarian if your pet develops any suspicious balding or crusty lesions. Although small animals such as dogs and cats will usually recover spontaneously from a ringworm infection, *The Merck Veterinary Manual* recommends treating them with anti-fungal medication to reduce the chance of spreading the infection to household members.

ROCKY MOUNTAIN SPOTTED FEVER

Known risk factors

Age:	?	Smoking:	No
Gender:	No	Drugs & medical procedures:	No
Race/ethnic group:	No	General health:	No
Family history:	No	Environment:	Yes
Diet:	No	Occupation:	No

Are you at risk?

Rocky Mountain spotted fever is an infectious illness transmitted by ticks carrying the organism, *Rickettsia rickettsii*. The disease, which is named for the area in which it was first identified in the late 19th century, has now been reported in Canada, Mexico, South America and all the states except Maine, Alaska and Hawaii. In recent years, the number of reported cases has been declining, from 1,200 in 1981 to 850 in 1985.

You are at risk for Rocky Mountain spotted fever when you work or play outdoors, especially during tick season. In the United States, that is ordinarily from April through September, but in the southern states, where the weather is warm, tick season may last all year. That may be why the highest number of cases in this country occur in North Carolina, Oklahoma, Missouri, South Carolina and Tennessee.

At least 60% of all cases of Rocky Mountain spotted fever occur in people younger than 20. It's not that children are more susceptible; it's that they are more likely to be playing with animals or in areas where the tick is plentiful and are less likely to be wearing protective clothing.

Early detection. If left untreated, Rocky Mountain spotted fever can cause pneumonia or circulatory failure, heart or brain damage, cardiac arrest and death.

The older you are, the more serious the illness is likely to be and the higher your chances of dying. However, treatment with anti-microbials has brought the death rate from Rocky Mountain spotted fever down from 20% to under 7%. Some experts believe it might be even lower if treatment were started promptly in all cases.

Rocky Mountain spotted fever is customarily diagnosed by a blood test or by its characteristic symptoms: severe headache, chills, prostration and muscular pains, high fever, rash on wrists, ankles, palms, soles and forearms, occurring after a tick bite or while you are in a part of the country where the ticks are known to be present.

To lower your risk of Rocky Mountain spotted fever

Wear protective clothing. The proper gear for a walk in woods that may be harboring ticks is a long-sleeved shirt tucked into long pants tucked into socks or boots. Light-colored clothes are a good idea because they show up the dark ticks.

Some experts also suggest using an insect repellent containing DEET on your pants, socks and shoes. Use sparingly as directed on the container.

Walk a cleared path or trail. Avoid the dense foliage where ticks may be hiding.

When you get home, conduct a serious search-and-destroy mission. Check clothes and body thoroughly for ticks. Don't forget to check the scalp: ticks can hide under hair.

The Animal Medical Center in New York recommends your wearing protective plastic or rubber gloves while searching for or removing ticks and cautions against using petroleum jelly, lighter fluid or matches to remove the ticks.

Instead, they recommend that if you find a tick that is engorged (swollen with blood after biting), grasp it with a pair of tweezers as close to the head and mouth as possible. Then pull straight up without squeezing the tick's body so as to remove the tick whole.

After removing the tick, save it in a closed container such as a small jar, and contact your doctor to determine if you need further treatment.

Check your pets. The tick that carries Rocky Mountain Spotted Fever can attach itself to household pets who can pass the tick along to you and are susceptible to the disease themselves. In general, you should bathe your pet regularly during the summer. Use a tick dip only as directed by your veterinarian.

According to the Animal Medical Center, tick repellents containing DEET (N,N-dimethyl-3-methylbenzamide) are considered reasonably safe for human beings but have been known to harm or even kill pets. They should be used only as directed by your veterinarian.

RUBELLA (GERMAN MEASLES)

Known risk factors

Age:	Yes	Smoking:	No
Gender:	No	Drugs & medical procedures:	Yes
Race/ethnic group:	No	General health:	No
Family history:	No	Environment:	No
Diet:	No	Occupation:	No

Are you at risk?

Anyone who has not had the rubella disease or been vaccinated with the rubella vaccine is at risk when exposed to someone who has rubella. The virus can be transmitted in the period lasting from one week before the rash appears to one week after it goes away.

Once a disease of young children, rubella is now more common among unvaccinated young adults, age 15 to 24. About 10 to 25% of all young adult women fall into this category, which raises the specter of their acquiring rubella during pregnancy. If the infection occurs in the first trimester, when fetal body organs are developing, the result may be a variety of birth defects that includes blindness from clouding of the cornea, deafness, malformation of bone and heart, mental retardation and retarded growth.

Babies who were exposed to rubella *in utero* have a higher-than-normal risk of brain damage, diabetes and seizures. In addition, the rubella virus will remain active in the baby's body and can be transmitted to others for as long as six months to two and one-half years after birth.

Early detection. Rubella is diagnosed by its characteristic symptoms: a low-grade fever, a red rash and swollen glands. In adults, the illness may also cause joint pains.

To lower your risk of rubella

Vaccination. Rubella vaccine is now given routinely to babies age 15 months as part of a vaccination known as MMR that also contains vaccines for measles and mumps. Rubella vaccine is not given to younger infants because they may be unable to form antibodies to the virus.

Women of childbearing age who have never been vaccinated, who have never had the disease, and who, when tested, do not have antibodies to the rubella virus in their blood should be vaccinated. After vaccination, they are usually advised to avoid becoming pregnant for at least three months lest the live virus in the vaccine cross the placenta and infect the baby *in utero.*

Like other live-virus vaccines, the vaccine for rubella may also be hazardous for people whose immune system is weakened or who are running a fever, going through radiation therapy or taking immunosuppressant drugs such as corticosteroids or anti-cancer medication.

SCHIZOPHRENIA

Known risk factors

Age:	Yes	Smoking:	No
Gender:	No	Drugs & medical procedures:	No
Race/ethnic group:	No	General health:	No
Family history:	Yes	Environment:	No
Diet:	No	Occupation:	No

Are you at risk?

Schizophrenia is a name used to describe a group of chronic and acute mental disorders other than mental retardation or organic brain disease that are characterized by psychotic episodes; disturbances in the ability to think, feel and behave normally; and an intense need for privacy.

Worldwide, schizophrenia affects about one in every 100 people. The rates are slightly higher in the United States and the USSR, not necessarily because more people develop schizophrenia but because more mental or emotional conditions are defined as schizophrenic. In the USSR, for example, political dissent has, at times, been described as abnormal social behavior characteristic of schizophrenia.

The risk of a schizophrenic incident is highest among young people, during the late teens or early 20s. Men and women are equally vulnerable. Although some researchers speak of a "schizophrenia gene," nobody really knows exactly what makes people susceptible to this illness.

On the one hand, as many as 90% of all people with schizophrenia do not have a schizophrenic parent, and as many as 80% do not have either a parent, brother or sister with the disease. On the other hand, schizophrenia may appear in several members of the same family, suggesting an inherited vulnerability that may be triggered by various individual psychological or social factors.

If you do have a close relative with schizophrenia, your own risk of schizophrenia is considered to be higher than normal. How much higher may depend on how close the relationship is. If one identical twin becomes schizophrenic, for example, there is a 65% chance that the other will too. Among fraternal twins, the risk of a second twin's developing schizophrenia is only 12%. Among children with one schizophrenic parent, the risk is 5 to 10%

Early detection. Schizophrenia is diagnosed when its symptoms (including psychotic episodes) have lasted for at least six months. This criterion helps to distinguish it from other mental illnesses and from transient psychotic reactions to drugs such as amphetamines and cocaine.

To lower your risk of schizophrenia

At present, there is no known way to reduce the initial risk of schizophrenia, but is it possible with specific drugs and therapy to reduce the incidence and severity of schizophrenic episodes so that people with schizophrenia may be able to create a tolerable life for themselves.

About one-third of all patients with schizophrenia recover completely, and most of the rest improve somewhat with treatment. Families with a schizophrenic member often find the situation devastating, but with support, perhaps from others in the same situation, they may be able to help the schizophrenic to live out life in peace.

SCURVY

Known risk factors

Age:	Yes	Smoking:	?
Gender:	No	Drugs & medical procedures:	No
Race/ethnic group:	No	General health:	Yes
Family history:	No	Environment:	No
Diet:	Yes	Occupation:	No

Are you at risk?

Scurvy is the nutritional disorder that develops when you are deficient in vitamin C.

Ordinarily, the person most at risk for scurvy is the one whose diet does not provide enough vitamin C. Examples include alcoholics, the elderly and food faddists. Others at risk include women who are pregnant or nursing; infants on commercial formulas who do not get supplements, citrus fruit or vegetables; and people with a gastrointestinal illness that either reduces their ability to absorb vitamin C or increases the amount they lose through feces. When you have an acute or inflammatory illness, are injured or burned, go through surgery or face environmental stress such as very cold or very hot weather, you may need more than the normal amount of vitamin C.

Paradoxically, you may also be at risk for scurvy if you are consuming doses of vitamin C in excess of the recommended dietary allowances (RDA) and then abruptly cut back.

Vitamin C is water-soluble. When you increase your consumption, your body steps up its excretion through urination. If you suddenly stop taking the large doses, your body will continue to excrete the larger amounts for a while. The result may be a short-term case of scurvy that will resolve itself when your body adapts to the new, lower dose.

Newborn babies whose mothers took large amounts of vitamin C while pregnant may face the same situation, a temporary case of scurvy at birth due to their needing more than the amount of vitamin C supplied in infant formulas.

Early detection. Scurvy is diagnosed by its symptoms: swollen or bleeding gums, small hemorrhages under the skin and pains in the joints. In severe, untreated scurvy, these symptoms may progress to anemia and bleeding into the muscles, joint swelling, loss of teeth and poor healing of wounds. These symptoms may resemble those of arthritis, some blood disorders or periodontal disease, each of which must be ruled out before confirming a diagnosis of scurvy.

To lower your risk of scurvy

Maintain a healthy diet. Scurvy is easily prevented by consuming adequate amounts of vitamin C. For healthy adults who are not pregnant or nursing, the RDA is 60 mg, just about what one medium-size orange provides.

Certain kinds of stress may increase the need for vitamin C. For example, in a 1973 study reported in the *South African Medical Journal*, researchers found that South African mine workers required 200 to 250 mg vitamin C a day in order to maintain body levels of the vitamin normally maintained when healthy adults consume 60 mg a day.

Smokers are another group whose requirements may be higher than normal. According to the National Research Council, people who smoke appear to metabolize and excrete vitamin C at a rate nearly 40% higher than that of non-smokers. Based on this, the NRC estimates that smokers may need twice as much vitamin C as non-smokers and sets the RDA for smokers at 100 mg (or more).

RDAs of Vitamin C

Age and Sex		RDA
Infants	to 6 mo.	30 mg
	6 mo.–1 yr.	35
Children	1–3	40
	4–6	45
	7–10	45
Males	11–14	50
	15–18	60
	19–22	60
	23–50	60
	51+	60
Females	11–14	50
	15–18	60
	19–22	60
	23–50	60
	51+	60
Pregnant women		70
Lactating women		95

Source: National Research Council, *Recommended Dietary Allowances*, Washington, D.C., National Academy Press, 1989.

SHINGLES (HERPES ZOSTER)

Known risk factors

Age:	Yes	Smoking:	No
Gender:	No	Drugs & medical procedures:	Yes
Race/ethnic group:	No	General health:	Yes
Family history:	No	Environment:	No
Diet:	No	Occupation:	No

Are you at risk?

Once you recover from chicken pox, the virus that caused the disease retreats along nerve pathways to remain in your body throughout your lifetime. Years later, it may be re-activated by an injury, an illness or a drug that impairs your immune system, emerging as the localized case of chicken pox we call shingles.

Shingles is not contagious, but people with shingles can pass on the chicken pox virus, and a chicken pox infection, to those not immune to it. Shingles may show up at any age, but is most common after 50. Those at highest risk are those who develop cancer or hepatitis or an immune system disorder such as arthritis or systemic lupus erythematosus or are immunized against hepatitis or take immunosuppressant drugs. In a young person at high risk for AIDS, a case of shingles may be the first sign of an otherwise asymptomatic infection with the HIV virus that causes AIDS.

Early detection. For most people, shingles is a painful but ultimately limited illness. But in those with weakened immune systems, it may cause such life-threatening complications as brain infections (encephalitis, meningitis) and pneumonia.

Depending on where the shingles occurs, the pain it causes may resemble that of appendicitis, kidney stones, gallbladder disease or colitis. Shingles is diagnosed by its symptoms (pain and a characteristic rash) combined with a history of chicken pox and isolation of the virus.

It is important to diagnose shingles and start treatment as early as possible. Acyclovir (Zovirax), the drug used to treat genital herpes, seems to shorten the course of a shingles episode but only if treatment starts within two days after the rash appears.

To lower your risk of developing shingles

At present there is no way to reduce the risk of developing shingles.

SICKLE-CELL DISEASE

Known risk factors

Age:	No	Smoking:	No
Gender:	No	Drugs & medical procedures:	No
Race/ethnic group:	Yes	General health:	No
Family history:	Yes	Environment:	No
Diet:	No	Occupation:	No

Are you at risk?

Sickle-cell disease is an inherited abnormality in hemoglobin, the oxygen-carrying pigment in red blood cells. People with sickle-cell disease have abnormally shaped ("sickled") red blood cells. These cells are so fragile that they are easily destroyed, resulting in a condition known as sickle-cell anemia. Because they are inflexible, they often cannot slide through the body's smallest blood vessels. They may obstruct these vessels, causing tissue damage and pain.

Sickle-cell disease is transmitted through a recessive gene. You must inherit one such gene from each parent in order to have the disease. Carriers (people who inherited only one sickle-cell gene) can pass it on to their children, but they will not have the disease themselves.

The person most likely to have sickle-cell disease is black. He may also have relatives with the disease, but in most cases there is no known family history of sickle cell.

In America, nearly one in every 400 newborn black babies will develop sickle-cell disease. Right now, it is estimated that there may be 50,000 black Americans with sickle-cell anemia and another 2 million carrying a single sickle cell gene. Sickle cell is most common among blacks of equatorial African descent. Less frequently, it affects people from the Mediterranean, the Middle East, India and the Central or South American countries.

Early detection. Sickle-cell disease is diagnosed with a blood test that shows the presence of the characteristic abnormally shaped red blood cells or that shows the presence of abnormal forms of hemoglobin, the red pigment in blood that carries oxygen to every cell in the body.

To lower the risk of sickle-cell anemia

Genetic counseling. When both parents are sickle cell carriers, there is a 25% chance with each pregnancy that their child will inherit two sickle-cell genes and develop sickle-cell disease, a 50% chance that he will inherit only one gene and become a symptomless carrier, and a 25% chance that he will not inherit the gene from either parent.

There are now simple blood tests to identify sickle-cell carriers. If both parents are carriers, a fetus with sickle-cell disease can be diagnosed prenatally by amniocentesis, an analyis of tissue from liquid inside the sac that holds the fetus, or chorionic villus sampling, an analysis of tissue from the chorion, the outermost membrane around the fetus.

SKIN CANCER

Known risk factors

Age:	Yes	Smoking:	No
Gender:	No	Drugs & medical procedures:	Yes
Race/ethnic group:	Yes	General health:	Yes
Family history:	Yes	Environment:	Yes
Diet:	No	Occupation:	Yes

Are you at risk?

Every year, more than 600,000 cases of skin cancer are diagnosed in the United States. Most are highly curable basal-cell or squamous-cell cancers, but at least 27,000 people can expect to hear a diagnosis of malignant melanoma, the most serious form of skin cancer. Malignant melanoma kills 6,300 Americans each year. Approximately 2,500 Americans die each year from other forms of skin cancer.

The person most likely to develop skin cancer is fair haired, fair skinned and light eyed; skin cancer is rare among blacks. Skin cancers occur at exactly the same rate in men and women, but men are two times as likely to die of a skin cancer because they are more likely to develop the most serious form of the disease, malignant melanoma, on the torso. For unknown reasons, melanomas on the torso are more likely to be fatal than melanomas on the arms or legs.

On the other hand, the number of moles you have on your legs may be an important predictor of your overall risk of developing melanoma in the first place. In 1989, *The Journal of the National Cancer Institute* published the results of a study by a team of researchers from Brown University in Providence, Rhode Island, and Harvard University, which suggested that people who have 12 or more moles on the leg, below the knee, may be two times more likely to develop melanoma than people who have 27 or more moles on the arm. Where the moles were did not seem to predict where on the body a melanoma might develop. It remains to be seen whether future research will confirm this intriguing theory.

The most important environmental risk factor for skin cancer is exposure to the sun's ultraviolet radiation. In general, the incidence of skin cancer goes up steadily the closer you get to the equator where the sun's rays are strong all year round. In the United States, for example, the rate of skin cancer increases steadily as you go south. In the Southwestern states Arizona and New Mexico, skin cancers are twice as common as they are in the Northeast. As you might expect, it is highest among people who court the sun or work outside. Several studies have suggested that a severe sunburn early in childhood dramatically increases your risk of melanoma as an adult.

A 1988 study of 1,389 patients at 16 medical centers in the United States suggests that people whose psoriasis is treated with the photosensitizing drug psoralen and exposed to ultraviolet light may have a higher-than-normal risk of the generally non-fatal skin cancers basal-cell carcinoma and squamous-cell carcinoma.

Early detection. Eighty percent of the people whose malignant melanoma is diagnosed before it has spread will be alive five years after their cancer is diagnosed; the rate drops to 39% if the cancer is found after it has metastasized. For people with other kinds of skin cancer, the overall five-year survival rate is 95%. A diagnosis of skin cancer is confirmed by a biopsy of the affected tissue.

To lower your risk of skin cancer

Know your own body. As with breast cancer and cancer of the testicles, self-examination can reduce the danger from cancers of the skin. Your first job is to know the warning signals of skin cancer. Basal-cell and squamous-cell cancers may begin as pale waxy bumps or red scaly patches, or, like melanomas, they may start as small moles or mole-like growths that get bigger or change color or crust or bleed.

Many cancer experts recommend your using the ABCD Rule as a guide to potential skin cancers:

A = asymmetry. If you draw an imaginary line down the center of a cancerous mole, the halves are likely to be differently shaped.

B = border irregularity. The edges of a cancerous mole are likely to be raggedy rather than smoothly drawn.

C = color. A cancerous mole is likely to be unevenly pigmented.

D = diameter. Cancerous moles are likely to be larger than 6 mm across. And their diameter is likely to change as they grow larger. Any mole that shows up after you are 30 should be checked by your doctor.

Remember: These rules are just a guide. Only your doctor can tell for sure whether or not your mole is a skin cancer.

Use a protective sunscreen. Chemical sunscreens such as PABA absorb the sun's ultraviolet rays; physical sunscreens, such as opaque clothes or titanium dioxide, reflect and block these rays. Both offer protection against radiation damage that triggers skin cancers.

Chemical sunscreens are rated according to a system known as the Sun Protective Factor (SPF), which is based on the amount of exposure to ultraviolet (UV) rays it takes to turn your skin red with and without a sunscreen. If it takes only 30 minutes in the sun for your skin to redden, a sunscreen with an SPF factor of 3 will allow you to stay three times as long (one and one-half hours) in the sun before you begin to redden.*

Paradoxically, sunscreens made with PABA may produce an allergic sensitivity that itself triggers redness and itching about 24 hours after the sunscreen is applied. If you think you are allergic to PABA sunscreens, apply the sunscreen to a small patch of skin and cover the patch with a small adhesive bandage. Wait 24 hours, then take off the bandage and expose the patch to sunlight for about 15 minutes. If the patch of skin is red and swollen the next day, it suggests that you are sensitive to PABA. In that case, the Food and Drug Administration (FDA) recommends your using a PABA-free sunscreen.

Chemical Sunscreens

PABA	Non-PABA
para-aminobenzoic acid	cinnamates (cinoxate, methoxycinnamate)
padimate O	methyl anthranilate
	benzophenones (oxybenzone, dioxybenzone, sulisobenzone)
	salicylic acid (homosalate, ethylhexyl salicylate)

Apply your sunscreen properly. The first rule is to apply your sunscreen evenly over your skin at least 30 minutes before you go into the sun. Apply the sunscreen to all exposed skin. If you wear make-up, use a nongreasy sunscreen underneath, as a cosmetic base; if you are bald, don't forget the top of your head. A cloudy day is no reason for stinting on the sunscreen. The sun's burning rays are completely blocked by ordinary window glass but they pass easily through light clouds or fog or even clear water. Snow and sand can intensify the effect by reflecting the rays up to your body.

Out of doors, reapply your sunscreen every two to three hours, more often if you are swimming or perspiring heavily because the moisture can wash away the protection. But no matter how often you reapply the sunscreen, its protection will not last longer than the SPF number says it will. In other words, three applications of a sunscreen with an SPF of 3 will not make the SPF 3 product as protective as a sunscreen with an SPF of 9.

---

*Some dermatologic researchers believe that this may be hazardous, not protective. They reason that if you do not see your skin turn red, you will not come in out of the sun, thus prolonging your exposure to potentially damaging ultraviolet radiation and increasing your risk of sun-triggered skin cancers.

Do not apply sunscreen to an infant's skin except with the advice and supervision of your doctor.

SLEEP APNEA

Known risk factors

Age:	Yes	Smoking:	No
Gender:	Yes	Drugs & medical procedures:	Yes
Race/ethnic group:	No	General health:	Yes
Family history:	No	Environment:	No
Diet:	Yes	Occupation:	No

Are you at risk?

Every night while they are sleeping, people with sleep apnea may suffer as many as several hundred episodes of interrupted breathing (apnea) that last 10 seconds or more. The result may be sleep deprivation that makes them drowsy and headachy all the following day. In some cases, the sleep deprivation may be severe enough to trigger changes in personality.

The most common cause of sleep apnea is obstructed breathing. A much smaller number of cases is caused by respiratory depression due to brain damage, brain tumors or too shallow breathing.

The person at highest risk for sleep apnea caused by obstructed breathing is an overweight middle-aged man. Sleep apnea is 10 to 15 times more common among men than among women; according to the Association of Professional Sleep Societies, one of every 20 adult American males has concentration and/or memory problems relating to sleep deprivation due to interrupted breathing. Snoring—the partially obstructed breathing that sometimes progresses to sleep apnea—is three times more common among overweight people than among people of normal weight, perhaps because the upper airway is narrowed by obesity. Enlarged tonsils or adenoids may also trigger sleep apnea by narrowing your upper airway. If you have sleep apnea, alcoholic beverages and sedative medications such as antihistamines, sleeping pills and tranquilizers are likely to make it worse.

Early detection. Sleep apnea may be diagnosed by observation of breathing patterns while a patient is sleeping in a hospital or sleep clinic setting. Early diagnosis of sleep apnea, combined with recommendations for changing your lifestyle or your body so as to avoid the problem, can improve memory and concentration, performance on the job and your everyday relationships with other people.

To lower your risk of sleep apnea

Keep your weight within normal bounds. If your sleep apnea arises from your being overweight, losing weight may reduce or even completely eliminate episodes of sleep disorder.

Adjust your bedding. Sleeping on your side or tilting the head of your bed upward may alleviate snoring. If your snoring is due to a chronic sinus infection or allergy, adequate medical treatment may relieve the obstructive stuffiness that makes you snore. Structural defects in the nose and throat may be amenable to surgery.

Consider a sleep clinic. Sleep clinics are laboratories designed to diagnose and treat sleep disorders. If your problem—insomnia, snoring, sleep apnea, sleepwalking—is making it hard for you to get a normal night's rest, the sleep clinic at a medical center near you may able to provide help.

SPINA BIFIDA (NEURAL TUBE DEFECTS)

Known risk factors

Age:	?	Smoking:	No
Gender:	Yes	Drugs & medical procedures:	Yes
Race/ethnic group:	Yes	General health:	Yes
Family history:	Yes	Environment:	No
Diet:	?	Occupation:	No

Are you at risk?

Approximately 33 in every 2,000 babies born live in the United States have a neural tube defect (a malformation of the brain or spinal cord). The most common neural tube defect is spina bifida, an incomplete closure of the spinal column that leaves the spinal cord exposed and malformed.

Ordinarily, the most important risk factor for producing a baby with a spina bifida is having a family history of this kind of birth defect. For example, if you have a brother or sister with a neural tube defect, your chances of producing a baby with some kind of neural tube defect is about one in 200. If your mother's sister had a baby with a neural tube defect, your chances of having such a baby are about one in 100; if your father's sister had a baby with a neural tube defect, your risk of having such a baby is about one in 300. If you have already had one baby with a neural tube defect, the risk that you will have another such baby is about one in 30.

Neural tube defects occur more frequently among white babies (one in every 700 births) than among black babies (less than one in every 3,000 births). According to the March of Dimes Birth Defects Foundation, the highest rates in the world occur in northern China, northern Ireland, southern Wales, in the Punjab (Sikh) region of India and in Alexandria, Egypt.

Early detection. Spina bifida and other neural tube defects in a fetus can often be detected via maternal blood tests, amniocentesis or ultrasound. Both the blood tests and an analysis of amniotic fluid withdrawn during amniocentesis are likely to show an elevated level of a substance called *alpha*-fetoprotein if the fetus has a neural tube defect.

However, there may also be high levels of *alpha*-fetoprotein if the pregnancy is further along than believed on the basis of menstrual history, or if a pregnant woman is carrying twins or is about to miscarry or if her fetus has a congenital kidney disease or certain other abnormalities.

In short, the maternal blood test for *alpha*-fetoprotein is only a screening test to identify pregnancies that may require more definitive diagnostic testing. A diagnosis of spina bifida or other neural tube defect may be confirmed by ultrasound (which shows the actual defect).

To lower the risk of a neural tube defect

Eat a balanced diet while you are pregnant. Studies of pregnant women in Great Britain, where the incidence of spina bifida and other neural tube defects is two or three times that in the United States, have suggested that simply supplementing a pregnant woman's diet with a vitamin (folic acid) and mineral supplement that provides the recommended dietary allowance (RDA) for healthy adults may reduce, but not entirely eliminate, her risk of having a spina bifida baby. This thesis was bolstered by a study of 24,000 pregnant women released in 1989 by researchers at Boston University's Center for Human Genetics.

While the evidence for the protective effects of these supplements and of a diet rich in green leafy vegetables is still not regarded as conclusive, the Boston researchers strongly suggested that pregnant women take an ordinary over-the-counter multi-vitamin tablet containing folic acid while trying to become pregnant and through at least the first six weeks of pregnancy.

There is no evidence at all to suggest that taking vitamin and mineral supplements in doses higher than the RDA offers any protection to a growing fetus. On the contrary, the National Research Council had reported that large (20,000 IU) daily doses of vitamin A during pregnancy may cause miscarriage or, if the fetus survives, malformations of the head, face, heart and central nervous system.

STOMACH CANCER

Known risk factors

Age:	Yes	Smoking:	No
Gender:	Yes	Drugs & medical procedures:	No
Race/ethnic group:	No	General health:	No
Family history:	Yes	Environment:	No
Diet:	Yes	Occupation:	No

Are you at risk?

In the past 50 years, the incidence of stomach cancer in the United States has gone down by about 75%. Nevertheless, the American Cancer Society (ACS) estimated that there would be 23,200 new cases diagnosed in 1990, and 9,400 deaths, down from the 24,800 new cases and 14,400 deaths in 1988.

The person most likely to develop cancer of the stomach is a man older than 50. Only one-fourth of all patients with stomach cancer are younger than 50; half are older than 60. Around the world, a man's risk of stomach cancer is about twice as high as a woman's. Cancer of the stomach is not inherited, but it is two to four times more common among people who have close relatives with the disease than among people who do not.

Perhaps the most interesting aspect of stomach cancer is its geographic distribution. There is an extremely high incidence in Chile, Iceland and Japan (where it is the most common cancer). In this country, it is more common in the North, among the poor and among blacks.

The common thread among these places and groups seems to be diet. It is easy to produce stomach cancers in laboratory animals by feeding them chemicals that contribute to the formation of nitrosamines (carcinogens created when nitrates that occur naturally in food are converted in the stomach to nitrites). This reaction, which may be triggered by some of the preservatives used in cured meat, can be inhibited by vitamin C, so the Food and Drug Administration (FDA) now requires the addition of ascorbic acid or other forms of vitamin C to foods that contain preservatives that can promote the formation of nitrosamines. In Japan and in Iceland, the high rate of stomach cancer is attributed to the high consumption of salted and smoked foods, which are also known to cause stomach tumors.

Having gastritis (an inflammation of the lining of the stomach) does not raise your risk of stomach cancer. Neither does having a gastric ulcer, although the ulcer will usually be biopsied to be certain it is not cancerous. Polyps in the stomach (gastric polyps) may be cancerous or they may occur along with cancer of the stomach, but most stomach cancers do not start as benign polyps. On the other hand, people with pernicious anemia do have a higher risk of stomach cancer because the anemia causes damaging, possibly pre-cancerous changes in the lining of the stomach.

Early detection. Because the early symptoms of stomach cancer may resemble those of benign gastric ulcer, early detection is rare and most stomach cancers are not found until they are well advanced and hard to treat.

As a result, fewer than 15% of all Americans with stomach cancer will survive five years after diagnosis. In Japan, on the other hand, mass screening is common, and more stomach cancers are diagnosed early enough to be treatable.

Screening tests for stomach cancer include blood tests that may discover iron-deficiency anemia due to bleeding from a lesion in the stomach and the guaiac test for hidden blood in the stool. Eighty percent of the people with stomach cancer will test positive in repeated guaiac tests.

The presence of a tumor can be confirmed by examination with an endoscope, a flexible lighted tube that allows your doctor to see the inside of your stomach, or by CT-scan. Ordinary X-rays may not detect small, early cancers.

A diagnosis of cancer is confirmed by a biopsy of tissue from the suspicious area.

To lower your risk of stomach cancer

If you are at high risk, ask your doctor about routine screening. If you are older than 40 and have pernicious anemia or stomach polyps, a family history of stomach cancer or were born in a country where stomach cancer is common, you are considered at high risk. For you, routine screening programs may be in order.

STROKE

Known risk factors

Age:	Yes	Smoking:	Yes
Gender:	Yes	Drugs & medical procedures:	No
Race/ethnic group:	Yes	General health:	Yes
Family history:	Yes	Environment:	No
Diet:	No	Occupation:	No

Are you at risk?

Stroke is the third leading cause of death in this country, right behind heart disease and cancer, and the most disabling of the neurologic diseases. According to the American Heart Association, in 1988, an estimated 500,000 Americans suffered a stroke and 150,300 died of stroke or its complications.

There are four major kinds of strokes. Cerebral thrombosis (a blood clot in a blood vessel in the brain) and cerebral embolism (a plug of foreign material in a blood vessel in the brain) are the most common kinds of strokes. Cerebral hemorrhage (bleeding from a ruptured blood vessel in the brain) and subarachnoid hemorrhage (bleeding into the space between the membranes surrounding the brain) are less common but more likely to be fatal.

People with heart disease or high blood pressure are two times more likely than others to have a stroke. You are at risk of a major stroke if you have a history of transient ischemic attacks (TIAs), also known as "little strokes." Only 10% of all the people who have strokes have TIAs first, but slightly more than one-third of all the people who have TIAs will later have a stroke.

Other risk factors include your age (the older you are, the higher your risk), your sex (men are at higher risk than women), your race (black Americans have a higher risk than white Americans) and having diabetes.

Smoking is a major, controllable risk factor for stroke. According to a study released in 1988 by researchers at the Harvard School of Medicine, women who smoke as little as half a pack of cigarettes a day have a risk of stroke twice that of women who have never smoked; those who smoke two packs a day have a risk six times higher. Earlier research has shown the same risk relationship for male smokers.

According to statistics released by the U.S. Department of Health and Human Services in 1984, for as-yet-unexplained reasons, the states with the highest death rates for stroke (60 or more per 100,000) among American white men age 35 to 74 are Alabama, Georgia, Indiana, Kentucky, Mississippi, North Carolina, South Carolina, Tennessee and West Virginia. The highest rates for black men (170 or more per 100,000) are in Arkansas, Georgia, Mississippi, North Carolina, South Carolina and Tennessee. The highest rates for white women (44.7 or more per 100,000) are in Arkansas, Georgia, Indiana, Kentucky, Mississippi, Ohio, Oklahoma, Tennessee and West Virginia. The highest rates for black women (120 or more per 100,000) are in Alabama, Arkansas, Florida, Georgia, Oklahoma and South Carolina.

Early detection. Stroke is diagnosed by its symptoms, ordinarily a loss of function on one side of the body due to a hemorrhage or blot clot in the brain. This may develop over a few hours or days or extremely quickly, within minutes. A CT-scan may be suggested to rule out a brain tumor or a hemorrhage or blood clot (hematoma) under the skull but outside the brain.

Immediate supportive care such as maintaining oxygen flow for a patient who cannot breathe on his own can keep a stroke victim alive, but the eventual outcome of a stroke depends pretty much on the body's ability to repair itself. People who start to improve quickly after a stroke have a better chance of surviving with less long-term damage.

To lower your risk of stroke

If you smoke, stop. Smokers who stop immediately reduce their risk of stroke by about half. After five years, their risk may be the same as that of non-smokers.

Control your weight; control your blood pressure. Sometimes, simply losing weight will lower blood pressure into the normal range. If it doesn't, your doctor may prescribe medication to control your hypertension and reduce the risk of stroke.

SUDDEN INFANT DEATH SYNDROME (SIDS)

Known risk factors

Age:	Yes	Smoking:	?
Gender:	Yes	Drugs & medical procedures:	No
Race/ethnic group:	Yes	General health:	No
Family history:	?	Environment:	No
Diet:	No	Occupation:	No

Are you at risk?

Sudden infant death syndrome (SIDS), once known as "crib death," is the leading cause of death among American babies younger than a year, killing as many as 6,000 to 7,000 live-born infants each year. SIDS occurs most often among babies two to four months old, and is more common among boys than among girls. In the United States, the risk is highest for black and Native American babies, lowest for Oriental infants. Premature birth increases the risk of SIDS, as does being born to a poor family or a family with several young children.

SIDS does not appear to be hereditary, but parents who have lost one child to SIDS may be at slightly higher risk of losing a second child to SIDS. Why this should be so is a matter of speculation. There is no hard evidence to prove that what a parent does before or after a baby is born has any effect on the infant's risk of SIDS, but some studies do suggest that anything that interferes with the flow of oxygen to a fetus in its mother's womb may imperceptibly damage the fetal brain and increase the risk of SIDS after the baby is born.

Among the things that may interfere with the fetus's oxygen supply are a woman's being anemic while pregnant (anemia reduces the amount of oxygen in the blood supply to the fetus), her smoking or using drugs while pregnant, the presence of more than one fetus in the womb, the placenta's being in an abnormal position in the uterus or pregnancies that occur less than a year apart, before the lining of the uterus has time to rebuild itself.

Early detection. Unfortunately, SIDS can only be conclusively diagnosed after death when an autopsy can rule out other possibilities such as brain hemorrhage, meningitis and heart damage.

To lower your baby's risk of SIDS

Because the exact causes of SIDS remain as mysterious as the exact mechanism by which it kills, there is at present no medically certain way to reduce the risk.

SUNBURN

Known risk factors

Age:	No	Smoking:	No
Gender:	No	Drugs & medical procedures:	Yes
Race/ethnic group:	Yes	General health:	Yes
Family history:	Yes	Environment:	Yes
Diet:	Yes	Occupation:	Yes

Are you at risk?

When you are exposed to the sun, cells in your skin known as melanocytes increase their production of the dark pigment melanin. The result is the darkening of the skin we call tanning. Because tanning offers some protection against the sun and the color of your skin determines how much melanin you can produce, skin color also plays a role in determining your risk of sunburn.

People with light skin are obviously more susceptible to the sun than people with dark skin but even those with the darkest, "black" skin are not immune and can be sunburned if they stay too long in the sun. The people at highest risk are the red-headed, light-skinned Irish and Scots who produce the uneven amounts of melanin we call freckles. These people are also more susceptible to the later effects of excess sun exposure: skin cancer and prematurely aged skin.

People with systemic lupus erythematosus have an increased sensitivity to sunlight. So do people who are taking any one of a number of drugs that act as photosensitizers, substances that make your skin more susceptible to the effects of sunlight.

The list includes antibiotics such as tetracyclines and sulfa drugs; the anti-cancer drugs dacarbazine (DTIC-Dome), fluorouracil (Adrucil), methotrexate (Mexate) and vincristine (Oncovin); the anti-depressants amitriptyline (Elavil), doxepin (Adapin, Sinequan) and protriptyline (Vivactil), among others; the anti-nausea drug promethazine (Phenergan); diuretics such as furosemide (Lasix), the thiazides and triamterene (Dyrenium); and oral contraceptives.

Cosmetics that may increase your sensitivity to sunlight include dandruff shampoos and perfumed products made with bergamot or the essential oils of citron, lavender, lime, sandalwood or cedar. Limes, parsley, celery and figs also contain natural photosensitizers that produce skin reactions in food handlers who harvest, pack and ship these foods.

Early detection. As your exposure to sunlight lengthens, your skin will eventually start to redden. If you ignore this warning sign and stay out in the sun, your skin may eventually swell or even blister, and a severe sunburn, like any other burn, can cause a wide range of physical symptoms including rash, infections, fever, chills, weakness and shock. Once the injured skin has healed, dried and peeled away, the new skin underneath will be especially sensitive to sunlight for weeks or even months afterward.

To lower your risk of sunburn

Use a protective sunscreen. Chemical sunscreens such as PABA absorb the sun's ultraviolet rays; physical sunscreens, such as opaque clothes or titanium dioxide, reflect and block these rays.

Chemical sunscreens are rated according to a system known as the Sun Protective Factor (SPF), which is based on the amount of exposure to ultraviolet (UV) rays it takes to turn your skin red with and without a sunscreen. If it takes only 30 minutes in the sun for your skin to redden, a sunscreen with an SPF factor of 3 will allow you to stay three times as long (one and one-half hours) in the sun before you begin to redden.*

Paradoxically, sunscreens made with PABA may produce an allergic sensitivity that itself triggers redness and itching about 24 hours after the sunscreen is applied. If you think you are allergic to PABA sunscreens, apply the sunscreen to a small patch of skin and cover the patch with a small adhesive bandage. Wait 24 hours, then take off the bandage and expose the patch to sunlight for about 15 minutes. If the patch of skin is red and swollen the next day, it suggests that you are sensitive to PABA. In that case, the Food and Drug Administration (FDA) recommends your using a PABA-free sunscreen.

Chemical Sunscreens

PABA	Non-PABA
para-aminobenzoic acid	cinnamates (cinoxate, methoxycinnamate)
padimate O	methyl anthranilate
	benzophenones (oxybenzone, dioxybenzone, sulisobenzone)
	salicylic acid (homosalate, ethylhexyl salicylate)

---

*Some dermatologic researchers believe that this may be hazardous, not protective. They reason that if you do not see your skin turn red, you will not come in out of the sun, thus prolonging your exposure to potentially damaging ultraviolet radiation and increasing your risk of sun-triggered skin cancers.

Apply your sunscreen properly. The first rule is to apply your sunscreen evenly over your skin at least 30 minutes before you go into the sun. Apply the sunscreen to all exposed skin. If you wear make-up, use a nongreasy sunscreen underneath, as a cosmetic base. If you are bald, don't forget the top of your head.

A cloudy day is no reason for stinting on the sunscreen. The sun's burning rays are completely blocked by ordinary window glass, but they pass easily through light clouds or fog or even clear water. Snow and sand can intensify the effect by reflecting the rays up to your body.

Outdoors, reapply your sunscreen every two to three hours, more often if you are swimming or perspiring heavily because the moisture can wash away the protection. But no matter how often you reapply the sunscreen, its protection will not last longer than the SPF number says it will. In other words, three applications of a sunscreen with an SPF of 3 will not make the SPF 3 product as protective as a sunscreen with an SPF of 9.

Do not apply sunscreen to an infant's skin except as directed by your doctor.

SYPHILIS

Known risk factors

Age:	Yes	Smoking:	No
Gender:	Yes	Drugs & medical procedures:	No
Race/ethnic group:	No	General health:	No
Family history:	No	Environment:	Yes
Diet:	No	Occupation:	No

Are you at risk?

In the United States, the incidence of syphilis has been riding a roller coaster for the last 50 years. The number of cases declined steadily each year from the 1940s right through the late 1970s, rose through the early 1980s and then fell once more. Now it has begun to rise again.

In 1984, there were about 52,000 cases of syphilis reported in this country. It is assumed that the actual figure was higher but that many cases were not reported to public health officials.

The syphilis organism, *Treponema pallidum*, is transmitted by contact with an infectious sore. This is most likely to occur during sexual intercourse, but on occasion kissing or close body contact may suffice. Syphilis may also (rarely) be transmitted in a transfusion of fresh blood from an infected donor, but this is rare because storing blood for 4 days (96 hours) at 4 to 10 degrees Celsius (39 to 50 degree Fahrenheit) kills the syphilis organism.

The more sexual partners you have, the higher your risk of acquiring syphilis will be. Syphilis is most common among men and women age 15 to 34, and male patients outnumber female patients by a ratio of approximately three to one. Until the advent of AIDS and the widespread adoption of safer sex practices such as the routine use of condoms, male homosexuals were the persons at highest risk, but the incidence of syphilis and other sexually transmitted diseases (STDs) has been dropping among these men. Infants born to women who have syphilis while pregnant are at risk for congenital syphilis acquired in the uterus.

Syphilis and other STDs are more common in urban areas, where they seem to affect blacks more often than whites, but this may be a statistical blip resulting from the fact that public clinics, which have a higher percentage of black clients, report their cases fully while private physicians, whose patients are more likely to be white, do not report all the cases they treat.

Early detection. The diagnostic test for syphilis is a blood test that detects the presence of an antibody to the syphilis organism. A single negative test may not totally eliminate the possibility of syphilis because it may take two to three weeks after infection for antibodies to show up. Drinking alcoholic beverages within 24 hours before the test can produce a false-negative reaction (a result that says you do not have syphilis when in fact your do). False-positive results may occur in people with arthritis, hepatitis, leprosy, malaria, mononucleosis and systemic lupus erythematosus (SLE), as well as pinta and yaws, two tropical diseases caused by organisms similar to the one that causes syphilis.

To lower your risk of syphilis

Practice safer sex. Limiting the number of people with whom you have sexual relations can reduce your risk of getting syphilis. But no form of contraception is considered truly protective against syphilis. The American Social Health Association (ASHA) urges anyone who has syphilis to refrain completely from sexual contact.

Ask your doctor about preventive antibiotic therapy. If you have been exposed to a person with syphilis or if you are in a high-risk group, your doctor may wish to treat you with antibiotics as though you have syphilis even before the diagnosis is confirmed.

SYSTEMIC LUPUS ERYTHEMATOSUS (SLE)

Known risk factors

Age:	Yes	Smoking:	No
Gender:	Yes	Drugs & medical procedures:	Yes
Race/ethnic group:	Yes	General health:	No
Family history:	Yes	Environment:	Yes
Diet:	No	Occupation:	No

Are you at risk?

Systemic lupus erythematosus, more familiarly known either as SLE or lupus, is an inflammatory disorder of the connective tissue that can affect many body organs, particularly the kidneys.

The person most likely to develop lupus is a young woman. Nearly nine out of every 10 lupus patients are women. Most cases occur in women younger than 40; lupus rarely develops after menopause. Having relatives with lupus raises your risk. Lupus is more common among blacks than among whites.

Contrary to popular belief, exposure to sunlight does not cause lupus, but it can exacerbate existing cases. When sunlight damages your skin, free DNA from injured cells enter your bloodstream. Healthy people have no problem eliminating this extra DNA from their bodies, but people with lupus produce an antibody to the DNA that causes an immune reaction similar to the reaction that occurs when someone eats a food to which she is allergic. Episodes of lupus may also be triggered by fatigue, emotional stress or the physical stress of fighting an infection.

Some drugs, including the heart medication procainamide and the anti-hypertensive hydralazine, may cause lupus-like symptoms in susceptible people.

Early detection. The screening test for lupus is a blood test designed to detect specific antibodies present in the blood of nearly 90% of all people with SLE.

To lower your risk of SLE

Today, there is no known way to lower your risk of lupus, but if you have lupus, you may be able to reduce the incidence and severity of flare-ups by controlling the various kinds of emotional or physical stress to which you are exposed.

TAY-SACHS DISEASE

Known risk factors

Age:	Yes	Smoking:	No
Gender:	No	Drugs & medical procedures:	No
Race/ethnic group:	Yes	General health:	No
Family history:	Yes	Environment:	No
Diet:	No	Occupation:	No

Are you at risk?

Tay-Sachs disease is an inherited metabolic disorder characterized by a deficiency in hexosaminidase A, an enzyme that allows the body to metabolize certain fatty compounds essential to nerve tissue. Without sufficient amounts of hexosaminidase A, these compounds accumulate in the brain, causing gradual paralysis, loss of mental and physical functions of all kinds, blindness and death, usually by the age of four.

The single most important risk factor for Tay-Sachs disease is being of eastern European Jewish descent. Tay-Sachs is about 100 times more common among these people than among people who are not Jewish. For unknown reasons, French-Canadians are also at higher risk.

Early detection. Tay-Sachs disease can be diagnosed prenatally by amniocentesis. After a baby is born, a diagnosis of Tay-Sachs can be confirmed by a blood test showing an absence of hexosaminidase A.

To lower your risk of Tay-Sachs.

Genetic testing. Approximately 3% to 5% of all people of eastern European Jewish ancestry carry the gene for Tay-Sachs disease. If both parents carry the gene, the risk of their having a Tay-Sachs baby is 25% with each pregnancy. The risk of their having a baby who carries one Tay-Sachs gene and can pass it along to his or her children is 50% with each pregnancy. (Babies who carry only one Tay-Sachs gene will not develop Tay-Sachs disease.) Whether or not you have the gene can be determined easily by genetic testing.

TEMPOROMANDIBULAR JOINT
DISORDER (TMD)

Known risk factors

Age:	Yes	Smoking:	No
Gender:	Yes	Drugs & medical procedures:	No
Race/ethnic group:	No	General health:	Yes
Family history:	No	Environment:	Yes
Diet:	Yes	Occupation:	Yes

Are you at risk?

The temporomandibular joint is the hinge on each side of your head where your lower jaw is connected to your skull. Pain in this joint is known formally as temporomandibular joint disorder, but most of us have known it simply as TMJ. Now it is more correctly called TMD.

TMD may seem to be one of those diseases-of-the-year that explode into prominence every once in a while and then fade into obscurity, but it is a real disorder with real pain and discomfort.

TMD may be triggered by osteoarthritis, inflammation or an injury to the

jaw. In the absence of this kind of physical damage, the single most important risk factor seems to be emotional stress. Under stress, your jaw muscles
tense and you may clench or grind your teeth. The ensuing muscle fatigue
can escalate into the painful muscle spasms of TMD. Your job, your personal relationships—anything that causes stress increases your risk of these
spasms. Your risk is also higher if you have poorly aligned teeth that make
you strain when you chew, if you are wearing poorly fitting dentures, or if
you chew something hard (such as French bread) when your jaw muscles
are beginning to tense.

For as-yet-unexplained reasons, women seem to be at higher risk than
men.

Early detection. As of the close of 1989, the American Dental Association had not yet established guidelines for diagnosing TMD, but the classic
symptoms are the pain and tension in your jaw muscles that limit your
ability to open and close your mouth, as well as a click or grinding sound
when you move your jaw. Because these symptoms resemble those you
might experience with arthritic degeneration of the jaw, your doctor may
request an X-ray to rule out the possibility that you have degenerative damage that would suggest arthritis rather than TMD.

To lower your risk of TMD

Deal with the underlying physical problem. If your TMD is caused by
arthritis or an inflammation or mis-aligned teeth or poorly fitting dentures,
treating or correcting these may eliminate the pain in your jaw.

Relieve stress. Exercise, meditation and anti-anxiety or anti-inflammatory medication—all the techniques used to relieve stress in other situations
may be helpful in preventing attacks of TMD.

TESTICULAR CANCER

Known risk factors

Age:	Yes	Smoking:	No
Gender:	Yes	Drugs & medical procedures:	No
Race/ethnic group:	Yes	General health:	Yes
Family history:	No	Environment:	No
Diet:	No	Occupation:	No

Are you at risk?

Testicular cancer was once the third leading cause of cancer deaths among
men age 14 to 35, but in the past few years, increasingly effective chemotherapy has pushed it far down the list.

In 1990, the American Cancer Society estimated that there would be 5,900 new cases of testicular cancer diagnosed in the United States and that 350 men would die of the disease.

Testicular cancer is almost always a young man's disease. You are most at risk between the ages of 15 and 35. If you were born with one or both testicles undescended, the risk of cancer in the undescended testicle is 2.5 to 20 times higher than in a descended testicle, even if the testicle is later brought down by surgery. You are also at higher risk if you had a case of mumps that involved the testes, if you had an inguinal hernia as a child or if you have already had cancer in one testicle. Cancer of the testicles is more common among white men than among black men.

Early detection. Survival rates for cancer of the testes are related to the type of cells the tumor contains. More than 80% of the men whose testicular tumors are seminomas (cancers that arise from sex cells) will be alive five years after diagnosis, even if the cancer had spread in the genital area before it was found. The five-year survival rate with choriocarcinoma (tumors comprised of many different kinds of cells) is very low. Survival rates with other kinds of tumors vary.

As with cancer of the breast, monthly self-examination can increase the possibility of finding cancers of the testes early on. The procedure is simple: Run the flat surface of your fingers over the surface of each testicle. Then, holding each testicle in your hand, gently squeeze to detect any mass inside the testicle. If you find a mass or any abnormality on the surface of either testicle, see your doctor right away. What you have found may be normal and expected, but only your doctor can tell for sure.

If there is a suspicious mass, the first step may be to rule out hydrocele (water in spaces inside the testicle), orchitis (an infection of the testicle), spermatocele (a cyst filled with sperm), syphilis or tuberculosis.

Urinalysis that shows increased amounts of sex hormones is suggestive of cancer of the testes, but the diagnosis can only be confirmed by a tissue biopsy.

To lower your risk of testicular cancer

At the moment, there is no medically certain way to reduce your risk of cancer of the testes.

TETANUS

Known risk factors

Age:	No	Smoking:	No
Gender:	No	Drugs & medical procedures:	Yes
Race/ethnic group:	No	General health:	No
Family history:	No	Environment:	Yes
Diet:	No	Occupation:	No

Are you at risk?

Tetanus is an acute infectious disease caused by a nerve toxin produced by *Clostridium tetani*, a bacteria whose spores are most commonly found in soil and animal feces.

Because the spores flourish in places where there is a short supply of oxygen, tetanus is most commonly associated with a puncture wound that pushes spores deep into tissues where there is less oxygen than there is on the surface of the skin. What makes the proverbial rusty nail dangerous is that it is almost always found on the ground or in a place where it is exposed to tetanus spores that are freed deep under the skin through a puncture wound.

Tetanus spores can also grow and produce their poison in any oxygen-starved, damaged or dying tissue, including burned tissues. If you have not been immunized against tetanus, your risk is highest if you are injured outdoors, suffer extensive burns, undergo surgery or if you are an intravenous drug abuser, constantly giving yourself puncture wounds with potentially dirty needles. Tetanus may also (rarely) occur *in utero*, after childbirth or in the newborn baby's umbilical cord.

Having tetanus once does not confer any immunity against future infections. The people most likely to die from an attack of tetanus are the very young and the very old.

Early detection. You don't have to suffer a dramatic injury to be exposed to tetanus. In fact, it can develop after an injury so small and apparently insignificant that you may not even have noticed it.

Tetanus is diagnosed by its symptoms: fever, headache and chills; irritability and restlessness; muscle spasms and rigidity, including the spasms of the mouth and throat muscles that make it hard to chew and swallow, giving tetanus its common nickname, "lockjaw."

These symptoms may show up from two days to six weeks after an injury. The faster they appear, the worse the prognosis is likely to be.

With tetanus, prevention is most important. Immunization is considered standard preventive medicine for all accident victims brought into hospital emergency rooms. If you are injured, but not severely enough to go to the hospital, ask your doctor about the need for a tetanus shot.

To lower your risk of tetanus

Immunization. Because immunization eliminates the risk of tetanus, young children are routinely immunized with tetanus toxoid, toxin that has been treated so as to make it non-poisonous but still retain its ability to stimulate the production of antibodies to the tetanus toxin itself.

Until the age of six, children are immunized with tetanus toxoid given along with the immunization for diphtheria and whooping cough (pertussis), a combination known as DTP. For immunized older children and adults, a booster shot that reactivates immunity is recommended every 10 years or immediately after an injury that carries the risk of exposure to the tetanus organism. Accident victims known to have been immunized more than five years prviously are given a tetanus booster shot. People who are unconscious or whose immunization history is uncertain, are given the toxoid plus tetanus immune globulin ("antitoxin"). Optimally the antitoxin is prepared from the blood of people who have had tetanus. Antitoxin made from horse or cow serum, which can cause serious allergic reactions in sensitive people, is used only if human serum is not available.

A pregnant woman who is immunized against tetanus can pass the immunity along to her baby who will be protected until about eight months after birth.

THALASSEMIA

Known risk factors

Age:	No	Smoking:	No
Gender:	No	Drugs & medical procedures:	No
Race/ethnic group:	Yes	General health:	No
Family history:	Yes	Environment:	No
Diet:	No	Occupation:	No

Are you at risk?

Thalassemia is an inherited blood disorder that interferes with the production of hemoglobin, the pigment in red blood cells that carries oxygen throughout your body. *Beta*-thalassemia, also known as Cooley's anemia, is transmitted by various recessive genes, but the usual distinction between dominant and recessive genes is blurred in thalassemia because you may develop the condition even if you get the gene only from one parent. How severe the condition is depends largely on whether you get a *beta*-thalassemia gene from each parent or only from one. People who inherit the gene for *beta*-thalassemia from both parents will usually have severe anemia that may require frequent blood transfusion. People who inherit a gene only from one parent typically have only mild, often asymptomatic anemia. Your risk of *beta*-thalassemia is higher than normal if you are black or if you or your parents come from the Mediterranean, northern Italy or southern Asia (Pakistan and India).

Alpha-thalassemia, a form of thalassemia most often found among blacks and people of Chinese, Filipino, Thai and other southern Asian heritage, is more truly the product of a recessive gene. You have to inherit the specific gene from both parents in order to develop the disorder. If you only get the gene from one parent, you can pass it along to your children, but you won't have *alpha*-thalassemia yourself.

Early detection. After a blood test showing reduced levels of hemoglobin and/or other abnormalities, thalassemia is diagnosed by a relatively inexpensive hemoglobin test.

To lower your risk of thalassemia.

Genetic testing. If both parents carry one gene for thalassemia, each time they conceive, there is a 25% chance that the child will get the gene from both parents, a 50% chance that it will inherit the gene from one parent, and a 25% chance that it will not inherit the gene from either parent.

If you are a member of a high-risk group or have a family history of thalassemia, when you are planning your family you may wish to consider the blood test that can detect asymptomatic carriers and to follow up with genetic counseling. Tests to detect the various forms of thalassemia in the fetus are widely available at major medical centers.

THYROID CANCER

Known risk factors

Age:	No	Smoking:	No
Gender:	Yes	Drugs & medical procedures:	Yes
Race/ethnic group:	No	General health:	No
Family history:	Yes	Environment:	No
Diet:	No	Occupation:	No

Are you at risk?

In 1990, the American Cancer Society (ACS) estimated that there would be approximately 12,100 new cases of thyroid cancer diagnosed in the United States, and about 1,000 deaths.

The risk factors for thyroid cancer depend on the kind of cancer involved. The most common thyroid cancer, papillary carcinoma, occurs most frequently among young people and affects women up to three times as often as men.

Your risk of follicular carcinoma of the thyroid, which is more common among the elderly, rises if your thyroid gland was exposed to radiation when your thymus gland was irradiated, a once-common, now discredited, practice no longer used.

Medullary carcinoma of the thyroid, which is most common among children younger than 15, sometimes seems to run in families, perhaps transmitted by a dominant gene. Anaplastic carcinoma of the thyroid occurs mostly among the elderly. It is slightly more common among women.

Early detection. Anyone who was given radiation to the thyroid as a child should be examined regularly for abnormalities of the thyroid gland. A swelling in the gland that does not disappear spontaneously within six months should be biopsied to confirm or rule out a diagnosis of thyroid cancer.

To lower your risk of thyroid cancer

The causes of thyroid cancer, other than radiation to the gland, are unknown, so there is no known way to reduce the risk of thyroid cancer.

TOOTH DECAY

Known risk factors

Age:	Yes	Smoking:	No
Gender:	No	Drugs & medical procedures:	No
Race/ethnic group:	No	General health:	Yes
Family history:	Yes	Environment:	No
Diet:	Yes	Occupation:	No

Are you at risk?

Cavities are the most common cause of tooth loss in people younger than 40. (After 40, periodontal disease moves into first place). The three most important risk factors for tooth decay are having the causative bacteria in your mouth, being susceptible to their effects and eating foods that promote bacterial activities.

Streptococcus mutans, the ubiquitous bacteria suspected to be the most important pathogen in the creation of tooth decay, does its damage by digesting sugars and excreting acids dissolve the calcium salts in your teeth. The sugar it uses most easily is sucrose (table sugar). It can also use fructose, which is found in fruit, and lactose, which is found in milk, but these two are less likely than sucrose to trigger the formation of cavities or contribute to the formation of plaque, the sticky substance that increases your risk of periodontal disease.

Because the structure of your teeth is determined by genetics, cavities may run in families.

Early detection. It is important to find cavities as early as possible because if you don't remove the decayed spot, the decay will continue to spread until it has destroyed the entire tooth.

Your dentist may identify cavities either by examining your teeth with a sharp pick that catches on any irregularity in the tooth surface or with X-rays that show small cavities between the teeth and illumine suspicious areas inside the tooth or on the surface below the gum line.

In 1989, a panel of dental experts at the Food and Drug Administration (FDA) issued new guidelines for dental X-rays. They suggest that a first set be taken at a child's first visit to the dentist. After that, children who have healthy teeth may require X-rays every one or two years; adults with healthy teeth may need them every two to three years; and adults who are at high risk for cavities or who have periodontal disease may need them more frequently.

To lower your risk of tooth decay

Drink fluoridated water; use fluoride dental products. Fluorine is an element that occurs naturally in soil and rocks and is a natural component of normal, healthy saliva. It helps harden bones and protects tooth enamel against acid attack. Fluoridation of the public water supply to a concentration of one part fluorine to every million parts water (1 ppm) has reduced the incidence of cavities among American children by as much as 70%.

Regular use of fluoride toothpastes, powders, gels and rinses can also increase the tooth's resistance to decay. According to the FDA's Review Panel on OTC Dentifrices and Dental Care Drug Products, these products are especially important in reducing the number of dental cavities that may develop in people who live in places where the water is not fluoridated. They are also important if you are drinking unfluoridated bottled water.

These products, which are categorized as drugs and regulated by the FDA, should be used only as your dentist directs, especially for young children who may swallow the toothpaste.

Eat a protective diet. Foods that stick to your teeth are more likely than other foods to support the bacteria that cause tooth decay. In other words, a raisin (which sounds healthy) may be more hazardous than a hard candy (which sounds like trouble).

Several foods, including cheddar cheese, cocoa and rice hulls, seem to contain an as yet unidentified substance that protects your teeth against cavities. Eating them at the end of the meal may neutralize the effects of sugars.

Raw fruits and vegetables, chicken, fish and beef, hard-boiled eggs, bean dips, unsalted nuts and unsugared coffee, tea, soft drinks, popcorn and candy are all considered neutral foods that do not promote cavities.

Chewing gum is a special case. Saliva helps prevent cavities by bathing your teeth in a mineral-rich solution. Recent research at the Indiana University School of Dentistry in Indianapolis suggests that the flow of saliva produced by chewing any kind of gum, sugared or not, helps neutralize the destructive acids produced by the bacteria that cause tooth decay.

That doesn't mean there are no special benefits to un-sugared chewing gums. In 1988, scientists at University of Michigan School of Dentistry found that xylitol, a sweetener often used in chewing gums made in Europe but not yet common in the United States, protects your teeth, perhaps because it kills harmful bacteria in your mouth. In the Michigan study, children who chewed xylitol-sweetened gum three times a day for two years had a significantly smaller number of cavities than children who chewed other kinds of gum; the protective effect seemed to last as long as two years after the children stopped chewing the xylitol-sweetened gum.

Practice good dental hygiene. Flossing, brushing, rinsing—all seem to reduce the incidence of cavities. Not everyone responds to the same technique, so your dentist's directions are your best guide.

Whatever regime you follow, get two toothbrushes per person so that each can dry out thoroughly between brushings. Replace your brushes on a regular schedule, every month or two or whenever they begin to look scruffy—bent or matted bristles won't clean properly.

TOXIC SHOCK SYNDROME (TSS)

Known risk factors

Age:	Yes	Smoking:	No
Gender:	Yes	Drugs & medical procedures:	Yes
Race/ethnic group:	No	General health:	No
Family history:	No	Environment:	No
Diet:	No	Occupation:	No

Are you at risk?

Toxic shock syndrome is an acute infectious disease caused by the toxin produced by *Staphylococcus aureus*. Although the first nationwide epidemic occurred in 1980 along with the introduction of new brands of super-absorbent vaginal tampons, TSS was not a new disease. It had occurred over the years, mostly among surgical patients, men as well as women and children, who had acquired a staphylococcus infection in the hospital.

What was new in 1980 was the target population (overwhelmingly female) and the site of the infection: the vagina.

About 70% of the TSS cases reported to the Federal Centers for Disease Control (CDC) during 1983 and 1984 occurred among menstruating women who were using tampons, primarily the new ones made of more absorbent synthetic materials that allowed women to leave them in place longer. The long use combined with the heightened absorbency may encourage the growth of *S. aureus* and increase the production of toxins. TSS has occasionally occurred among women who were using contraceptive diaphragms or sponges, perhaps because they were left in place longer than recommended, thus encouraging the growth of *S. aureus*.

Having sexual intercourse with a person who has TSS may raise your risk. Although is not considered a sexually transmitted disease (STD), there have been a few reports of two sexual partners developing TSS at the same time. The risk of TSS remains higher for women than for men, but with the change in the construction of vaginal tampons, statistics from the Federal Centers for Disease Control show that the incidence of TSS has dropped from a high of 890 cases in 1980 to 61 in 1989.

Early detection. The early warning signs of TSS resemble flu symptoms: a sore throat, a sudden high fever (above 102 degrees F by mouth), muscle pains and diarrhea. Or you may develop a rash that makes your skin look sunburned or experience a sudden drop in blood pressure that makes you feel dizzy or even causes you to faint when you stand up.

TSS may progress from these early symptoms to irregular heartbeat, disorientation and/or coma, and respiratory distress. These symptoms may resemble those of several other infections, including blood poisoning (septicemia), an infection of the brain or Rocky Mountain spotted fever. They are signs of a potentially fatal illness that requires immediate medical attention.

To lower your risk of TSS

Use the least absorbent tampons necessary. In 1990, the Food and Drug Administration (FDA) released standardized label terms for tampons to allow a woman to compare the absorbency (in grams of liquid) of different brands of tampons.

Tampon Absorbency

Label Term	Absorbency (in grams of liquid)
Junior absorbency	6 and under
Regular absorbency	6 to 9
Super absorbency	9 to 12
Super plus absorbency	12 to 15

Source: *FDA Consumer*, February 1990.

Use sanitary napkins in place of tampons. Using sanitary pads rather than tampons, or alternating tampons with napkins, may reduce the risk of TSS.

TUBERCULOSIS (TB)

Known risk factors

Age:	Yes	Smoking:	No
Gender:	No	Drugs & medical procedures:	No
Race/ethnic group:	Yes	General health:	Yes
Family history:	Yes	Environment:	No
Diet:	?	Occupation:	No

Are you at risk?

From 1963 through 1985, the number of new cases of tuberculosis diagnosed in the United States declined each year except for 1980, after a sudden influx of emigrants from Southeast Asia, where TB is common. In 1986, however, cases of TB began to rise again in this country; by 1988, TB was being reported at a rate of 22,000 new cases a year. Worldwide, it is estimated that there are 10 million to 15 million people with active tuberculosis, and as many as 1 billion who may be harboring the TB bacillus but have no symptoms of disease.

In America, the risk of TB is higher among the very young, the very old, and the very poor. You are also at higher risk if you have a disease that attacks your immune system. According to the Federal Centers for Disease Control (CDC), as many as half the Americans with TB also harbor HIV, the virus that causes AIDS. You are also at higher risk if you are taking immuno-suppressant drugs such as steroid drugs or anti-cancer medication.

At every age, the number of non-white Americans with TB tends to be twice as high as the number of whites. Immigrants from Africa, Central America, South America and Southeast Asia, many of whom are resistant to one or more of the drugs used to treat tuberculosis, are at high risk. So are people who work or live in close contact with a person who has active tuberculosis or who have once had TB but were not adequately treated. This last may explain the prevalence of TB in nursing homes among the elderly who were exposed to TB as children and have harbored dormant bacilli, which are reactivated by stress or another infection.

Exactly how nutrition raises or lowers your risk of TB is still unclear, but the incidence of tuberculosis is known to increase dramatically in areas where the general resistance to disease is lowered by famine. TB is also spread by milk from cows infected with bovine tuberculosis. This is rare in the United States, where the Public Health Service's Grade A Pasteurized Milk Ordinance requires that milk cows be certified free of disease and that their milk be pasteurized before being sold to consumers.

Early detection. The symptoms of tuberculosis are similar to those for other low-grade infections: a loss of appetite followed by weight loss and fatigue; a steady, low-grade fever; chills and coughing. People with TB may also wake up during the night drenched in sweat. Because these symptoms are so common, many TB patients discover their illness only by accident, for example, when they have a routine chest X-ray film during an otherwise unexceptional annual check-up.

The screening test for tuberculosis is a skin test that demonstrates sensitivity to tuberculin (a culture of TB organisms). A diagnosis is confirmed by a culture of bacteria from the patient's sputum. Getting the results of this test may take as long as three to six weeks.

To lower your risk of tuberculosis

If you are at risk, ask your doctor about a TB test. If you test positive (even without symptoms of active disease) or if you live in a household with a person who has active TB or if you had TB and your immune system is now compromised, your doctor may recommend treatment with an anti-TB drug, which may be important to forestall or cure active disease.

TYPHOID

Known risk factors

Age:	No	Smoking:	No
Gender:	No	Drugs & medical procedures:	No
Race/ethnic group:	No	General health:	No
Family history:	No	Environment:	Yes
Diet:	Yes	Occupation:	No

Are you at risk?

Typhoid fever is an infectious disease caused by consuming food or water contaminated with human feces that harbor the typhoid organism, *Salmonella typhi*, a bacteria that can survive freezing and drying.

Typhoid is often spread by people working as food handlers who carry the infection but show no symptoms of the disease. The most likely typhoid carriers are people with urinary tract infections or chronic gallbladder disease (the bacteria can hide in gallstones). Because these latter illnesses are more common among women, typhoid carriers are more likely to be female, the best known being New York City's infamous "Typhoid Mary."

Not surprisingly, your risk of typhoid is highest in places where the sanitation is poor, where milk is not pasteurized, and where public health laws do not control typhoid carriers. Over the last 100 years, as public sanitation improved in the United States, the incidence of typhoid moved steadily downward. Today, fewer than 500 cases a year are diagnosed in this country. More than two-thirds of the Americans who get typhoid fever get it traveling to places such as Mexico and India where the disease is endemic.

Early detection. The symptoms of typhoid fever are similar to those of many other infectious diseases: sore throat, fever, headaches, joint pains, constipation, loss of appetite and abdominal pain. If typhoid is not diagnosed and treated, the patient's temperature will begin to rise, producing fevers as high as 103 or 104 degrees F. Heartbeat may slow. Blood and liver abnormalities, and bloody diarrhea or coma may develop.

A diagnosis of typhoid is suggested when all these symptoms appear after exposure to *Salmonella typhi*-contaminated food or water or to a typhoid carrier. During the first two weeks of the illness, a diagnosis of typhoid can be confirmed by culturing *S. typhia* from blood; later, from samples of stool or urine.

To lower your risk of typhoid

Vaccination. Typhoid vaccine provides only partial protection. As a result, it is generally used only for people known to be at risk: those who live in a household where there are people with active typhoid or are traveling to a place where typhoid is endemic or medical researchers working with the typhoid bacteria. The vaccine is administered in two doses not less than four weeks apart. In 1989, the Food and Drug Administration approved an oral typhoid vaccine.

Travel smart by eating with care. When traveling or living in areas where typhoid is endemic, avoid all raw fruits and vegetables. Don't drink water that has not been boiled. Pass up the ice cubes. Turn down unpasteurized milk. Avoid eggs, meat, poultry, fish, milk products and prepared foods stored without refrigeration and any prepared dishes served at room temperature.

ULCERS (PEPTIC ULCER)

Known risk factors

Age:	Yes	Smoking:	Yes
Gender:	Yes	Drugs & medical procedures:	Yes
Race/ethnic group:	No	General health:	No
Family history:	Yes	Environment:	No
Diet:	No	Occupation:	No

Are you at risk?

Peptic ulcer (which most of us simply call ulcers) may affect as many as one in every 50 Americans. According to the National Center for Health Statistics, more than 4 million new cases were diagnosed in 1987.

Duodenal ulcers (ulcers in the first part of the small intestine) are four or five times more common than gastric ulcers (ulcers in the stomach), but their incidence has been declining over the past decade. If you are a man, your risk of a duodenal ulcer is two times a woman's risk. The older you are, the higher your risk; although ulcers can show up at any age, they are more likely after age 35.

Ulcers are now believed to be caused by the action of bacteria named *Helicobacter pylori* (formerly *Campylobacter*), but exactly what triggers or exacerbates their attack on the lining of the stomach or the duodenum is still

unclear. Stomach acid seems a logical villain, but some people with duodenal ulcers produce low levels of acid while others who produce copious
amounts never develop ulcers. Experts speculate that the real relationship
may lie in the relative ability of the mucous membrane lining of your intestines to resist the erosion caused by stomach acid. The stronger the resistance, the less likely you may be to end up with duodenal ulcers.

An individual's production of stomach acid has no effect on his risk of
gastric ulcers. The stomach, after all, is designed to release acid so as to
begin the digestion of the food you eat. People with gastric ulcers have
about the same concentration of stomach acid as healthy people. Men have
a slightly higher risk than women; in both sexes, the risk is higher after 50.

Ulcers may run in families. If you have close relatives (mother, father,
sister, brother) with duodenal ulcers, your risk is about three times higher
than it would be if your relatives were free of ulcers. For unknown reasons,
people with duodenal ulcers are more likely than the rest of us to have
blood type O.

Does what you eat affect your risk of ulcers? Probably not. Every controlled study of ulcer patients has shown that foods do not cause ulcers and
that neither the type nor the consistency of the food you eat will interfere
with the healing of an ulcer. The exceptions to this rule are cocoa, coffee
and tea (regular and decaffeinated), alcoholic beverages and perhaps the
spices that can irritate the gastrointestinal tract: hot peppers, cloves and
nutmeg. Obviously, even if you don't have an ulcer, you should avoid any
food that upsets your stomach.

Long-term use of aspirin and the non-steroidal anti-inflammatory drugs
(NSAIDs) raises your risk of ulcers. These drugs may erode the lining of the
gastrointestinal tract, thus accounting for the higher-than-normal incidence
of ulcers among people with arthritis. The same may be true of large doses
of corticosteroids, the anti-hypertensive drug reserpine and the diuretic
ethacrynic acid (Edacrin).

Smoking doubles your risk of ulcer, reduces the rate at which existing
ulcers heal and increases your risk of a relapse. Emotional turmoil is unlikely to cause an ulcer, but psychological or physical stress may exacerbate
an existing one.

Early detection. The characteristic symptom of a duodenal ulcer is pain
three or four hours after eating or in the middle of the night. The pain is
relieved by eating. The opposite is true of gastric ulcers: eating causes pain.
Duodenal ulcers are almost invariably benign; gastric ulcers may be malignant.

A diagnosis of ulcers is confirmed by X-rays taken after you have swal-
lowed a barium solution or by endoscopy, an examination of the intestinal
tract with a flexible lighted tube that lets your doctor see the surface of the
intestines.

To lower your risk of ulcers

Because so little is known for certain about the causes of ulcers, there is no medically certain way to avoid an ulcer in the first place, other than to exercise discretion and check with your doctor when using drugs known to erode the intestinal lining.

URINARY TRACT INFECTION (UTI)

Known risk factors

Age:	Yes	Smoking:	No
Gender:	Yes	Drugs & medical procedures:	Yes
Race/ethnic group:	No	General health:	Yes
Family history:	No	Environment:	No
Diet:	No	Occupation:	No

Are you at risk?

Urinary tract infections are exceedingly common, second only to respiratory infections as a reason for visits to the doctor.

The organisms that cause urinary tract infections ascend into the bladder through the ureter, the tube that runs from the urethral opening to the bladder. Because a woman's ureter is about seven inches shorter than a man's and her urethral opening is closer to the anus and the vagina, both potential sources of bacterial contamination, her risk of a urinary infection is about 10 times higher than a man's.

One out of every five women will have a UTI at some time in her life. Women who develop recurring urinary tract infections may be harboring larger than normal numbers of bacteria at the opening to the vagina.

Among men, the most likely risk factor for chronic UTI is a chronic prostate infection. Recent research suggests that routine circumcision of baby boys may decrease the incidence of UTI by removing the foreskin under which bacteria can hide. In 1989, the American Academy of Pediatrics reversed its earlier position against routine circumcision on the grounds that circumcised men may be as much as 11 times less likely than uncircumcised men to develop urinary tract infections.

Being sexually active significantly increases the risk of a urinary infection because it increases the number of bacteria around the urethral opening. Using oral contraceptives raises the risk because the hormones make the vagina more hospitable to bacteria. A badly fitted diaphragm may cause repeated irritation, leading to infection. Using sanitary pads rather than tampons may increase the risk of UTI because the pad acts as a bridge for bacteria from the anus to cross to the urethra.

The risk of a UTI rises if you are hospitalized, particularly after abdominal surgery if you are given a urinary catheter. Urine that collects in the bladder for long periods of time supports the growth of bacteria, so any medical condition that prevents you from completely emptying the bladder will increase your risk of UTI. Examples of these conditions are cystocele (a hernia of the bladder), a prolapsed urethra or uterus that presses against the bladder, and an injury to the spinal nerves that control urination.

Urinary tract infections are likely occur more frequently as we get older and are most common among the institutionalized elderly.

Early detection. Untreated urinary tract infections may lead to serious kidney damage.

The screening test for a urinary tract infection is a urinalysis test that examines color (infection may darken your urine), odor (an infection can make your urine smell unpleasant), clarity (if you have a UTI, your urine may be clouded by excess blood cells, micro-organisms, fat and protein), pH (healthy urine is acidic) and protein levels (excess amounts may indicate infection).

A diagnosis of UTI is confirmed by finding pathogens (bacteria, yeasts, etc.) in the urine.

If you are taking medication, tell your doctor before you have a urinalysis. Some medicines may alter the properties of your urine and affect the results of a urinalysis. For example:

Drugs that change the color of urine: Red-orange-yellow: deferoxamine mesylate (Desferal), oral anti-coagulants, phenazopyridine (Azo Gantanol, Azo Gantrisin, Pyridinium, Thiosulfil, Urobiotic), quinacrine (Atabrine), riboflavin (vitamin B1), rifampin (Ritadin, Rifamate, Rimactane), sulfasalazine (Azufidine). *Brown-black:* furazolidone (Furoxone), iron salts, nitrofurantoin (Furadantin, Macrodantin). *Blue:* Methylene blue. *Dark:* Chlorpromazine, levodopa (Laradopa, Sinemet), metronidazole (Flagyl).

Drugs that impart an odor to urine: Antibiotics, paraldehyde, and some vitamins.

Drugs that make urine more alkaline: Acetazolamide (Diamox), amphotericin B (Fungizone, Mysteclin-F), sodium bicarbonate and potassium citrate.

Drugs that make urine more acidic: Ammonium chloride, diazoxide (Proglycem), methenamine (Hiprex, Urex, Urised, Uro-Phosphate), vitamin C.

Drugs that may increase white blood cells in urine: Allopurinal (Lopurin, Zyloprim), ampicillin, aspirin, kanamycin (Kantrex).

Drugs that may increase the amount of protein in your urine: Amikacin (Amikin), amphotericin B (Fungizone, Mysteclin F), gold preparations, kanamycin (Kantrex), phenylbutazone (Butazolidin), streptomycin, trimethadone (Tridione). Acetazolamide (Diamox), cephalothin (Seffin), nafcillin (Unipen), sodium bicarbonate, tolbutamide (Orinase) and tolmetin (Tolectin) may cause a false-positive result for protein in your urine, suggesting that protein is present when it is not. Penicillin and the sulfonamides can cause both protein in the urine and a false-positive result.

Drugs that may cause blood in urine: Amphotericin B (Fungizone, Mysteclin F), coumarin derivatives, methenamine (Hiprex, Urex, Urised, Uro-Phosphate), para-aminobenzoic acid (Mega-B), phenylbutazone (Butazolidin), sulfonamides.

Drugs that cause casts (cylindrical particles that suggest the presence of an infection): Amphotericin B (Fungizone, Mysteclin F), aspirin, ethacrynic acid (Edecrin), furosemide (Lasix), griseolfulvin (Fulvicin, Grisactin), isoniazid (INH), kanamycin (Kantrex), penicillin, radiographic agents, streptomycin, sulfonamides.

To lower your risk of urinary tract infections

Drink an adequate amount of water. The more fluids you drink, the more urine you will produce. Be sure to empty your bladder completely each time you void. Don't ignore your body's signals. The longer you wait, the longer the urine sits in your bladder, the more likely it is to support the growth of the organisms that cause urinary tract infections.

Keep your genital area clean. Ordinarily, this means washing once a day with warm soapy water. It is safer to avoid commercial bubble baths, bath salts and bath oils that may irritate the urinary tract. Empty your bladder completely before and after sexual intercourse. After a bowel movement, the most protective procedure for women is to wipe from front to back to avoid bringing bacteria from the anal area up to the urethral and vaginal openings.

Wear loose-fitting undergarments. The best are cotton underpants loose enough to allow air to circulate through to your skin to dry perspiration and discourage the growth of bacteria.

VAGINAL CANCER

Known risk factors

Age:	Yes	Smoking:	No
Gender:	Yes	Drugs & medical procedures:	Yes
Race/ethnic group:	No	General health:	No
Family history:	No	Environment:	No
Diet:	No	Occupation:	No

Are you at risk?

Cancers of the vagina account for about 1% of all gynecological malignancies. Ordinarily, vaginal cancers occur most commonly among middle-aged women, 45 to 65. The exception to this rule is clear cell cancer of the vagina, which accounts for about 5% of all vaginal cancers. This tumor is most likely to occur in young women, some still in their teens, who were exposed to the synthetic estrogen diethylstilbesterol (DES) while still in their mothers' wombs.

In the years between 1947 and 1971, DES was widely used in the United States in an attempt to prevent miscarriage; some estimate that as many as 3 million fetuses may have been exposed.

Young women whose mothers took DES while pregnant have a higher-than-normal rate of cervical and uterine abnormalities, as well as vaginal cancers. Boys who were exposed to DES *in utero* have a higher-than-normal rate of abnormalities of the testicles and the epididymides, the tiny tubes through which sperm move inside the testicle. They are also more likely to suffer from oligospermia, a decreased number of sperm in the seminal fluid.

The risk factors for other forms of vaginal cancer are still a mystery, although some suspect that exposure to human papilloma virus, which has already been linked to cervical cancer and cancer of the penis, may play a role.

Early detection. The early signs of cancer of the vagina include vaginal bleeding and discharge, which are also early warning signs of endometrial cancer. A diagnosis of vaginal cancer is confirmed by a biopsy of the affected tissues.

To lower your risk of vaginal cancer

Because so little is known about the causes of vaginal cancer, there are no medically certain ways to reduce your risk of developing it. However, yearly gynecological examinations, especially if you were exposed to DES while your mother was pregnant, may enable your doctor to find any such cancer in an early, curable stage.

VAGINITIS

Known risk factors

Age:	Yes	Smoking:	No
Gender:	Yes	Drugs & medical procedures:	Yes
Race/ethnic group:	No	General health:	No
Family history:	No	Environment:	No
Diet:	No	Occupation:	No

Are you at risk?

Vaginitis is an infection of the tissues in or around the vagina. It may be the most common gynecological complaint of women in the reproductive years, so common, in fact, that it is reputed to be the number-one diagnosis among women visiting clinics that treat sexually transmitted diseases (STDs).

Vaginitis is caused by any one of a number of different organisms. In childhood, the most common kind of vaginitis is an infection caused by *Escherichia coli (E. coli)*, an organism normally found in the anal area. During the reproductive years, the most common forms of vaginitis are yeast infections and protozoal infections. Bacterial and fungal infections are more common after menopause.

Women who are being treated with long-term courses of antibiotics, such as low-dose tetracycline therapy to control acne, have a higher-than-normal risk of vaginal yeast infections. The risk of a vaginal yeast infection also rises if you are using oral contraceptives because the hormones alter the pH (acid/alkaline balance) in the vagina and encourage the growth of yeast-like organisms such as *Candida albicans*, which produce a thick, white discharge. Recurring candida infections may be caused by sexual intercourse with an infected partner. These infections are most likely to re-appear right before your period or when you are using antibiotics that eliminate bacteria and allow yeasts to flourish.

The most common form of protozoal vaginitis is the one caused by *Trichmonas*, a one-celled parasite that can be transmitted during sexual intercourse. Every year, as many as 100 million women worldwide (including 3 million in the United States) will acquire trichmonal vaginitis. Trichmonal vaginitis is most common among sexually active women younger than 25. Their risk is directly related to their sexual activity; virgins and celibate woman rarely get trichmonas.

Wearing tight, non-porous underpants may encourage the growth of yeasts and fungi. So does frequent douching with prepared douche solutions that may upset the normal balance among the bacteria, yeasts and other organisms commonly present in the healthy vagina. Vaginal sprays, harsh soaps, bubble baths and bath salts or oils may irritate vaginal tissues. Some women are also sensitive to specific chemical spermicides, as well as latex diaphragms or condoms.

Early detection. The most common symptom of a vaginal infection is a thick itchy discharge. (A thin, watery or bloody discharge may be a symptom of endometrial or vaginal cancer).

A diagnosis of vaginitis is confirmed by finding any one of the various vaginitis organisms in a sample of discharge examined under a microscope.

To lower your risk of vaginitis

Keep your genital area clean. Ordinarily, this means washing once a day with warm soapy water and drying the vaginal area thoroughly afterwards. This ordinarily prevents vaginal odors and allows you to avoid potentially irritating prepared douches and vaginal deodorant sprays. It is also safer to avoid commercial bubble baths, bath salts and bath oils that may irritate vaginal tissues. After a bowel movement, the most protective procedure for women is to wipe from front to back to avoid bringing bacteria from the anal area up to the vagina.

Wear loose-fitting undergarments. The general consensus is that the best are cotton underpants loose enough to allow air to circulate through to your skin.

Practice safer sex. Some of the organisms that cause vaginitis may be transmitted during sexual intercourse. Your partner's using a condom every time you have intercourse may reduce your risk of a vaginal infection.

The correct use of condoms begins with storing them properly in a cool, dry place to protect the latex from drying out. The condom should be put on gently to avoid tearing. Leave room at the tip to accommodate the ejaculate. After ejaculation, your partner should withdraw the penis with the condom still in place, holding it close against the base of the penis to avoid spilling any ejaculate. Discard all used condoms; never try to wash them out and use them again.

According to the American Social Health Association, you may increase the protective effect of a condom by using a spermicidal foam that contains nonoxynol-9. In laboratory studies, nonoxynol-9 appears to kill many of the organisms that cause sexually transmitted diseases. But the two contraceptives must be used in tandem; on its own, the foam is not considered adequately protective.

VARICOSE VEINS

Known risk factors

Age:	Yes	Smoking:	No
Gender:	?	Drugs & medical procedures:	No
Race/ethnic group:	No	General health:	No
Family history:	Yes	Environment:	No
Diet:	No	Occupation:	Yes

Are you at risk?

Varicose veins are nature's revenge for our daring to stand up on our hind legs rather than walking on all fours like any sensible animal.

The veins in our legs carry blood up against the pull of gravity from our feet to our heart. As blood is pushed up by muscles in your legs, the walls of the veins and a series of one-way valves keep it from flowing backwards down the vein. Sometimes the valves weaken and the blood does flow backward, pooling in the vein. The resulting bulge is a varicosity.

About 10% of all adult Americans have varicose veins serious enough to cause discomfort. Another 30% to 40% have small varicosities or the tiny stretched "spider" veins somewhere on the body that may look unattractive but don't cause any discomfort. Exactly why this happens in some people but not others is still a mystery, but fluctuating hormone levels and pressure in the abdomen are known to play a part.

Women are more likely than men to develop varicose veins, but statistics showing that women patients outnumber men by about three or four to one may be skewed by the facts that we wear different clothes (skirts show varicose veins; slacks hide them) and that women are more likely than men to visit the doctor.

It may also represent a different pattern in the ages at which men and women develop varicose veins. Women are most likely to get them during the childbearing years, before age 49; men, between the ages of 70 and 79.

Women who do develop varicose veins are most likely to develop them during the second half of the menstrual cycle, or while they are pregnant.

In the early weeks of pregnancy, a woman's body produces hormones that relax ligaments in muscles, including the smooth muscle in the walls of the blood vessels. This allows the uterus to expand enough to hold the developing fetus and it enables blood vessels to expand to hold the increased supply of blood for mother and baby.

Some pregnant women also develop a weakness in the valves in the veins that keep blood from flowing backward down the leg. As a result, the blood pools in the veins, creating the swelling known as varicose veins. Pregnancy doesn't cause this; it just aggravates a pre-existing condition, the tendency to varicosities. Most varicosities that pop up during pregnancy are temporary; nine out of ten will smooth down after the baby is born.

Varicose veins seem to run in families. As many as 80% of all patients with varicose veins have relatives with varicosities, so you can safely figure that if your relatives have varicose veins, you are likely to, as well. The problem may be a genetic defect in the valve system that controls the flow of blood through veins or you may have inherited a body with fewer valves than normal.

Spending long hours on your feet may also raise your risk of varicose veins. So will being obese (weighing 30% more than most weight tables say you should).

Early detection. Varicose veins are easy to diagnose simply by their appearance. Left untreated, their progress is uncertain. Some may eventually break down and ulcerate or produce blood clots that can travel as far as the lungs. Others will never cause any serious problems.

To lower your risk of varicose veins

Stay in shape. Because the tendency to varicose veins is inherited, you can't totally avoid the problem if it runs in your family. However, if you are susceptible, you can help your body fight off varicosities by staying trim.

Regular walking or swimming tones the muscles in your legs that help force blood upwards.

Be kind to your legs. Put your legs up on your desk or, more modestly, use a reclining chair or a footstool whenever you can, especially if you are pregnant. Both promote circulation of blood through the veins in your legs.

Don't wear garters or sit with your legs crossed at the knee. Doing this cuts down the flow of blood. If you have to sit in one place for a long time flex your leg muscles regularly from time to time. On a long plane flight, get up and walk around the cabin.

Ask your doctor about support hose, especially if your work requires you to stand a lot. The stockings are designed to augment the pressure your leg muscles exert against the veins in your leg and keep the blood flowing smoothly upward. The best stockings are those made to your personal measurements.

VENEREAL WARTS

Known risk factors

Age:	Yes	Smoking:	No
Gender:	No	Drugs & medical procedures:	No
Race/ethnic group:	No	General health:	No
Family history:	No	Environment:	No
Diet:	No	Occupation:	No

Are you at risk?

Venereal warts are among the most common of sexually transmitted diseases. In 1981, for example, about 1 million Americans went to the doctor for treatment for venereal warts.

The warts are caused by the human papilloma virus (HPV), which is transmitted during sexual intercourse. Although venereal warts are most likely to appear in the genital area, if you have oral sex with a person who is carrying the virus, you can develop them in the mouth and throat.

As you might expect, your risk of catching venereal warts is higher if you are sexually active. The people at highest risk are young adults, age 20 to 24. A baby born to a woman who has venereal warts while pregnant (when the HPV is more likely to flourish) can pick up the virus as he travels through her infected vaginal canal.

Early detection. Because the virus that causes venereal warts has been linked to changes in tissues leading to cancer of the cervix and found in cells taken from patients with bladder cancer, it is important to find and treat the warts as early as possible. If you have already had venereal warts, follow-up treatment is a must to deal with relapses that frequently occur.

Visible venereal warts are often diagnosed by their appearance: soft, pink or red swellings on the genitals, anus or rectum that can cause pain during intercourse or when urinating or defecating. Venereal warts that occur in the throat can make swallowing painful.

Because venereal warts may sometimes resemble syphilitic lesions, your doctor may wish to confirm a diagnosis of warts by testing you for syphilis so that he or she can rule that out.

To lower your risk of venereal warts

Practice safer sex. A human papilloma virus (HPV) infection is a chronic disease. The virus can be transmitted even when there are no visible symptoms of infection. To reduce your risk of transmitting or acquiring venereal warts, use a condom every single time you have sexual intercourse.

The correct use of condoms begins with storing them properly in a cool, dry place to protect the latex from drying out. The condom should be put on gently to avoid tearing. Leave room at the tip to accommodate the ejaculate. After ejaculation, the penis should be withdrawn with the condom still in place, held close against the base of the penis to avoid spilling any ejaculate. Discard all used condoms; never try to wash them out and use them again.

According to the American Social Health Association, you may increase the protective effect of a condom by using a spermicidal foam that contains nonoxynol-9. In laboratory studies, nonoxynol-9 appears to kill many of the organisms that cause sexually transmitted diseases on contact. But the two contraceptives must be used in tandem; on its own, the foam is not considered adequately protective.

WARTS

Known risk factors

Age:	Yes	Smoking:	No
Gender:	No	Drugs & medical procedures:	Yes
Race/ethnic group:	No	General health:	Yes
Family history:	No	Environment:	Yes
Diet:	No	Occupation:	Yes

Are you at risk?

Warts are viral infections caused by human papilloma viruses that spread from one person to another or from one part of the body to another by direct contact and enter through a minute break in the skin. The viruses are ubiquitous. We are all exposed to them time and again, but most of us don't get warts. This suggests that personal immunity plays an important role in determining whether or not you get warts, although the more frequently you are exposed to the virus, the more likely you are to develop warts. For example, according to the American Academy of Dermatology, dermatologists have a higher-than-normal incidence of warts.

The person most likely to have warts is a child age 12 to 16; one of every 10 school children in this age group have at least one wart. If you have an illness that depresses your immune system or are getting anti-cancer chemotherapy or taking post-transplant drugs that suppress your immune system, you are more than ordinarily susceptible to warts. Warts are least common among the healthy elderly who, presumably, have developed immunity to the virus through repeated exposure over the years.

Because the wart viruses survive on damp surfaces, your risk of warts goes up if you share towels with someone who has a wart or if you use public showers or swimming pools. People who work as butchers and meat cutters are at higher-than-normal risk, perhaps because they are exposed to bovine papilloma viruses or because they have multiple breaks in the skin through which the human papilloma virus can enter easily.

Early detection. Most warts disappear spontaneously, but about one-third of all the people whose warts disappear after treatment will develop warts again within a year.

Warts are diagnosed by their appearance. If there is any question, a biopsy will rule out the possibility that what looks like a wart is really a squamous-cell skin cancer.

To lower your risk of warts

Practice good hygiene. The virus that causes warts is an infectious agent, just like the virus that causes colds. It spreads easily from person to person and from place to place on the body. It's virtually impossible to avoid, but you may be able to reduce your risk of spreading or catching it doing some of the same things you do to avoid colds. If you don't have warts, be cautious. Don't share unlaundered towels or clothes with someone who has warts.

WHOOPING COUGH (PERTUSSIS)

Known risk factors

Age:	Yes	Smoking:	No
Gender:	No	Drugs & medical procedures:	No
Race/ethnic group:	No	General health:	No
Family history:	No	Environment:	Yes
Diet:	No	Occupation:	No

Are you at risk?

Whooping cough is a highly infectious disease caused by an organism known as *Bordella pertussis*.

According to the Federal Centers for Disease Control (CDC), there were 3,745 cases of whooping cough reported in the United States in 1989, up from 3,450 cases in 1988. The CDC estimates, however, that only 5% to 10% of all cases of whooping cough are actually reported, so that the actual number of cases may be as high as 60,000 a year.

Your risk of catching whooping cough depends on whether or not you have been immunized against it. If you have, your risk is almost zero. If you have not, your risk is high. As many as nine of every 10 susceptible people living in close contact with someone who has whooping cough will catch it. Having had whooping cough does not make you immune, but if you catch it again, it may be so mild as to pass unnoticed.

Whooping cough is found everywhere in the world. Most cases occur in children younger than two who have not been immunized and do not have protective antibodies. In the United States, 42% of all cases occur in children younger than one year; 25% in children aged one to four.

Early detection. Early diagnosis of whooping cough is important because erythromycin, the anti-microbial used to treat it, is more effective early on.

The early symptoms of whooping cough look like those of any other upper respiratory infection: a low grade fever, runny nose, sneezing and a cough.

What tells the doctor it's whooping cough is the characteristic dry, hacking, forceful cough that develops about 10 days into the illness and usually lasts anywhere from one week to a month. The "whoop" that gives the disease its name occurs when a child tries to breathe in through an airway narrowed by a paroxysm of coughing. The diagnosis is confirmed by finding the whooping cough micro-organism in nasal mucus.

To lower your risk of whooping cough

Immunization. Until the 1980s, cases of whooping cough steadily declined as the whooping cough vaccine was routinely given to young children as part of the immunization known as D (diphtheria) P (pertussis) T (tetanus). The Immunization Practices Advisory Committee of the CDC recommends whooping cough vaccination as part of the diptheria-pertussis-tetanus (DPT) injections given to infants at three months, five months, seven months and 19 months.

But whooping cough vaccine, whose common side effects include redness and tenderness at the site of the injection, may also cause severe allergic reactions, blood disorders, convulsions, encephalitis, fever, very low or very high blood pressure and sudden infant death syndrome (SIDS).

Consequently, an increasing number of parents have refused to allow their children to get the pertussis component. The inevitable result has been a rise in the number of American children with whooping cough.

Many experts suggest that the benefits of vaccination outweigh the risk of side effects except among children who have had a reaction to the first shot in the DPT series or who have an underlying neurological disorder or who are older than seven, when the risk of reactions goes up. In 1990, researchers at the Vanderbilt University School of Medicine in Tennessee released a study of 38,171 Tennessee children who had gotten a total of 107,154 DPT vaccinations. The study showed that while a small percentage of the children had suffered from high fevers and fever-triggered seizures after vaccination, there had been no increase in the incidence of epilepsy or other neurological problems among the children and no deaths. This study, combined with previous ones, has provided information about 230,000 American children who were given a total of 713,000 immunizations for whooping cough. The conclusions of all the studies is that there is no link between the vaccine and brain damage.

Whether or not you choose to give your child the whooping cough vaccine will depend on how you and your doctor balance the equation between risks and benefits.

YELLOW FEVER

Known risk factors

Age:	No	Smoking:	No
Gender:	No	Drugs & medical procedures:	No
Race/ethnic group:	No	General health:	No
Family history:	No	Environment:	Yes
Diet:	No	Occupation:	No

Are you at risk?

The virus that causes yellow fever is transmitted from person to person by the bite of a female mosquito that has previously fed on someone who has yellow fever. Your risk of getting yellow fever depends on your being in an area where mosquitoes can find people with yellow fever and then fly on to you. This is most likely to happen if you live or travel in places where yellow fever is endemic, such as Africa and Central and South America.

Having yellow fever once gives you life-long immunity.

Early detection. The symptoms of yellow fever include a sudden fever that may go as high as 104 degrees F, a pulse that is rapid at first and then slows (the slow pulse plus the high fever are known as Faget's sign), flushed face and a tongue that is red at the edges and furry in the middle, upset stomach (nausea, vomiting, constipation, pain), headache and muscle pains, restlessness and irritability.

In susceptible people, these symptoms appear less than a week after being bitten by a carrier mosquito. After a week, the illness may spontaneously disappear or it may progress, after a short remission, to jaundice, bloody vomit, albuminuria (higher than normal amounts of protein in the urine), mental confusion and coma.

A diagnosis of yellow fever is suggested by Faget's sign and confirmed by finding either the yellow fever virus or a high level of antibodies to it in a blood specimen.

To lower your risk of yellow fever

Vaccination. Immunization with live virus yellow fever vaccine protects you against yellow fever. If you are traveling to an area where yellow fever is endemic, vaccination may be required before permission for you to enter the country is granted, but countries vary in their vaccination requirements.

The yellow fever vaccine is administered only at U.S. Public Health Service (USPHS) Yellow Fever Vaccination Centers. For current information on vaccination requirements and the address of the vaccination centers nearest you, contact the USPHS or your state or local health department.

BIBLIOGRAPHY

Books

AMA Drug Evaluations, 5th ed. Chicago: American Medical Association, 1983.

The American Dietetic Association. *Handbook of Clinical Dietetics*. New Haven, Connecticut: Yale University Press, 1981.

The American Pharmaceutical Association. *Handbook of Nonprescription Drugs*, 8th ed. Washington, D.C.: The National Professional Society of Pharmacists, 1986.

Berkow, Robert, ed. *The Merck Manual*, 15th ed. Rahway, N.J.: Sharp & Dohme Research Laboratory, 1987.

Braunwald, Eugene, et al., eds. *Harrison's Principles of Internal Medicine*, 11th ed. New York: McGraw-Hill Book Company, 1987.

Briggs, George M., and Calloway, Doris Howes. *Nutrition and Physical Fitness*. New York: Holt, Rinehart and Winston, 1984.

Carper, Jean. *Health Care U.S.A.* New York: Prentice Hall Press, 1987.

Chemotherapy & You. Bethesda, Md.: National Cancer Institute, 1987.

Diamond, Seymour, and Epstein, Mary Franklin. *Coping with Your Headaches*. New York: Delair Publishing Company, 1982.

Ford, Regina Daley, ed. *Diagnostic Tests Handbook*. Springhouse, Pennsylvania: Springhouse Corporation, 1987.

Gilman, Alfred Goodman; Goodman, Louis S.; and Gilman, Alfred. *The Pharmacological Basis of Therapeutics*, 6th ed. New York: Macmillan, 1980.

Krupp, Marcus A.; Chatton, Milton J.; and Tierney, Lawrence M. *Current Medical Diagnosis and Treatment 1986*. Los Altos, California: Lange Medical Publications, 1986.

Long, James W. *The Essential Guide to Prescription Drugs*. New York: Harper & Row, 1987.

Windholz, Martha, ed. *The Merck Index*, 10th ed. Rahway, N.J.: Merck & Co., 1983.

Zapsalis, Charles, and Beck, R. Anderle. *Food Chemistry and Nutritional Biochemistry*. New York: John Wiley & Sons, 1985.

Zimmerman, David R. *The Essential Guide to Nonprescription Drugs*. New York: Harper & Row, 1983.

Pamphlets, Periodicals & Press Releases

About Muscular Dystrophy. New York: Muscular Dystrophy Association, 1980.

Ackerman, S. J. "Flu shots. Do you need one?" *FDA Consumer*, October 1989.

Altman, Lawrence K. "Physicians See a Familial Link in Ovarian Cancer." *New York Times*, September 5, 1989.

———. "Pregnancy Problem Linked to Hormone." *New York Times*, November 13, 1990.

———. "Research Links Diet and Infertility Factors to Ovarian Cancer." *New York Times*, July 25, 1989.

"ALS." New York: Muscular Dystrophy Association, 1989.

Andres, R., et al. "Impact of Age on Weight Goals."

Annals of Internal Medicine, December 1985.

Annual Cancer Statistics Review. Washington, D.C.: National Cancer Institute, January 1988.

"Asthma Death Rate Reported Up 30%." *New York Times*, August 2, 1990.

Athlete's Foot. Evanston, Illinois: American Academy of Dermatology, 1988.

"Babies and Barbells: Make Your Choice." *Science News*, February 27, 1988.

Beil, L. "One-Third of Pregnancies May Miscarry." *Science News*, August 6, 1988.

———. "Some Neurons Predisposed to Huntington's." *Science News*, August 20, 1988.

Blakeslee, Sandra. "New Tests Can Detect Viruses that Signal Risk of Cervical Cancer." *New York Times*, October 20, 1988.

"Blood Cells Yield Cystic Fibrosis Clues." *Science News*, February 18, 1989.

Bower, Bruce. "Alcoholism's Elusive Genes." *Science News*, July 30, 1988.

———. "New Bone Loss Risk Factors in Young Women." *Science News*, November 18, 1987.

———. "Platelets Enter into Alzheimer's Disease." *Science News*, October 29, 1988.

———. "Schizophrenia: Genetic Clues and Caveats." *Science News*, November 12, 1988.

"Breast Cancer: Low-Fat Finding." *Science News*, n.d.

"Breast Cancer: New Trend On Age and Family History." *New York Times*, November 16, 1990.

"Breast Implants Hinder X-Ray Mammography." *Wall Street Journal*, June 14, 1989.

Brody, Jane. "Oral Cancer Specialists Warn that Cigarettes and Alcohol Are a Perilous Combination." *New York Times*, April 13, 1989.

Brower, Vicki. "Circumcision's Comeback?" *American Health*, September 1989.

———. "Need Those X-rays?" *American Health*, June 1989.

Cancer Facts & Figures—1990. New York: American Cancer Society, 1990.

Cancer in the United States: Is There an Epidemic? New York: American Council on Science and Health, June 1988.

"Cancer Prevention: Not All Fiber Helps." *Science News,* December 3, 1988.

Cathy Carlson, ed. "Questions and Answers about Amyotrophic Lateral Sclerosis." *MDA Newsletter,* August 1987.

"Cereal: Breakfast Food or Nutritional Supplement?" *Consumer Reports,* October 1989.

Childhood Asthma. Danville, Pennsylvania: Geisinger Medical Center, August 16, 1989.

"Circadian Effect Seen in Cancer Therapy Trial." *Medical World News,* May 13, 1985.

Cold Air and Asthma: No Reason to Stay Indoors. Madison, Wisconsin: University of Wisconsin-Madison, Center for Health Sciences, November 1988.

Condoms, Contraceptives and Sexually Transmitted Disease. Research Triangle Park, N.C.: American Social Health Association, 1989.

"Deaths from Measles Are The Most Since '71." *New York Times.* December 26, 1989.

A Dermatologist Talks about Warts. Evanston, Illinois: American Academy of Dermatology, 1988.

Diabetes: Facts You Need to Know. Alexandria, Virginia: American Diabetes Association, n.d.

Drink a Little and Help Your Heart? Scientists Find a Possible Reason. American Heart Association: Dallas, Texas, November 19, 1987.

"Drug Shows Promise in Sickle Cell Anemia." *Science News,* June 3, 1989.

Eckholm, Erik. "Health Benefits of Lifelong Leanness Are Challenged by New Weight Table." *New York Times,* August 6, 1985.

Edwards, D. D. "Exposing Lung Cancer as a Genetic Disease." *Science News,* June 4, 1988.

Eisenberg, S. "Biting Down on the Culprit Causing Gum Disease." *Science News,* January 9, 1989.

———. "Smoking Raises Female Heart Attack Risks." *Science News,* November 28, 1987.

"Enzymes and Alcoholism: Blood Simple?" *Science News,* January 30, 1988.

Eron, C. "Cold Facts on Diabetes." *Science News,* August 20, 1988.

———. "Double Trouble: Risks of Psoriasis Therapy," *Science News,* September 10, 1988.

Evidence for an "Obesity Gene" Emerges from Family Studies. American Heart Association: Dallas, Texas, November 18, 1989.

Fackelmann, K. A. "Dairy Sugar Linked to Ovarian Cancer." *Science News,* July 22, 1989.

———. "Early AZT Use Slows Progression to AIDS." *Science News,* August 26, 1989.

———. "More Cervical Cancer in Passive Smokers." *Science News,* March 18, 1989.

Facts about SIDS. National SIDS Foundation: Columbia, Maryland, July 1989.

Farley, Dixie. "Preventing TSS." *FDA Consumer,* February 1990.

Fink, Aaron. "To Circumcise or Not to Circumcise?" *Stanford Medicine,* Spring 1988.

French, Howard W. "Asthma Deaths Center on 2 Groups, Experts Say." *New York Times,* May 12, 1989.

Frouman, Jane. "Stress Can be a Jawbreaker." *Business Week,* September 11, 1989.

"Future Obesity Set by Age 3 Months?" *Science News,* March 5, 1988.

Gallstone Disease Fact Sheet. New York: Lobsenz-Stevens, May 16, 1988.

Gergen, Peter J., and Turkeltaub, Paul C. National Center for Health Statistics. *Percutaneous Immediate Hypersensitivity to Eight Allergens, United States 1976–1980.* Washington, D.C.: Government Printing Office, July 1986.

"Genetic Basis of Colon Cancer." *Science News,* September 17, 1988.

Gilman, Lois. "Shedding Light on Jet Lag." *American Health,* June 1989.

Gossel, Thomas A. "The Common Cold: New Defenses Against an Old Enemy." *U.S. Pharmacist,* January 1987.

———. "Use of Sunscreens to Prevent Sun-Damaged Skin." *U.S. Pharmacist,* May 1989.

Hair Loss. Evanston, Illinois: American Academy of Dermatology, 1988.

Health Hotlines. Washington, D.C.: National Library of Medicine, January 1990.

Health United States 1984. Hyattsville, Maryland: U.S. Department of Health and Human Services, December 1988.

Henderson, Doug. "Early Detection the Key to Success against Testicular Cancer." *FDA Consumer,* December 1988–January 1989.

Hendricks, M. "Estrogen Receptors Detected in Bone Cells." *Science News,* July 2, 1988.

"Heredity and Drinking: How Strong is the Link?" *Newsweek,* January 18, 1988.

Horner, J., Heyman, A., and Dawson D. "The Relationship of Agraphia to the Severity of Dementia in Alzheimer's Disease." *Archives of Neurology,* 1988.

How to Help Patients Stop Smoking. U.S. Pharmacist, March 1989.

James, Melissa. "What's Your Osteoporosis I.Q.?" *Arthritis Today*, March–April 1988.

Jones, Dawn L. *Cold Triggers Raynaud's Phenomenon*. Madison, Wisconsin: University of Wisconsin–Madison, Center for Health Sciences, November 1988.

Kolata, Gina. "Menopause Hormone Linked to Breast Cancer." *New York Times*, August 3, 1989.

———. "Researchers Find Link Between Endometriosis and Bone Development." *New York Times*, March 8, 1988.

———. "Sharp Cut in Serious Birth Defects is Tied to Vitamins in Pregnancy." *New York Times*, November 24, 1989.

———. "Studies Link Age to AIDS Development." *New York Times*, May 21, 1989.

———. "Whooping Cough Vaccine Found Not to be Linked to Brain Damage." *New York Times*, March 21, 1990.

Knox, C. "The Air You Breathe May Hurt Your Ears." *Science News*, November 19, 1988.

Landau, Janet. "Varicose Veins." *U.S. Pharmacist*, July 1987.

"Leg Moles? Get Out the Sunblocker." *Science News*, July 8, 1989.

Loupe, D. E. "Hepatitis C May Spread Heterosexually." *Science News*, September 2, 1989.

Lyme Disease: A Hazard for Humans and Their Pets Flourishes in Warm Weather. New York: Animal Medical Center, n.d.

Mayo Clinic Health Letter: "Duodenal Ulcers," September 1989; "Gallstones," May 1989; "Hair Loss," June 1989; "Infertility," medical essay, June 1989; "Late Effects of Polio," August 1989; "Lyme Disease," October 1989; "Occupational Jet Lag," April 1987; "Pneumonia," September 1989; "Red Measles," April 1989; Sudden Infant Death Syndrome," April 1989; "TMJ Disorder," October 1988; "Varicose Veins," September 1983.

McNamara, Judith R., et al., "Effect of Gender, Age and Lipid Status on Low Density Lipoprotein Subfraction Distribution," *Arteriosclerosis*, September/October 1987.

Memory and Aging. Chicago, Illinois: Alzheimer's Disease and Related Disorders Association, 1987.

"A Method to Detect Alzheimer's Disease." *New York Times*, June 10, 1989.

Miller, Sarah J. "The Role of Diet in Three Chronic Diseases." *U.S. Pharmacist*, August 1986.

"More Bad News for Sun Worshipers." *Science News*, November 12, 1988.

"New Link between Pill and Cancer Reported." *New York Times*, May 6, 1989.

"New Test Developed for Early Ovarian Cancer." *New York Times*, December 5, 1989.

"New Test Finds Signs of AIDS at Earlier Point." *New York Times*, July 11, 1989.

Noise, Ears & Hearing Protection. Washington, D.C.: American Academy of Otolaryngology—Head and Neck Surgery, 1987.

NYU Medical Center Health Letter: "Aggressive Approach Needed to Combat Antibiotic Resistant Gonorrhea," June 1989; "New Drug Therapy Proves Safe and Effective Against Shingles," May 1989.

1990 Heart and Stroke Facts." Dallas, Texas: American Heart Association, 1989.

"Passive Smoke: Risk to Nonsmokers Only?" *Science News*, June 6, 1987.

Patlack, Margie. "The Puzzling Picture of Multiple Sclerosis." *FDA Consumer*, July–August 1989.

"Periodontal Disease." *American Health*, September 1989.

Pray, W. Steven. "The Link between Diabetes and Obesity: Diabesity." *U.S. Pharmacist*, November 1988.

"Prostate Cancer Drug Approved." *FDA Consumer*, April 1989.

Psoriasis? 3 Million People Aren't Laughing. Portland, Oregon: National Psoriasis Foundation, 1988.

Questions and Answers about Epilepsy. New York: Epilepsy Foundation of America, 1987.

Questions and Answers about Psoriasis and Its Treatment. New York: Lobsenz-Stevens Inc., n.d.

"Rad Risks in Young Breasts." *Science News*, November 11, 1989.

Raloff, J. "Smallest Aerosol Pollutants Linked to Disease." *Science News*, May 6, 1989.

Reporter's Handbook for the Prescription Drug Industry. Washington, D.C. Pharmaceutical Manufacturers Association, 1989.

"Research Group Reports Success in Finding Gene for Cystic Fibrosis." *New York Times*, August 23, 1989.

Rosenthal, Elizabeth. "Physicians Pin Ulcers on New Suspect: A Germ." *New York Times*, April 26, 1990.

Schmeck, Harold M. Jr. "Depression and Anxiety Seen as Cause of Much Addiction." *New York Times*, November 15, 1988.

———. "Hereditary Link Studied as Colon Cancer Causes." *New York Times*, January 21, 1988.

———. "Schizophrenia Study Finds Strong Signs of Hereditary Cause." *New York Times*, November 10, 1988.

Schoenfield, Leslie J. and Bean, Kristine J. eds. *Clinical Symposia, Gallstones.* Summit, N.J.: CIBA-GEIGY, 1988.

Scientists Revise Estimates on Prevalence of Alzheimer's Disease. Bethesda, Maryland: National Institute on Aging, November 9, 1989.

Scientists Unveil Laser Instrument Designed for Early Detection of Cataracts. Atlanta, Georgia: Research Communications Office, Georgia Institute of Technology, April 6, 1989.

"Second Neural Tube Defects." *Science News*, December 10, 1988.

Seligman, Jean. "Checking Up on a Killer." *Newsweek*, June 12, 1989.

———. "Getting a Grasp on Asthma's Grip," *Newsweek*, September 4, 1989.

"Sickle Cell Yes, Malaria No." *Science News*, June 17, 1978.

Silburner, J. "Smoking and Cancer: Value in Paradox." *Science News*, September 14, 1985.

Sleep Disorder Harms Concentration, Memory. Rochester, Minnesota: Association of Professional Sleep Societies, 1987.

"A Smart Skin Patch That Checks for Cystic Fibrosis." *Business Week*, March 14, 1988.

"Smoking of Cigarettes Is Linked for First Time to a Form of Cataracts." *New York Times*, September 14, 1989.

Some Questions and Answers about Chlamydia. Palo Alto, California: American Social Health Association, 1984.

Something Can Be Done about Acne. Evanston, Illinois: American Academy of Dermatology, 1987.

"Spina Bifida Survival Rises." *New York Times*, April 25, 1989.

"Spousal Promiscuity Emerges as Cervical Cancer Risk Factor." *Medical World News*, March 14, 1988.

Stehlin, Dori. "The Silent Epidemic of Hip Fractures," *FDA Consumer*, May 1988.

Stanaszek, Walter F., and Carlstedt, Bruce C. "Prevention Strategies for Migraine Headaches." *U.S. Pharmacist*, July 1988.

"State Vaccination Requirements for School Entry Reduce Mumps Incidence." *The Double Helix*. The National Foundation for Infectious Diseases, July/August 1989.

"Strokes in Women Linked to Smoking." *New York Times*, March 14, 1988.

"Study Says Quitting Smoking Reduces Risk of Stroke by 50%." *New York Times*. January 20, 1988.

Sugars and Your Health. New York: American Council on Science and Health, May 1986.

Sullivan, Walter. "New Studies Link Exercise to Delays in Menstruation—and Less Cancer," *New York Times*, January 16, 1988.

"Sunglasses to Be Labeled." *New York Times*, May 18, 1989.

"Surge in Mumps Is Easing, but Victims Are Now Older." *New York Times*, June 13, 1989.

Talan, Jamie. "Alcohol: The Danger to Women." *Newsday*, February 23, 1988.

"Task Force says Circumcision has Benefits." *Science News*, March 11, 1989.

"Top 25 Most Frequently Performed Surgeries." *HealthWeek*, June 20, 1988.

"Toxic Shock Toll Plummets." *New York Times*, July 5, 1990.

Tufts University Diet & Nutrition Letter: "Caffeine Suspected in Impaired Fertility," April 1989; "Can Diet Affect Premenstrual Syndrome?" October 1988; "Can Eating the 'Right' Food Cut Your Risk of Cancer?" April 1988; "The Good News about Morning Sickness," September 1989; "Is an Eating Disorder Developing in Your Family?" May 1989; "The Latest on Diet and Breast Cancer," June 1989; "Need for Food Increases During Menstrual Cycle," September 1987.

"Up to 60,000 a Year Get Whooping Cough." *New York Times*, February 6, 1990.

"Urine Test Detects Bladder Cancer at Early Stage." *New York Times*, October 1, 1988.

"Vitamins May Reduce Neural Tube Defects." *Science News*, December 10, 1988.

Wallace, Lance A. "Major Sources of Benzene Exposure." *Environmental Health Perspectives*, October 1989.

"Weak Bones Linked to Anorexia." *New York Times*, April 18, 1989.

Weiss, R. "Bone Density Drops with Thyroid Therapy." *Science News*. June 4, 1988.

Weiss, Rick. "TB Trouble." *Science News*, February 6, 1988.

What You Should Know about Toxic Shock Syndrome (TSS). Lake Success, N.Y.: Tambrands, 1988.

Wickelgren, I. "Firming the Figures on Mental Illness." *Science News*, November 12, 1988.

―――. "MS Gene Discovery: A Piece of The Puzzle." *Science News*, July 8, 1989.

―――. "Mutation Revealed for Adult Tay-Sachs," March 18, 1989.

―――. "Vitamins C and E May Prevent Cataracts." *Science News*, May 20, 1989.

Willis, Judith Levine. "Mumps Make a Comeback." *FDA Consumer*, July–August 1989.

Women Suffering More Than Men from Alzheimer's and Its Consequences. San Francisco: University of California, San Francisco, December 12, 1987.

INDEX